RISE AND GROWTH OF ARYA SAMAJ MOVEMENT

(1863-1947)

RISE AND GROWTH OF ARYA SAMAJ MOVEMENT (1863-1947)

Brij Kishore Sharma

PATHAK PUBLISHER AND DISTRIBUTORS
Delhi (India)

Rise and Growth of Arya Samaj Movemen in 1863-1947

Author : Brij Kishore Sharma

ISBN : 978-93-91952-20-4

Price : ₹ 1595/-

First Edition: 2022

Published by :
PATHAK PUBLISHER AND DISTRIBUTORS
E-6/33c & 34, Ground Floor, Sangam Vihar
New Delhi-110080
E-mail: pathakppd@gmail.com

Type Setting by
G. R. Sharma
(M) 9968281826

Printed by
R. K. Offset, Delhi

Contents

Preface

The religious and social reform movement of nineteenth century in India was the outcome of India's reaction to western challenge. Initially the British imperialism adversely affected the political and economic life of India. But when the British Empire got sound footing in India then the British tried to colonize or subdue the Indian culture. Such British efforts resulted in cultural conflict between the British rulers and Indian people. It was a kind of politico-cultural conflict because the British were using their political authority to overpower the Indian culture. Thus, the vibrant movements for social and religious reforms during the nineteenth century were the first all India response to the cultural and moral challenges posed by the colonial rule.

A very modest beginning was made by Raja Ram Mohan Roy through the Brahamo Samaj. He discovered the ancient Indian knowledge and wisdom in the light of western knowledge. The Arya Samaj movement belongs to radical stream, which had wide influence in northern India. It had modest presence in erstwhile princely states of Rajputana and the British territory of Ajmer-Merwara. Since the inception Swami Dayanand had attraction towards the princely states of Rajputana. The arrival of Swami Dayanand in Rajasthan has great significance because he brought a ray of hope in the colonial and feudal atmosphere. When he step out for the first time from the territories of Gujarat he arrived at Mount Abu in 1852 and it was a coincidence that he breathed his last at

Ajmer on 30th October, 1883. He visited the princely states and Ajmer-Merwara many times and had left deep impact on social, cultural and even political life of the area presently known as Rajasthan. Though, the Arya Samaj had its presence in all the princely states but due to many factors Ajmer emerged as the main centre of Arya Samaj movement in Rajasthan.

The establishment of the Arya Samaj proved a miracle for Rajasthan as it initiated the process of social and religious reforms. The educational efforts of Arya Samaj created social, cultural and national awakening in Rajasthan. It had initiated crusade against evil religious and social practices and at the same time it propagated the message of *Swadeshi* which facilitated the growth of nationalism on all India level and Rajasthan became its' immediate beneficiary. In Rajasthan the Arya Samaj movement could spread among all the sections of the society, but newly emerged educated urban intelligentsia remained in the role of its vanguard. Though, it's activities initially were based in urban areas but its influence was deeply spread in the rural areas in a systematic way.

Though, sizable works has been done on the history of Arya Samaj movement in India. But most of these works are of general nature or focuses on erstwhile British provinces of Punjab and United Provinces. Few of these have given scanty informations about Rajasthan. Therefore, the history of Arya Samaj movement in Rajasthan cannot be ignored for a long time. The present work is an effort to bridge the gap existed in the history writings on Arya Samaj. The religious, social and political contribution of Arya Samaj in Rajasthan has been focused in this study.

The study is based on wide range of primary and as well as on secondary sources procured from national Archives of India, Rajasthan State Archives and various libraries. The printed and unprinted reports and records of the Arya Samaj organizations has also been used as primary source material, which were collected mainly from the library of Paropkarini Sabha (Vedic Pustakalaya), Ajmer. Many valuable reports, documents and records has also been collected from various Arya Samaj organisations and institutions located at Jaipur, Udaipur, Jodhpur, Ajmer, Mount Abu, Bharatpur and Alwar. The contemporary newspapers mainly the Arya Samaj journals has also been consulted for this study. The important and core works of Swami Dayanand has been widely used to study the theological aspects of the Arya Samaj. The leading biographies of Swami Dayanand Saraswati and official histories published by Arya Samaj institutions have also been utilized as authentic sources. The published books and unpublished works on the subject have been used as secondary sources. The study is based on historical method of research.

The study has been sponsored and financially supported by the Indian Council of Historical Research, New Delhi under the Senior Academic Fellowship scheme. I express my sense of gratitude and obligation to the authorities and staff of the ICHR, New Delhi for this valuable support and contribution.

I gratefully extend my thanks to the researchers and scholars whose works has been consulted and used for this study. I am highly thankful to the authorities and staff of the National Archives of India, New Delhi, Rajasthan State Archives, Bikaner, Library of Paropkarini Sabha, Ajmer, Central Library, University of Rajasthan, Jaipur, ICHR Library, New Delhi, Arya Samaj Library, Adarsh Nagar, Jaipur and the Arya Samaj organisations and institutions situated at Ajmer, Mount Abu, Jaipur, Udaipur, Jodhpur, Bharatpur and Alwar for the generous cooperation and hospitality extended to me in providing the necessary facilities for collection of source-material.

At more personal level, I appreciate the cooperation and timely support of my wife Dr. Shail Bala Sharma, without her incalculable and untiring support this work would not have been possible.

Jaipur

Prof. (Dr.) Brij Kishore Sharma
Senior Academic Fellow
Indian Council of Historical Research
New Delhi-110001

1

Introduction and Review of Literature

The Nineteenth Century is known for Indian Renaissance. The religious and social reform movements made it a reality. These movements were not limited to theology but had broad religious, social, cultural and political spectrum. Therefore, it was the century of the rise of cultural nationalism. This remained an important component of the Revolt of 1857. The destruction of Indian polity, the transformation of its economy and attacks upon its social system and culture, threatened to reduce this ancient people to political subservience forever, but also to the status of an economic colony and a cultural province of the west. Therefore, a protest arose against this political dependence and intellectual slavery in the form of cultural nationalism. This also seems right that when efforts to dislodge the political authority of England proved futile, attention naturally turned to the cultural and social aspects of western domination.

The British tried to justify their rule by propagation that their duty is to civilize the barbaric Indians. In fact they tried to subdue or colonize the Indian culture and such efforts resulted into cultural conflict between the British rulers and Indian people. The impact of the west did not operate in a normal peaceful manner, but was consequential upon military conquest, which determined the relations between the bearers of the two cultures. Inherent in the conquest was pride of empire and sense of superiority, on the part of the conquerors and resentment on the part of conquered. It produced also a feeling of inferiority and a longing for self assertion. The insolent claim to a monopoly of wisdom in devising measures for the people's welfare and an intolerable arrogance of behaviour towards the inhabitants of India evoked among them hatred towards the west.

The vibrant movement for social and religious reform in the 19th century was the first all-India response to the cultural and moral challenge posed by the colonial rule. The movement was initiated by the educated middle classes in the backdrop of an ideological and cultural conflict between the British imperialists and the Indian intelligentsia. The cultural confrontation was provoked and preceded by an unabashed indictment of the Indian social and cultural practices by the Christian missionaries and English utilitarians. The Indian intelligentsia unearthed the true and pure Hindu religion as they were of the firm view that the true nature of Hindu society and religion should not be evaluated from its prevalent forms because its true form lay buried under a mass of irrationalities and superstitions. Therefore, they called the people to return to the origin and purity of faith. They took their ideas from scriptures, Vedas, Upanishads, Bhagwat Geeta and other *shastras*. Through scriptural knowledge and philosophy they established the superiority of Hindu religion, culture and society. The negative views of Christian missionaries, British administrators and educationists, western thinkers and others regarding Indian society, culture, moral, intellectual and physical faculties of the Indian encouraged the Indian intelligentsia for affirmative action against dubious efforts of the west. These movements fostered a rational outlook and developed a logical and critical thinking. Even the attitude of those conservatives who continued to stick firmly to Indian tradition, was changed from uncritical acceptance to justification by reason. Thus, the cultural and religious consciousness combined with political and economic factors provided a powerful basis to the growth of nationalism.

Arya Samaj played an important role in the Religious and social reform movement of 19th century. Raja Ram Mohan Roy was the first who initiated the process of the religious and social reform under the influence of western education and culture. But the challenge of the west to the basic ideas and institutions of India was unprecedented because the British were exploiting this in the expansion and strengthening of their colonial interest. The political subordination of India to the British led to the decline of Indian social system and culture. Raja Ram Mohan Roy was highly influenced by the western education and culture. No doubt that the spirit of the new age was represented by the Brahma Samaj in Bengal and subsequently, the Prarthana Samaj came into being in Bombay as an offshoot of it. These were the middle class reformist movements led by pro-western educated class whom illiterate rural population regarded as Christian and looked to them with profound suspicion. These movements could not attract mass support. But the Arya Samaj movement initiated by Swami Dayanand Saraswati attracted the large mass following because he was the first reformer whose appeal was much wider and he openly criticised the British rule which was the root cause of social and cultural decay of India. He was scholar of great stature of Indian language, philosophy, theology, religion and culture. He took Vedic and Sanskrit education on Gurukul pattern.

Obviously, the numerical and geographical influence of Arya Samaj Movement was very large. It became much popular in the Hindi heart land of Northern India. It has modest presence in Maharashtra, Gujarat and Bengal while it has made rich presence in Bihar, U.P., Punjab, Haryana, Rajasthan and Madhya Pradesh. In the areas of its influence it was joined by the mass of peasants, dalits, merchant classes etc.. Moreover, the conscious and educated people joined it. The Arya Samaj was the first to propagate the idea of *Swaraj*. Dayanand Saraswati considered the colonial subservience responsible for degeneration of Indian culture. He questioned that how could a people as sublime as the Vedic Aryans, who predated all other men and created civilization, sink to such depth of ignorance and dependency.

The Arya Samaj has also played decisive role in the emergence of nationalism which finally culminated into freedom struggle. All religious, cultural, social, economic and national aspects of the Arya Samaj movement will be discussed in the future chapters of the present study. Here it is pertinent to review the existing literature on Swami Dayanand and the Arya Samaj Movement.

Review of Literature : Works of Swami Dayanand Saraswati

Swami Dayanand himself was a prolific writer, thinker debater and orator. He has authored about 32 *Granthas* on various themes and subjects in Hindi and Sanskrit.[1] All his compositions were based on scriptures and religious literature. He also did *shastrarthas* (debates and discussions) with Sanatani, Jain, Islamic and Christian theologists. Most of his spiritual and theological discourses were also based on his ideology of restoring Vedic society, culture, religion and politics. Thus, his *shastrarthas* and spiritual discourses were equally of high level that enriched the Vedic and scriptural tradition of India. Some of his *shastrarthas* and speeches were also composed in the form of *granths*, therefore, the number of books written by Swamiji touched the sixty. Among these writings the Satyarth

Prakash is prominent as the Arya Samjists accepts its authority as superior book of knowledge and theology. They gave the Satyarth Prakash a status of Veda. And also they saw Swamiji as the *Rishi*.[2] One foreign scholar Keneth W. Jones designated the Satyarth Prakash as Bible of Arya Samaj.[3] Another foreign scholar Chritophe Jaffrelot has narrated the fact as follows : In 1883, he (Guru Dutt) had been sent by the Arya Samaj of this city (Lahore) to Dayananda who lay dying in Ajmer. He returned transformed by this experience. From 1883 onwards, he started interpreting Dayanand's writings in a very religions light : he thus turned him into a *rishi* and the *Styarth Prakash* into a scripture.[4]

Satyarth Prakash (1875) was printed and published in Harvansh Lal's Star Press, Benares (Varanasi).[5] Till 1874 Swami's work was confined to oral discourses and religious debates. In June 1874 one of his devotee Raja Jaikishendas (district collector of Aligarh) suggested that Swamiji's teachings should be embodied in a book.[6] The result was the Satyarth Prakash. Raja Jaikishendas appointed one Pandit Chandrashekhar to take dictation from Swamiji and write the same. Thus, the composition of the Satyarth Prakash began on 12th June, 1874 and the same completed within six months duration. It got published in 1875 A.D. with the financial assistance of Raja Jaikishendas. All it happened before formal establishment of the Arya Samaj on 10th April 1875 in Bombay. Among of all Swamiji's works the most important and most widely known is the Satyarth Praksash. It is looked upon by the Arya Samaj in the same light as is the Bible by the Christians. It embodies the teachings of Swami Dayanand Saraswati in almost all matters, religious, social, educational and moral; his beliefs, his teachings, and the way of all life he prescribed for men. The Vedas can be studied only by the highly educated people, who know Sanskrit well. The Satyarth Prakash being in Hindi, is for all the educated and the common folk. It is read by all men, women and grown up children and is cited at the meetings of every Arya Samaj. It gives to the people the gist of what Swamiji wishes everyone to know. It contained principles and rules of conduct for all.[7]

Any enquiry into the theology and history of Arya Samaj cannot be initiated and completed without going through the Satyarth Prakash. Due to some ambiguities in the first edition of the Satyarth Prakash Swamiji himself revised the same in 1882 A.D.. He completed this task in Udaipur city with the support of Maharana Sajjan Singh of Mewar. The anomalies in the first edition were erupted due to communication gap between Swamiji and writer of the manuscript. Swamiji himself has confessed the same as follows : At the time when the first edition of this book, called Satyarth Prakash, was published and before that, I spoke Sanskrit and made use of the same in reading and writing, while my mother-tongue was Gujarati : For this reason I had a poor knowledge of the language (i.e. Arya Bhasha)[8] in which this book is written. Consequently, the language of the edition was very defective. Now that I have acquired fair practice in speaking and writing the Bhasha, I have corrected the language in accordance with the rules of grammar and brought out this second edition. The book has been carefully revised, and misprints, which had crept into the first edition, have been carefully corrected.[9] The printing of the revised edition was done by the Vedic Yantralaya, Allahabad.

The second edition is divided into fourteen chapters contained in two parts. Out of these the first ten constitute the first part, while the remaining four form the second part. While, there were only twelve chapters in first edition and last two chapters were incorporated in the second edition and in the end Swamiji added "A Statement of my beliefs". The chapter first is an exposition of Om and other names of

God. The second chapter deals with the birth and the home education of children, with pregnancy, conception, diet of the expectant mother, and the instruction and training of infants. Emphasis is laid on what the parents should do or not do, so that the infants mind becomes strong. The chapter third is on education which treats of Brahmacharya, the duties and qualifications of students and teachers, good and bad and the scheme of studies. It also says that the Vedas should be studied by women and the Sudras, for they are for all men and women.

The fourth chapter treats of marriage, the age of marriage, Varna or caste to be determined by conduct and action, change of caste, duties of the four varnas and treatment of women. Five great duties; Truth, Duty to parents and preceptors and sages, practice of truth, qualifications of teachers, re-marriage, patriotism, sacrifices, household duties and other things. It shows the necessity and the great merits of the Grihastha Ashram. The chapter fifth treats of Vanaprastha (the order of Asceticism) and Sanyas Ashrama (the order of Reunion). The chapter sixth is on Raj Dharma or science of Government. In this Swamiji has given an extensive discourse on *Rajniti* and its all the aspects including civil, military, law and justice, punishment, war and peace, neutrality etc. based on Indian traditions and values. Thus, he has suggested an ideal statecraft.

The chapter seventh deals with the Vedas and God in which all the philosophical questions and issues has been explained lucidly. Chapter eight deals with the creation, sustenance and dissolution of the universe. Chapter ninth deals with the philosophical questions like knowledge and ignorance, and emancipation and bondage. Chapter tenth treats of conduct desirable and undesirable and diet, permissible and forbidden.

First ten chapters of part I of the Satyarth Prakash are inter related with the Vedic knowledge and practices, which proved as the basic foundation of the establishment of Arya Samaj. The

Arya Samaj movement initiated by Swami Dayanand Saraswati was in fact a revival of Aryan culture and society. Thus, Swamiji composed the Satyagrah Prakash based on knowledge of Vedas blended with the requirement of nineteenth century.

The part II consists of four chapters viz. eleventh, twelfth, thirteenth and fourteenth are quite different from the Vedic knowledge and beliefs. Though, all the issues and aspects of these chapters has been dealt through the tools of Vedic philosophy. The last four chapters are contented with discourse on religions of India and world. Swamiji has established that the Vedic religion is far superior from all other religious practices. He has repeatedly mentioned that it is an established fact that about five thousand years ago there was no other religion except the Vedic. According to him Vedic principles are all consistent with science. Swamiji writes that : There are four main anti-vedic religions, Pauranism, Jainism, Christianity and Islam coming one after another in succession. At present the branches of these four religions are not less than one thousand. The object of writing this book is to give facilities to the followers of these religions, their disciples, and all other persons in the investigation of truth. Whatever has been written in this book in the advocacy of true beliefs and refutation of false beliefs is meant for the enlightenment of all. I have thought it best to put before the public all that I have understood after a study of the original scriptures of these religions according to my intellect and my knowledge, as knowledge one lost cannot be easily recovered. Truth and untruth will be clear to those who will read it with an unprejudiced mind. Then it will be easy for all to accept the truth and reject the untruth according to their own lights.[10]

Swamiji has himself wrote that in the eleventh chapter that we have elucidated the merits and demerits of those cults which have branched off from the Puranas etc., in this country of the

Aryavartta. The chapter twelfth presents extensive discourse on Charvaka, Buddhist and Jain religions. The chapter thirteenth is an examination of the doctrines of Christianity and the chapter fourteenth is an examination of the doctrines of Mohammedanism.

As has already been told that last two chapters on Christianity and Islam were not the part of the first edition and these were incorporated in the second edition of the Satyarth Prakash. Therefore, Swamiji has humbly submitted that: If you are not inclined to appreciate my work, never mind. At best do not oppose it. My object is not to injure anybody or to oppose him, but only to ascertain the truth. It is incumbent upon all men to look upon things with eye of justice. The sole purpose of being born as man is to learn what is truth and what is untruth, and not to uphold wrangling.

Learned men of unprejudiced mind alone can calculate the harm done in past, being done in present, and likely to be done in the future religious hostilities. As long as if mankind is not freed from the habit of falsely denouncing each other's religion, the world cannot be happy. It is not impossible, for all and especially for learned persons to be able to accept the truth and reject the untruth, if they give up their presuppositions and ascertain the truth with open mind. It is certain that the differences of the learned people are the cause of the differences among the common people. If learned men rise above their selfish motives and work for the welfare of all, they can be united today and be of one religion.[11]

Swamiji has stressed on truth repeatedly. He has written that my chief aim in writing this book is to unfold truth. He has said that, I have incorporated into this book whatever is true in all religions and in harmony with their highest teaching but have refuted whatever is false in them. I have exposed to the view of men - learned or otherwise - all evil practises whether resorted to secretly or openly. This will help my readers to discuss religious questions in a spirit of love and embrace the true religion. Though I was born in Aryavarta and still live in it, yet just as I do not defend the evil doctrines and practices of the religion prevailing in my own country on the other hand, expose them properly in like manner I deal with alien religion. I treat the foreigners in the same way as I treat my own countrymen in recognition of our common humanity. It behoves all the rest to act likewise. Had I taken the side of one of the prevailing religions of India, I would have but followed the example of sectarian who extol, defend and preach their own religion and decry, refute and check the progress of other creeds. In my opinion, however, such things are beneath the dignity of man.[12]

Moreover, Swamiji has written that, should a man act like an animal, which is strong, oppressed the weak and even puts them to death, he is more an animal than a man. He alone can rightly be called a man who being strong protects the weak. He that injures others in order to gain his selfish ends, can only be called a big animal.[13]

Finally Swamiji has written in his conclusive remarks that : There are many people who, through bigotry and wrong-headedness, misconstrue the meaning of the author. The sectarians are the greatest sinners in this respect because their intellect is wrapped by bigotry. Just as I have studied the Jain and Buddhist scriptures, the Puranas, the Bible and the Quran with an unbiased mind and have accepted what is good in them and rejected what is false, and endeavourer for the betterment of all mankind, it behoves all good men to do likewise. I have very briefly pointed out to the defects of these religions. The perusal of this book will help men to sift truth from falsehood and to embrace the former and renounce the latter. It does not become the wise to mislead people. The ignorant are sure to misinterpret what I say, but if the wise will realize what may aim is in writing this book, I shall consider my labour amply rewarded. I place this work before all men in the hope that they will embrace the truth and make my labour fruitful. I consider it the first and the foremost duty of every man to proclaim the truth without fear or favour.[14]

The Satyarth Prakash became the holy book of Arya Samaj as it contents the essence of the ideas and thoughts of Maharishi Dayanand Saraswati. He has presented it as a book of universal knowledge. Sanskar Vidhi is another important work of Swamiji in which he has explained the famous sixteen sanskaras.[15] Veda Bhashya has been written by Swamiji as a commentary of Vedas. His other works include the Bhagavata Khandanam, Advaitamat Khandanam, Vedavirudh mat Khandana, Aryoddheshya Ratnamala, etc. . His important shastrarthas has also been published in form of books. Swamiji has composed massive literature but for the purpose of research on Maharishi Dayanand Saraswati and Arya Samaj the Satyarth Prakash is an important source without which one cannot proceed further.

In addition to the writings of Swamiji there are various types of writings on Swamiji and Arya Samaj. Among these writings the biographical accounts have central place because these accounts are main sources of study of the rise and growth of Arya Samaj movement. These also explained the ideological and intellectual growth of Swamiji. Next to biographical accounts the books on the history of Arya Samaj and its role in the National and freedom movement are important. In future pages I have studied and reviewed some of the selected works.

Biographies

The first biographical account of Swami Dayanand Saraswati is found in the form of a kind of autobiographical details revealed by Swamiji during his spiritual discourses in Poona during July-August, 1875 after the foundation of the Arya Samaj in Bombay on 10 April, 1875. Swamiji delivered a series of 15 lectures, which had began on 4th July and concluded on 4th August. His fifteenth and concluding lecture was autobiographical in nature. Here it is interesting to note that in one particular lecture Swamiji referred to Martin Luther's role in exposing the Roman Pope's malfeasance. He called himself the Martin Luther of India. He termed the Brahimins Popes and declared that they had distorted the pristine religion of the Vedas. He further said that, they were Brahmins by accident or birth not by merit. Therefore, irritated Brahmins began to spread rumors about Swamiji. Thus, to refute the malicious rumors he revealed the facts about his early life. Moreover, his admirers wanted to know about his early life. This narrative was published in Marathi and later on it was published in Hindi. Thus, this autobiographical narrative was first authentic account of early life of Swamiji up to 1860.

Second biography of Swamiji Dayanand Saraswati was published by Theosophical Society in its journal Theosophist. Here it is pertinent to mention that the founders of the Theosophical Society Conl. H.S. Olcott and Madame H.P. Blavatsky were highly impressed with Swamiji. It is believed that it was an autobiographical account written in Hindi by Swamiji and its English translation was published in the Theosophist in three instalments : Vol. I (October 1897), pp. 9-13; Vol. I (December 1879), pp 66-68; Vol. II (November 1880), pp 24-26. The Hindi version was recovered by the Paropkarini Sabha, Ajmer, and was published with the English version from the *Theosophist* in Paropkari 17, No. 5, March 1975. A noted scholar on Arya Samaj Prof. K.C. Yadav edited the Autobiography of Dayanand Saraswati in 1976 and was published by Manohar Publication, New Delhi.

The autobiography edited by Prof. Yadav is an enlarged edition which took final shape in 1987. This gives many details about the personality and works of Swamiji. Thus, this is an important source of history.[16]

First serious attempt to write the biography of Dayanand Saraswati was made by Pandit Lekh Ram. The Arya Prathinidhi Sabha, the apex body of the Punjab Arya Samaj appointed him on 1st July, 1888 to write the biography. Lekh Ram made extensive tours, interviewed many people and carried out detailed research, using also newspapers and journals as source material. He took extensive tours of Gujarat, Maharashtra, U.P. and Rajasathan. Pt. Lekhram was also a preacher, so he took the task of writing of biography of Swami Dayanand Saraswati with a Zeal. He collected massive source material within a period of seven years, but due to his preoccupation in the preaching work his mission of biography writing got delayed. When he was in the process of finalising the material and arranging the material in chronological order he was murdered on 6 March, 1887. The *Punjab Samachar* of 6 March, 1887 reported that Pandit Lekhram had been murdered, assassinated by a muhmmadan who was living with Lekh Ram under the pretension of becoming a Hindu again.[17] He could not complete his work of biography writing. Even, he could not arrange the source material and left a heap of raw material behind him. But his labour did not go in vain as the material got transferred to famous scholar and worker of Arya Samaj Shree Master Atma Ram Amritsari. No doubt it was difficult work to enter in to the idea of Pt. Lekh Ram because he himself had the mental picture of the biography, only he knew the chronological order of the events, and how much of a particular version was to be accepted or rejected. After all odds master Atma Ram Amritsari with the support of his associates accomplished the work. The title of this biography is *Dayanand-Charit* and the language is Urdu. Later on its Hindi version came. The first edition of the book in Urdu was published on 25 October, 1897 from Lahore by the Arya Pratinidhi Sabha, Pubjab. The said book under the title of *Maharishi Dayanand Saraswati ka Jivan Charitra* translated from original Urdu in Hindi by Kaviraj Raghunandansingh 'Nirmal' and edited by Pandit Harshchandra Vidyalankar, Delhi, 1972.

The biography composed by Pandit Lekh Ram and Master Atmaram Amritsari is the first work on the biography of Swami Dayanand and also on the early history of Arya Samaj movement. Pandit Ghasi Ram a noted Arya Samaj scholar has said that said *Charit* in Urdu is mine of knowledge. None of the biographer of Swamiji cannot put a step ahead without the help of this. Thus, the said work became a basis of future writings on Arya Samaj and its founder. Only this has made it possible to continue the writings on Swamiji and Arya Samaj.[18] Even today it is equally important and relevant to the researchers on the History of Arya Samaj movement.

The most authentic biography of Swamiji is considered written by Babu Devandranath Mukhopadhyay and Pandit Ghasi Ram. In fact the writing of this was initiated by Shri Mukhopadhyay and accomplished by Pandit Ghasi Ram. But Pandit Ghasi Ram has humbly submitted that I have nothing of mine in the composition of this biography as I have only assembled the works of Pt. Lekh Ram, Swami Satyanand (Shrimad Dayanand Prakash) and material collected by Babu Mukhopadhyay. But this is most authentic *Jivancharit* of Swami Dayanand Saraswati. The history of the composition of this biography is itself very interesting.

A non-Arya Samaji Babu Devendranath Mukhopadhyay was highly impressed with the life of Swami Dayanand Saraswati. In 1894 he published a booklet in two parts in Bengali language in the title *Dayanand Charit.* Pt. Ghasi Ram came to know about this publication. He read it and wished to do it's *Arya-Bhasha* (Hindi) translation. Devendranath Babu himself was not satisfied with his booklet and he planned to write a detailed biography of Dayanand Saraswati. He began to collect the material for the same through field work and he extensively travelled all over India in the areas of the activities of Swamiji. He also visited Meerut in the connection of material collection, where he came into contact of Pt. Ghasi Ram. Pt. Ghasi Ram translated the Bangla booklet and got it published in 1913 with the permission of Devendranath babu. By 1915 or 1916 Babu Devendranath Mukhopadhyay completed the work of collection of material. He could write introduction and four chapters of *Dayanand-Charit* in Bangla and died due to physical ailment. Thereafter, the written and unwritten material of this work came into hands of Pt. Ghasi Ram in 1917-18.[19]

Pt. Ghasi Ram took the task into his hands to complete the work initiated by Devendranath Mukhopadhyay. By that time Swami Satyanand an Arya Samaji activist composed *Shrimad Dayanand Prakash* a *Granth* of devotion and *Bhatki.* The fact has also been mentioned by Pt. Ghasi Ram that Shrimad Dayanad Prakash was not written with historical point of view and was purely a devotional work. But he used it as a source of writing and Pandit Ghasi Ram finally composed the *Maharishi Dayanand Saraswati Ka Jivan Charit* in 1933.

The said biography is contented with the introduction by Pandit Ghasi Ram and preface & introduction by Devendranath Mukhopadhyaya. The main text is divided into twenty eight chapters and in the end five appendixes has been included. No doubt it is one of the extensive and authentic work on the biography of Swami Dayanand Saraswati. In the present form it is printed in 736 pages of big size. The narrations in this book are in their natural condition and no manipulation has been made by Pt. Ghasi Ram. Moreover, it has been composed with historical point of view and in unbiased manner as neither over exaggeration nor criticism has been made.

A noted work on the biography of Swami Dayanand Saraswati is of Bawa Chhajju Singh. The same was published in 1903 under the title *"Life and Teachings of Swami Dayanand Saraswati."*[20] Baba Chhajju Singh and Baba Arjun Singh both were brothers and prolific writers who contributed to the Arya Samaj literature. Bawa Arjun Singh was the first editor or Arya Patrika an English organ of Arya Pratinidhi Sabha, Punjab. The Arya Patrika was first published from Lahore in the month of June, 1885 as a weekly magazine. First it was brought out by Arya Samaj, Lahore, but after the bifurcation of the Arya Samaj in Lahore it went to Mahatma Party or the Gurukul section of the Samaj. After the untimely death of Bawa Arjun Singh, his elder brother Bawa Chhajju Singh became the editor of the Patrika.[21]

The second Reprinted edition of the biography of Swami Dayanand Saraswati by Bawa Chhajju Singh was published in 1971. The said book is in two parties. The part first has thirty six chapters containing in one hundred seventy one pages. In the end of first part fifty nine pictures based on photographs, portraits and sketches related to the life of Swamiji has been printed. The pictorial presentation is a special feature of this work. The second part of this book has eleven chapters containing one Hundred Eighty Five pages. In the end of second part appendix has been given detailed as under :

(i) The places where Swami Dayanand Saraswati paid visits in various dates.

(ii) Some important events of Swami Dayanand's Life.

(iii) A few elegant religious debates of Swami Dayanand Saraswati.

(iv) Homage to Swami Dayanand Saraswati by world's Great Personalities.

(v) Principales of Arya Samaj.

The first nine chapters of part first depicted the early life from his birth upto his meeting with Swami Virajanand and becoming his disciple. An independent chapter has been given on completion of studies undere Swami Virajanand. Remaining twenty seven chapters of part first throw ample light on the activities of Swami Dayanand Saraswati which included his visits of various places, his spiritual discourses, *shastrarthas etc.*

The second part began with the establishment of Arya Samajs in the U.P. and has covered the following topic : The Kumbha fair of 1879, tours in the UP and Bihar, the Barelli Shastrarth, the Arya Sanmarg Darshini Sabha, Tour in Rajasthan, the Jains and Swami Dayanand, Swami Dayanand and the Theosophical Society, illness and death, Great teacher and reformer as others saw him, Personality and character, works and teachings.

The efforts of Bawa Chhajju Singh are appreciable as he ably composed this volume like a serious researcher. He has thoroughly observed objectivity in his narrations. It has covered all the aspects of the life and works of Dayanand Saraswati with historicity. Thus, it is an exhaustive work on the History of Arya Samaj movement during the life time of its founder. Therefore, its importance as a source for writing and research on Arya Samaj is obvious.

In the category of biographical writings the works of Lal Lajpat Rai is worthy to mention. In 1914 his work entitled "A History of the Arya Samaj" (An Account of its origin, Doctrines and Activities with a Biographical Sketch of the Founder) was published by Orient Longman, London.[22] The book under review is not merely the biography but a complete analytical history of the Arya Samaj and it covers the period upto 1914. Thus, it has also covered the events of thirty one years after the death of Swamiji. And also the publication of this work is a land mark of Arya Samaj literature. It was great departure from the devotional literature as Lala Lajpat Rai wrote this work on the lines of modern historiography accepted internationally. He also took the assistance of some of his British friends in finalising the book. In the introduction he had specially mentioned two British scholar as follows : I am, besides, very grateful to Professor Sidney Webb, LL.D., for having read my manuscript and written for it a preface. It is to his learned wife and himself that I am indebted for the encouragement which has stimulated me to write this book, and it is they who impressed upon me the necessity for such a work in the interest of the Arya Samaj. My thanks in addition are due to my friend, Mr. W.F. Westbrook, for having read the manuscript and made valuable suggestions.[23]

The first Indian edition of 1967 is a revised form of the book written by Lajpat Rai. It has been edited by Sri Ram Sharma. Some extracts from editor's preface are worthy to mention here as under[24] :

In bringing out this revised edition, the text has been thoroughly revised, additional notes have been added where necessary. Citations of authorities have been checked and provided where needed. The divisioin of the book into three parts has been discarded and the arrangement of chapters recast. I have omitted the text of the Vedic mantras in Devnagri characters as it could not be of any interest to non-Sanskritists. Three appendixes have been added. The first, "Swami Dayananda and the Vedas", reproduces an article contributed by Aurobindo Ghosh to the *Vedic Magazine,* Haridwar. The second, "A Red Letter Day", reproduces an article I contributed to the *Indian Express,* on the D.A.V. College Foundation Day

(1 June). The last chapter was originally written by me for a seminar held in 1964 by the Delhi University on Indian Thought in the Nineteenth Century and Its Impact on Contemporary Civilization. The third appendix tries to throw some light on the author's own part in Indian politics which led to his deportation. The Bibliography has been revised and brought up to date.

I am grateful to the editorial department of Orient Longmans Ltd. for their help on bringing out this revised edition.

Despite much that has since been written on the Arya Samaj, this book continues to provide an overall view of the Arya Samaj, a critical biography of Swami Dayanand and an analytical account of the work it has been doing till 1914 when the book was first published. Its history since then has been mostly one of expansion of the tasks it had then undertaken. I have traced the outlines of that story till the death of Mahatma Hansraj in 1942 in *Mahatma Hansraj : A Maker of Modern Punjab.* The Bibliography includes some of the recent works that cover the post - 1914 period.

Following the author's plan, I have confined the Bibliography to works in English alone.

I have left the concluding chapter as the author wrote it. To revise it or to bring it up to date would have been a sacrilege which I thought I should not be guilty of.

The above statement of the editor gives a clear picture of the making of the present book under review. The book by Lala Lajpat Rai was written for use both in India and abroad. He felt that the English press was creating wrong notion among the English and European people towards Arya Samaj. Therefore, the demand for the Arya Samaj literature in English had been growing. He has written that, until recently, the Arya Samajas were quite content to continue their work of reform among their own people, and had no desire to attract the notice of the outside world. They have been drawn into the world arena much against their will. Circumstances have forced their hands, and they have learnt in the school of adversity and by bitter experience that quiet, unassuming work is liable to serious misconstruction and misrepresentation. So long as the Arya Samaj was attacked in India alone, it could not afford to ignore those attacks.[25] Therefore, to defend the activities of the Arya Samaj in the right perspective the book under review was written. Thus, a book based on sound analytical judgements came into being. The book is divided into fifteen chapters covering a wide range of aspects of the Arya Samaj movement and containing two hundred and seventeen printed pages.

The worth of the book written by Lala Lajpat Rai is proved with the fact that the author himself was devotee, worker and leader of the Arya Samaj. His sentiments and spirit behind this book which he has expressed in the introduction are worthy to read. Some extracts from the same are as follows :

The present work is an attempt to meet the need which we have explained. No one is more conscious of its defects than the writer himself, who can lay no claim either to profound knowledge or to excellence in style. His sole claim for being heard on the subject is that he has been in the movement ever since he was a boy of eighteen (A.D. 1882); that he has given the best part of his leisure time to the movement; that he has taken the lead in organizing several of its activities; that he owes a great deal of what may be considered old in him to its influence; and that the Samaj has passed through a serious political crisis on account of his connection with it. In the absence of abler and better qualified hands, having time and inclination to devote to the work, he has tried to do it from a sense of duty to and love for the Arya Samaj.

If the fact be considered that I have played some part in making the Samaj what it is, I shall perhaps be excused if I venture to recommend this book to those who, within a brief space, wish to make acquaintance with the society and its founders, and have a bird's eye view of its activities in the past. This book is meant for circulation both in and outside India - a fact which has contributed not inconsiderably to its bulk. Certain matters have been dealt with in detail for the benefit of non-Indians which might will have been omitted from a book intended for the use of Indians only; and *vice versa.* There is another matter which I should like to mention in connection with the preparation of this book : viz. that the whole of it was conceived, sketched and written in the course of not more than eight weeks, in London, far from the scene of the activities covered by it : and without the inestimable advantage of consultation with the leaders of the Samaj. My constant endeavour has been to take a detached, unbiased successful in doing so, since it must view of all things : but I do not know if I have been quite successful in doing so, since it must be admitted to be difficult to take a detached view of affairs in which one has been so intimately involved. This work is the first of its kind, and might be improved in subsequent editions, if it should be so fortunate as to find favour with those for whom it is meant.[26]

It is clear from the foregoing that it was very ambitious project of Lala Lajpat Rai which he accomplished efficiently. In a way it was a sort of nationalistic writings by which he could disseminate his own ideas and thoughts regarding the Arya Samaj and its founder. Thus an unique book could be written.

Life of Dayanand Saraswati (1945) by Har Bilas Sarda is a celebrated, detailed and authentic biography of Swamiji. It was published by the Propkarini Sabha, Ajmer. It's IInd edition has also been published by the Propkarini Sabha, Ajmer in 1968.[27]

The book contained in four parts and thirty three chapters. Part first entitled 'Life of Dayanand' contains nine chapters, second part is on 'works of Dayanand Saraswati' which contains four chapters, Part third 'Teachings of Dayanad Saraswati' is divided into six chapters and part four is on 'Religions and Sects in India' contains three chapters. This is very huge volume contained with vast material on the history of Arya Samaj movement. The volume bears an introduction of ninety pages, while main text contains six hundred nineteen pages.

Har Bilas Sarda himself was a staunch devotee, worker and leader of Arya Samaj. In the preface he has mentioned about only to biographies written by Pt. Lekh Ram and Babu Devendranath Mukhopadhyay. He has not made any reference of the books written before him by Bawa Chhajju Singh and Lala Lajpat Rai. Really it is an amazing fact. May be some internal matter of Arya Samaj people. Sarda has told that the Paropkarini Sabha celebrated the half century of Swami Dayanand Saraswti's death at Ajmer in October, 1933. The lack of an adequate Life of Swamiji in English was felt and some friends suggested that I should write it. In his own words he has underlined the need of his book as follows : Late in 1942 A.D. an occasion arose when the question of writing a life of Swami Dayanand Saraswti again pressed itself on my attention. And I began seriously to consider the matter. I remembered that when as a child I had gone with my father to have Swamiji's *darsana* in Fatehmal Bhadagtiya's garden at Ajmer, I had the inestimable privilege of exchanging a few words with him, and he had placed his hand on my head and blessed me. I also remembered that on the dipawali day S. 1940 (30 October, 1883 A.D.) I was present at the Bhinai House, Ajmer, where he breathed his last : that the next day I followed Swamiji's bire from the Bhinai House to the cremation ground at Malusar and present when the last rites were performed;

that I had the honour of listening to his lectures during the two of his visits to Ajmer, some sentences of which still ring in my ears. The sight of him sitting on the dias and deliver his discourses dominating the audience as I have seen no one else do is as fresh as ever. When I thought of all these and other memories crowding in my mind and I remembered that my life and beliefs had been greatly influenced by Swamiji's teachings, and that I owed a debt to him, my mind was made up and I decided that feeble and old as I was, and humble as my contribution in the circumstances would be, I should take up the work without further hesitation and pay my humble tribute ot him. Accordingly, during the last three years, 1943 to 1945 A.D., I have devoted all my energy and the little power of work that I still possessed to this work.[28]

The above statement indicates that the work under review was composed by Har Bilas Sarda out of his devotion as his homage to Swami Dayanand Saraswati. Apart from his devotion he has given his best and contributed a detailed volume on the biography of Swamiji. No doubt in my view it is best among all other biographies. He has put the matter in a very systematic manner. One thing which I wish to express that this volume contains maximum information and details about the history of Arya Samaj movement in Rajasthan. Har Bilas Sarda being resident of Rajasthan has unearthed many details regarding the activities of Swamiji and Arya Samaj in Rajasthan. I must say that this is the only published source of information about the Arya Samaj in Rajasthan. In all respect the book by Sarda is of worth reading. The ninety pages introduction of this book is part of essential readings, which is essence of thoughts and action of Swami Dayanand Saraswati. But being output of a devotee may raise some questions because the author has explained the thoughts and action of Swamiji as a devotee and he has justified everything related to Swami Dayanand Saraswati. But irrespective of all the book under review is a treasure of Arya Samaj theology and history. Thus, a combination of theology and history took excellent shape in form of "Life of Dayanand Saraswati" by Har Bilas Sarda.

A Most notable and noticeable work on the biography of Swami Dayanand Saraswati has been done by a foreigner J.T.F. Jordens (1978). His work entitled "Dayanand Sarasvati, His life and Ideas", published by the Oxford University Press, Delhi in 1978 has been well accepted in the academic circles.[29] It has been the first biography of Swamiji written by a non-devotee of Arya Samaj and non-Indian author. Jordens has analysed the early biographical writings and has also identified the shortcomings of such writings. On the biographies of Pt. Lekh Ram and Devendranath Mukhopadhyay J.T.F. Jorden has commented that : These two had done valuable pioneering work in tracking down oral and printed sources, and had collected a mass of data that otherwise would have been utterly lost. Lekh Ram's volume did not really get beyond the collating stage : the documents and testimonies are not even arranged chronologically. However, in many ways his work has to value of a primary source because it contains numerous verbatim reports of eyewitnesses' stories, and also several transcripts of the Swami's discussions. Mukhopadhyay added new first-hand material to this as the result of his tireless travels in search of documents, and witnesses : but he too was unable to finish his task.[30] In his view the effort of Pt. Ghasiram was not more than presenting the vital raw material for a historical biography and the material too was confined to the activities and sayings of the Swamiji. Moreover, he has commented that practically all subsequent biographers simply used that work and went very little beyond its narrow confines. Even Har Bilas Sarda's extensive English biography adds little to that of Ghasiram.

The biography of Dayanand Saraswati written by J.T.F. Jordens is considered as one of the best biography. He is of the view that most of biographers themselves belonged to the Arya Samaj and they portraited their guru the Swamiji as an object of their beliefs. Therefore, they did not question any thought and action of Swamiji. Jordens has asked a question about such biographers that : Although they describe the success of Dayanand in the Doab, in Calcutta, in Bombay, in Panjab, and in U.P., they have written in an isolated manner as they have not seen the activities and thoughts of Swamiji in the perspective of a nineteenth century phenomenon of social and religious movement. Jordens has specifically stated that : These writers do not ask the important question why the Swami spent the last years of his life in Rajputana, or why he became involved in the movements for the promotion of cow-protection and of Hindu.[31]

The biography entitled "Dayanand Saraswati, His Life and Ideas" written by J.T.F. Jordens contains twelve chapters, covering main aspects of Swamiji's life. In addition to preface and introduction it is contained in 368 pages. The author has applied the historical method of enquiry. Therefore, its value as a historical work is immense. The book under review may also serve the purpose of source material for writings and research on the history of Arya Samaj movement. One more fact which I wish to mention here is that Jorden has contributed a full separate chapter on Rajputana in the title "The Ultimate Effort: The Princes of Rajputana".

J.T.F. Jordens (1998) has also got published another important work on Dayanand Saraswati.[32] His work entitled "Dayanand Sarasvati, Essays on His Life and Ideas" is a collection of his essays on various themes. It is a collection of thirteen essays divided into four thematic parts as follows : Part I : Biographical; Part II : Doctrinal; Part III : comparative ;

and Part IV : Arya Samaj. In the end a detailed bibliography and Index is given. The same is well documented work. The essays are not limited to the period of Swamiji's life and it has covered larger period than that. The volume under review is also useful for understanding of Arya Samaj movement in right perspective. It may also serve as an important source for future writing and research.

One more work of J.T.F. Jordens (1981) is of worth mention which is on the biography of Swami Shraddhananda a leading figure after Swami Dayanand Saraswati. The book entitled "Swami Shradhananda, His life and Causes", deserves appreciation because this has added immensely to the knowledge and history of Arya Samaj.[33] The author himself has underlined his objective behind writing this as follows : After having written a work on Swami Dayanand Sarasvati I decided to continue my study of the Arya Samaj from the eighteen eighties into the third decade of the twentieth century. Swami Shraddhananda seemed to be a most appropriate figure to focus upon. He not only played a leading role in the new developments inside the Samaj, and became the major initiator of a new concept of Arya education, but he also emerged as a key figure in Congress politics and in the *shuddhi* and *sangathan* movements of the twenties. Thus he played a mojor part in the great transformation that changed the social composition of the Arya Samaj, and brought its members into both Congress politics and the movement for Hindu *sangathan.*[34]

The book under review on Swami Shraddhananda covers a major period of the Arya Samaj Movement and as well as the freedom movement of India. Swami Shraddhananda entered in the independence movement in 1917. He also participated in the nationwide protest against the Rowlatt Act. He presided over the Amritsar session of Indian National Congress in 1919. In 1923 he took the leadership of *Suddhi* movement and became the president of Bhartiya Hindu Shuddhi Sabha. On 23 December 1926 he was assassinated by a fanatic Muslim. He is also well known for his work for the emancipation of untouchables. Thus, the Swami Shraddhananda phase of Arya Samaj movement was an important phase contained with multifarious activities. Therefore, the work under review is an important and useful source of enquiry into the history of Arya Samaj movement.

The book by Jordens on Swami Shraddhanda contains six chapters and 210 pages. In the end of the book a detailed bibliography is appended for the help of future researchers.

In the category of biographical writings the work of Bhawanilal Bhartiya (1983) entitled "Navajagaran Ke Purodha: Dayanand Saraswati" in Hindi is of worth mention.[35] It is considered as one of the best biography of Swamiji written in Hindu after the work of Babu Devendranath Mukhopadhyay accomplished by Pt. Ghasiram. Bhawanilal Bhartiya wrote this book on the occasion of hundredth death anniversary of Swami Dayanad Saraswati. Bhartiya has been a devotee and follower of Arya Samaj and out of his faith and devotion he authored and brought out this work. Moreover, Bhartiya is a prolific author of Arya Samaj literature. As per his own statement he is engaged in writing on the themes of Dayanand since sixty years and he has contributed about 75-80 books in the form of authored, edited and translated works. The popularity of the book under review is evident from the fact that its second edition in two volumes published in 2009.[36] The title of second edition is "Nava Jagaran ke Purodha : Maharishi Dayanand Saraswati." Both the volumes contain one thousand pages. Though, there is no major change in main text contents including numbers and titles of the chapters. The new material and informations has been added in introductory part in the beginning and concluding part in the end. There are seven items in the appendix of first edition, while the number reached upto twelve in the second edition. The introduction of the first edition has been written by Satyaprakash Saraswati, which is also the part of second edition. While, the second edition bears a preface, written by T.N. Chaturvedi the Governor of Karnatka. In the same manners a conclusion of one and half pages written by author Bhawanilal Bhartiya has been attached in the extreme end. The photos and maps in both the editions are different. Therefore, both the editions are useful for readers and writers both.

The book by Bhartiya is an exhaustive work written in Hindi language. The author is not critical in approach but he has given serious thought to each description and he has also discovered various new facts which are not available in other works. Thus, the book is an essential readings for the future researches and writers.

Here I would like to mention about one more biographical work which I read in the beginning of this project during the process of preparing the proposal. The book entitled "Svami Dayanand : A Biography" authored by J.M. Sharma (1998) deserves appreciation.[37] The author has also clarified in the beginning that he is in the third generation of a family of Arya Samajists. Thus, his faith in the thoughts and action of Swami Dayanand Saraswati is self proven and undisputed. The author himself is neither an academician nor a theologist but out of his devotional spirits he produced this book. By underlining the need of his book the author stated that : one cannot fully understand Hinduism in its present form without comprehending the vital role played by Svami Dayanand in according a new direction and a new dimension to this centuries old religion. A large number of reformers have worked towards the restructuring of Hinduism, but the name of Dayanand stands out among them. Unfortunately very little is known about this remarkable individual, especially to the English - educated Indians. This volume seeks to fill that lacuna.[38] In addition to preface, context and prologue the book contains two hundred eighty three pages and the book bears twenty chapters. In the introduction the author has made clear about the theme of book that : This book attempts to recount the story of an extraordinary man who converted ethnic Hinduism into a missionary religion. It seeks to unravel the travails of this individual who liberated the Vedas from the custody of Brahmins and opened them to women, Shudras, ati-Shudras (the lowest castes); nay, in fact, to all humankind. It reveals how one determined crusader rescued Hinduism from the stranglehold of otherworldliness and infused it with the positive, globally valid philosophy of the Vedas. He was a reformer who rekindled a political will among Hindus, and gave the slogan of self-rule, ten years before the birth of the Indian National Congress and at a time when the country's political leaders were agitating merely for a greater share in the government. During the course of his life, he made the greatest contribution to the promotion of Hindi as the national language. He was the one who gave us the popular greeting *Namaste.* On the basis of his vast and varied experiences, he revived the Vedic ritual of *agnihotra* (fire sacrifice), now an essential feature of almost all Hindu ceremonies. This man was Svami Dayanand Sarasvati, the founder of the Arya Samaj. During his lifetime, Hindu orthodoxy, Christian missionaries and Muslim Mullahs were all ranged against him. He was abused, assaulted and even attempts on his life were made, but he remained steadfast in his beliefs.[39]

The book by J. M. Sharma is mainly based on secondary sources which evident from the references and bibliography. Before writing this book the author has gone through other biographies composed by many biographers. Thus he has extracted all such biographical and historical literature to produce this book. He has put the things in logical and chronological order. Therefore, the book is in smooth rhythm and easily understandable. Thus, the book is comprehensive in nature. It gives an analytical insight to the reader. Hence, the book deserves a status of reference and resource book.

The last work which I have to mention in the series of biography of Swami Dayanand Saraswati is an edited work by Suresh K. Sharma (2009). This is a collection of Sixty one articles in two volumes. The title of the book is "Swami Dayananda and the Arya Samaj Movement". In volume one there are 35 articles on Biographical Aspect and volume two bears 26 articles on Religious, Social and Educational aspects. These articles may serve the purpose of reference material. But, this book has one drawback that titles and authors of these collected articles has been mentioned, but the sources from which these has been copied has not been mentioned completely. However, this may serve the purpose of study on the Arya Samaj movement.

Books on Arya Samaj

"The origin, Scope and Mission of the Arya Samaj" by Ganga Prasad Upadhyay (1940) is a foremost compact book written on the history and theology of Arya Samaj. In a very brief preface the author has underlined his objective as follows : These days religion is looked upon as a bugbear. Yet mankind has not been able to give up religiosity. To banish religion is one thing; to try to free it from the bondage of pretenders quite another. We entirely agree with the view of the great modern scientist Max Planck *that the religions element in his nature must be recognised and cultivated if all the powers of the human soul are to act together in perfect balance and harmony.* True religiosity is the only bed-rock on which the great fabric of human progress can be built in safety. It is to expound this view that the books of the Religious Renaissance Series are being written.[40]

The author has further more explained the objective of the book under review as follows : The Arya Samaj is a well known organisation founded by Swami Dayanand Saraswati on April 7, 1875 in Bombay. In these sixty-five years, the society has made a great progress and at present there are no less than two thousand Arya Samajs all over India, and a few hundred in Burma, Africa, Baghadad, Fiji and Southern America. Its adherents according to the last Census Report were about 10 lacs in India and States. That the Arya Samaj is a mighty movement very few realise. Even those who are in close contact with it are unaware of its potentials. That the fact remains that from its very birth, it has been influencing almost every department of human life in India. There is hardly any political party, religious and social movement of the country which does not have its vital inspiration to the Arya Samaj. And that there are few who are prepared to acknowledge it. There are many group of people who look on the Arya Samaj with a hostile eye.

This hostility is differently expressed in different circles. Some persons have special misgivings about the movement. But even such persons have borrowed much from the Arya Samaj, though unknowingly. The Arya Samaj has thus benefited all, directly and indirectly, and the more people come to understand the movement, the more they will learn to support this cause. The present book proposes to put before the public a brief survey of the movement, its objects and activities.[41]

The book 'The Origin, Scope and Mission of the Arya Samaj'. Under review is a brief history of Arya Samaj movement in India from 1875-1940. The book contains sixteen chapters and one hundred eighty pages. Thus, the book is worthy even for advance readings as it has covered the major aspects. The author has his own methodology and the work is based on primary and secondary sources. Though, the author is not critical in his approach but his analytical insight is reflected in his logical presentation. Therefore, it may also serve that purpose of a resource book. Conclusively, this is a periodical work and a land mark in the writing of history of Arya Samaj. Thus, the work under review created a basis of writing the history of Arya Samaj.

An exhaustive and official history of the Arya Samaj appeared in 1957 written in Hindi by Indra Vidyyavachaspati. Indra Vidyavachaspati was a man of multifarious talent and specialities. He was son of Swami Shradhanand a noted Arya Samaj leader and freedom fighter. He has good qualities as a journalist, educationist, historian ad politician. The title of the book by Indra Vidyavachaspati is "Arya Samaj ka Itihas", Pratham Bhag Evam Dwitiya Bhag (1957 A.D., V.S. 2013).[42] It has been published by the Sarvadeshik Arya Pratinidhi Sabha, therefore, its status as official history of Arya Samaj is self proved.

The author has made it clear that in the year 1917 Swami Shraddhanand decided to prepare the history of Arya Samaj. Accordingly he began the collection of source material, but due to his over busyness he could not begin the writing work. Before his death he verbally expressed his will to get the work accomplished by Indra Vidyavachaspati or he made his will in favour of Vdyavachaspati to write the said history. Thus, he got the responsibility of history writing in succession. Swami Shraddhanand was assassinated on 23 December, 1926. The author could not fulfil the resolution of writing history even after twenty years of said demise of Shraddhanandji. But his effort could remain continue and could be completed in 1957. Thus, the work under review took about forty years in completion. Both of the volumes of the said book have been published together and as per the introduction it is the first complete history of Arya Samaj upto 1957.

The part one contains 360 pages, six sections, forty eight chapters and ten annexures. It bears a lucidly written introduction in historical reference. The preface of the book is written by Dr. Gokulchand Narang a noted scholar on Arya Samaj. In the same manner the part two contains 376 pages, seventy one chapters, six sections and two annexures. No doubt it is an unparallel work on the history of Arya Samaj. It's value as primary source of history is self proved.

Radhe Shaym Pareek's (1965) work entitled "Contribution of Arya Samaj in the making of Modern India 1875-1947" is an outcome of Ph.D. thesis in political science.[43] The book contains 375 pages and eight chapters. This also bears a glossary of technical terms, Abbreviations and an extensive bibliography. The chapter I, India on the eve of the Establishment of Arya Samaj, discusses the social, economic, political and cultural conditions. The organisation of Arya Samaj is depicted in chapter II and chapter III discusses the Arya Samaj as a movement of Religious Reforms. The chapter IV is on Social Reform of the Samaj, while, the contribution of the Arya Samaj to Education is discussed in the chapter V. The political Thought of Dayanand formed the chapter VI and the Political Thought after Dayanand has been discussed in chapter VII. The Arya Samaj and the National movement has been narrated and analysed in the last, i.e. chapter VIII. There is no consolidated conclusion of the study but each chapter bears separate conclusion. The work is based on wide range of primary and secondary sources in a balanced manner. It is a kind of macro level study, therefore much detail on the contribution of Arya Samaj in Rajasthan are not available in this book. The said book talks more on general trends on the subject. Being a research and reference book it is useful for future research and writings.

The book entitled "The Arya Samaj and Indian Nationalism (1875-1920)", by Dhanpati Pandey (1972), is also a by product of Ph.D. thesis in History.[44] In addition to forward, Preface, Abbreviation and contents the book contains 203 pages and seven chapters. In the end it bears a general conclusion and bibliography. The forward of this book is written by Padama-Bhushan Dr. Dukhan Ram, the President of the International League of the Arya Samaj. Dr. Ram has reacted that in his (author) opinion, the Samaj's main aim was to emancipate India from the British Yoke. It is the effort of the author to show that long before the Indian National Congress, took up the programme of Swadeshi, Boycott, national education, national language and social amelioration, the Samaj and its founder, Swami Dayanand Saraswati had already stressed on these national aspects and reforms.[45] The author has underlined the differences between Swami Dayanand and his contemporary reformers as follows : But Swami Dayanand, the founder of the Arya Samaj, stood against Western influences. He was the first reformer to depart from this tradition and gave an indigenous orientation to Indian nationalism.[46] Thus, the author has looked at the role of Arya Samaj in the rise and growth of Indian Nationalism. But again this work is also of macro and general type as it did not took cognizance of the influences and activities of Arya Samaj at regional and local level. The author has discussed the general trends, concepts and theory or say thoughts but analysis of action is absent. Irrespective of all shortcomings the book under review is an important contribution in the history of Arya Samaj movement.

Kenneth W. Jones (1976) an American Professor of history at Kansas State University, Manhattan has worked on the Arya Samaj in Punjab and brought a book entitled "Arya Dharm : Hindu Consciousness in 19th Century Punjab."[47]This is the first micro level study which focuses on regional level activities and events occurred in Punjab in reference to Arya Samaj. It is printed on the jacket of the book that : The major focus of this book is on modernizing movements - social, religious, and cultural - among Punjabi Hindus from the 1860s through world war I. The Arya Samaj, one such volume, as it dominated a half century of change in the Punjab. Jones begins with an account of the earliest individual attempts of reformers to adapt their cultural tradition to the new world of the British Empire. He examines the development of new ideologies, the creation of group consciousness based on them, and the resultant expression of an overt Hindu politics. He demonstrates that the process underlying cultural interaction between the British and Punjabi Hindus, beginning in a particularistic manner, found expression by the twentieth century in the demands of politicized Hindu elite. He also delineates the pattern of communal conflict among Hindus, Muslims, and Sikhs and the dynamic of the British Raj that contributed to this conflict.

Prof. Kenneth in the opening para of the preface of the book has stated that : Cultural interaction between the British and South Asians, between rulers and ruled, dominates the history of nineteenth century British India. The conquest of South Asia and the establishment of the British Raj brought western civilization through the medium of British culture into direct contact with the Indo-Muslim civilization of South Asia. From this confrontation emerged a new colonial culture neither wholly English nor completely South Asian, but a unique way of life peculiar to the British Raj.[48]

It evident from the above that Kenneth has big ideological canvas. The author has seen the rise of nationalism in terms of rise of Hindu consciousness or Hindu nationalism, which is highly defective and unacceptable. Though, element of cultural nationalism is there but not in communal terms. The facts and events in this book seem authentic but their analysis is not unbiased. No doubt that the religious and social reform movement or renaissance of 19th century gave birth to cultural nationalism, later on which became the basis of economic and political nationalism. But the stream of cultural nationalism remained parallel to the political and economic nationalism. Thus, the use of this book requires serious precautions. Irrespective of some shortcomings the book makes the part of essential readings for writers and researchers on Arya Samaj. Movement.

On the occasion of Maharishi Dayanand Death centenary celebrations in 1983 the Paropkarini Sabha, Ajmer, published the "Dayanand Commemoration Volume" (Maharishi Dayanand Nirvan-Shati Smritigranth), Edited by Svami Satya Pakash Sarasvati.[49] It is a huge collection of articles written in English and Hindi. The articles are not in bilingual form as some of the articles are in English and some in Hindi. Most of the articles are contributed by followers of Arya Samaj. Thus, these are the kind of devotional articles paying homage to the founder of the Arya Samaj. But at the same time these contains various important facts and information. The material available in these articles is useful for research and writing on the Arya Samaj.

K.C. Yadav and K.S. Arya (1988), Jointly wrote the book entitled "Arya Samaj And The Freedom Movement, Volume one : 1875-1918" which is also an important work on a vital theme.[50] The Arya Samaj movement had been in the background of the rise of national consciousness in India during the 19th century. And particularly it has played important role in northern India. The book is mainly concentrated on Punjab and has also reported some events and development occurred in United Provinces. It lack the informations related to Rajasthan, while there the Arya Samaj activities were in abundance. In a chapter on Arya Samaj and the Revolutionary Movement the author has mentioned about the revolutionary activities of Govind Guru and Keshari Singh Barhath, who belongs to Rajasthan.[51]

I have seen the file of Govind Guru at the National Archives of India and he has no association with the Arya Samaj. Yes, Keshari Singh Barhath was a revolutionary but he too have no direct link with the Arya Samaj. Therefore, as far as the Rajasthan is concerned the book under review has no substantial information and material related to the Arya Samaj Movement.

The book by K.C. Yadav and K.S. Arya under review contains 394 pages, three parts and nine chapters. The main text on the theme of book divided into eight chapters in part first. The part second includes the chapter nine which is on eminent Arya Freedom Fighters, 1875-1918 and the part third bears the Appendices, Bibliography and index. The book is intensively concentrated on the theme without any deviation which is evident from the chapters as follows : Swami Dayanand ; His political Message and Impact, Arya Samaj's contributions to political Awakening and National consciousness, Arya Samaj and the Swadeshi Movement, British Government's Hostility towards Arya Samaj and Pubjab Disturbances, Persecution of Arya Samaj, 1875-1918, Arya Samajists and unrest in the Army, Arya Samaj and the Congress movement and Arya Samaj and the Revolutionary Movement.

The work under review is a fine product created by the mature scholars' based on wide range of source material. This may guide the future researches and writings.

Another official history of Arya Samaj after Indra Vidyavachaspati has been composed by Satyaketu Vidyalankar as author and chief Editor. The book entitled "Aryasamaj Ka Itihas" has been published in Seven Volumes (1985-1988).[52] The book under review is a treasure of informations on the Aryasamaj as it is prepared under an ambitious scheme of history writing of Sarvadeshik Arya Pratinidhi Sabha. Its first volume has been published in 1985, while the last volume seven came out in 1988. For the purpose of preparing the history a editorial board was constituted. This included Satyaketu Vidyalankar as chief Editor and among the members Priyavrat Vedavachaspati, Prithvi Singh Mehta, Haridutt Vidyalankar, Bhawani Lal Bhartiya, Dhanpati Pandey, Rajendra Jigyasu, Kshem Chhandra Suman and Vedpratap Vedic are included. The basic drawback of this work is vary serious as it has lacked the references of source material. Therefore, many details looks like concocted. Thus, this is not merely a drawback rather it is basic defect.

The collected works of Lal Lajpat Rai edited by B.R. Nanda (2003-2010) are also important source of the history of Aryasamaj.[53] This is a set of 15 volumes which include the articles, speeches, letters, memorandums etc. of Lal Lajpat Rai. Being an Aryasamajist he has written extensively on various aspects of the Arya Samaj. When the Aryasamajists and their organisations were being targeted by the British during the Swadeshi movement and onwards then Lajpat Rai was the sole defender of Arya Samaj. Therefore, his writings proved very useful source of information for the researchers and writers on Arya Samaj.

Sangeeta Sharma's (2010) work "Women's Liberation : The Arya Samaj Movement in India" deserves cognizance and appreciation as it is an extensive research work on one of the most progressive activity of Arya Samaj.[54] The author has stated that : The present work explores the decisive and unique contribution of Dayanand Saraswati and Arya Samaj in the realm of social reform, particularly the comprehensive, structured and multi-layered programme that they initiated for women's liberation. The primary campaign of the Arya Samaj were in the realm of women's education wherein they were able to translate the theoretical debates of the nineteenth century into concrete programmes.

The Samajist success was most noteworthy in the sphere of rehabilitation of of widows wherein they displayed exceptional commitment in formulating strategies and programme for amelioration of their deplorable lot. This work is therefore focused on the holistic perspective, multi pronged strategies and whole hearted enthusiasm of the movement on issues like women's education and widow remarriage.[55]

Sangeeta Sharma's book included the chapters like women in the nineteenth century : context and Perspective, Indian Renaissance, Tradition, Dayanand and the Vedas, women in the Vedic Age, Dayanand's concept of womanhood, issues of widowhood : Samajist Perspective, liberating women : Marriage, Caste and *Purda,* Pioneer of women's Education etc. The book is based on Ph.D. thesis which presents the problem in right perspective. The author has tapped wide range of primary and secondary sources to complete this study. The study of this book will certainly give and insight to the future researchers and writers.

Writings on the Arya Samaj Movement in Rajasthan

It is clear from the forgoing description that sizable works has been done on the history of Arya Samaj movement. But most of these works either are of general nature or focuses mainly on Punjab and United Provinces. Few of these have given information about Rajasthan (erstwhile Rajputana). After going through the biographical works on Swami Dayanand Saraswati it is ascertained that the book of Harbilas Sarda throws ample light on the activities and achievements of Swamiji and Arya Samaj in Rajasthan upto 1883.

Author has not come yet across any work of worth mention on Arya Samaj movement in Rajasthan. Even there is not a single introductory booket in existence on Arya Samaj in Rajasthan as part of Arya Samaj's propaganda literature. As far as the research work on Arya Samaj in Rajasthan is concerned the first attempt has been made by K.S. Saxena (1971) in his work 'The Political Movements And Awakening in Rajasthan (1857-1947)' has contributed about eight pages on the role of Arya Samaj in the growth of political awakening in Rajasthan.[56] Subsequently, Richard Sission (1972) in his work 'The Congress Party in Rajasthan' has also contributed four pages on the political growth of Jat community under the influence of Arya Samaj.[57] In the same manner Shyamlal (2008) in his book 'Ambedkar and Dalit Movement has contributed six pages on the efforts of Arya Samaj in eradication of untouchability and emancipation of Dalits in Rajasthan.[58] Myself Brij Kishore Sharma (2008) in the book 'Social, Economic and Political Contribution of Caste Associations in Northern India (A case study of All India Jat Mahasabha)' has discuss the role of Arya Samaj in social emancipation of Jat community also in Rajasthan.[59] In my work Mass Movements and Freedom struggle in Rajasthan (2013). I have precisely traced in brief the contribution of Arya Samaj in the freedom movement of Rajasthan.[60] Now it is clear from the foregoing narration that the field of research on Arya Samaj in Rajasthan largely remained unexplored. Thus, an effort has been made in the present study to fill up the gap existed.

Apart from published books on the Arya Samaj movement in Rajasthan the work in the form of published articles is also insignificant. Prof. V.K. Vashishtha's (1978) research article 'Arya Samaj Movement in Rajasthan during Nineteenth Century' is the only well researched article.[61] But it has also its limits as it is confined to the nineteenth century. Being a brief article it could not address all the aspects and issues related to Arya Samaj movement in Rajasthan. Thus, it could have only presented an outline for future researchers. The article by Prithvi

Singh Mehta (1986) entitled *'Swatantrata Andolan : Mewar aur Arya Samaj'* is written in Hindi is a sort of memoir as it has no reference.[62] It seems based on oral sources. The author is himself anArya Samajist and he has also authored a book in Hindi 'Hamara Rajasthan' (1950). Thus, the article under review is an introductory one and lack the historical methodology. Tej Kumar Mathur and Meghna Sharma's (2005) research article 'The efforts of Arya Samaj in elevating the condition of women folk in Rajasthan : In light of its publications (1875-1950)', superficially reveals the facts relating to the contribution of Arya Samaj in emancipation of women.[63] The source-material of this article is limited to the published material of Arya Samaj. Moreover, being very brief article it could not address all the aspects of the emancipation of women. N.K. Sharma's article (2005) entitled *"Shaikshnik Kshetra mein Arya Samaj ka Yogdan (1865 se 1949 Tak)"*, written in Hindi gives and introductory outline regarding the educational activities of Arya Samaj in Rajasthan.[64] Professor V.K. Vashishtha's (2012) article entitled *'Bhartiya Swatantrata Andolan Mein Ajmer-Merwada Mein Arya Samaj ka Yogdan'* is well document and well researched.[65] The said article covers the period of freedom movement from 1905-1947.

The foregoing account of research articles on the Arya Samaj Movement is not encouraging. Therefore, the research and writing on the subject is much more needed.

Relevance of the Present Study

In the scenario of foregoing review of literature the relevance of the present study is self-explanatory. Moreover, the Rajasthan witnessed the early activities of Swami Dayanand Saraswati and Arya Samaj, and Ajmer became the centre of Arya Samaj movement but no work of worth mention on the history of Arya Samaj movement in Rajasthan has been done. Hence, the present study is a humble and modest effort in this direction. This study shall bridge gap existed in the knowledge of Arya Samaj Movement in Rajasthan.

The establishment of Arya Samaj organisations in Rajasthan proved a miracle because in the arch reactionary feudal setup it rise as ray of hope. Before the Arya Samaj there was not a single organisation founded on the modern lines. Indeed, in the background of the rise of nationalism the socio-religious reform movements played an important role in the rise of nationalism in India, but in the context of Rajasthan these created general awareness. The people began to discuss their social, political and economic surroundings which impressed them to think beyond the existing situations. Hence, the establishment of Arya Samaj organisation initiated the process of modern thinking. Therefore, the present study may prove its worth.

The social, religious and educational activities awakened the masses in Rajasthan. The people began to come out of their conservatism and religious darkness and the Arya Samaj made the people politically conscious of their rights and duties. It created spirit of self-respect, self-confidence and self-esteem among the people and also generated a new consciousness in all spheres of national life. Thus, the Arya Samaj became a vehicle of political and national regeneration of the country in general and Rajasthan in particular. In this way the contribution of Arya Samaj has been evaluated and analysed in the future pages of the present work.

Notes

1. Bhawanilal Bhartiya, *Navjagaran ke Purodha Dayanand Saraswati,* Vedic Pustakalaya, Paropkarini Sabha, Ajmer, V.S. 2040 (1981 A.D.), pp. 582-83. Prof. Vithal Rao the Secrtary of Sarvadeshik Arya Pratinidhi Sabha, Delhi Claims that he (Bhartiya) wrote 66 books spanning some 17000 pages.

2. *Arya Patrika,* 9 August, 1887.
3. Kenneth W. Jones, *Arya Dharm,* Manohar Publications, New Delhi, 2006, Reprint (First Ed. 1976), p. 127.
4. Christophe Jaffrelot, *Religion, Caste and Politics in India,* Primus Books, 2018 Reprinted (First Ed. 2010), p. 83.
5. Har Bilas Sarda, *Life of Dayanad Saraswati,* Paropakarini Sabha, Ajmer, 1968, Reprinted, IInd Edition (First Editioin 1945), p. 401.
6. Kenneth W. Jones, (p. 35) writes him as collector of Aligarh while Har Bilas Sarda has mentioned him (p. 400) as Deputy Collector of Banaras.
7. Har Bilas Sarda, *op.cit,* p. 400.
8. The name Swamiji gave to Hindi.
9. Introduction to the Second Edition of the *Satyarth Prakash* by Swamiji, P.X. An English translation by Chiranjiva Bhardwaja, Published by Sarvdeshik Arya Pratinidhi Sabha, New Delhi, 2015 (Reprinted). The title of this translated version is "Light of Truth".
10. Sub-Preface to the Part II of the above translated edition of *Satyarth Prakash.*
11. *Ibid.*
12. Introduction by Swamiji to the Second Edition of *Satyarth Prakash,* translated by Chiranjiva Bhardwaj, p. XIII.
13. *Ibid,* pp. XIII-XIV.
14. *Ibid,* pp. XVII.
15. First edition of the *Sanskarvidhi* was published in 1877 by the Asiatic Press, Bombay and second edition was published in 1884 by the Vedic Yantralaya, Prayag.
16. K.C. Yadav (Ed.), *The autobiography of Dayanand Saraswati,* First Edition 1976, Manohar Publications, New Delhi.
17. *Punjab Samachar,* March 6, 1897.

18. Devendranath Mukhopadhyay, *Maharishi Dayanand Saraswati ka Jivan Charit,* Reprinted 2013, Hindaun City, first published in Banlga in 1916 and again published in Hindi in 1933 with an introduction and translation by Pandit Ghashi Ram, pp. 2-3.
19. *Ibid,* pp. 3-4.
20. Bawa Chhajju Singh, *Life and Teachings of Swami Dayanand Saraswati,* Reprinted Second edition 1971 (First edition 1903), Jan Gyan Prakashan, New Delhi.
21. *Ibid,* the introductory note about the author.
22. Lala Lajpat Rai, *A History of the Arya Samaj (An Account of its Origin, Doctrines and Activities with a Biographical Sketch of the Founder),* Orient Longmans (Longmans, Green And Co. Ltd.), London, 1914. I have got the revised and enlarged edition, first publication in India in 1967 by the Orient Longmans, New Delhi.
23. *Ibid,* p. 6.
24. *Ibid,* pp. V-VI .
25. *Ibid,* p. 2.
26. *Ibid,* pp. 3 and 5.
27. Har Bilas Sarda, *Life of Dayanand Saraswati,* Propkarini Sabha, Ajmer, IInd Editioin, 1968.
28. *Ibid,* p. F and G of Preface.
29. J.T.F. Jordens, *Dayanand Saraswati, His Life and Ideas,* Oxford University Press Delhi, 1978.
30. *Ibid,* p. XIII.
31. *Ibid,* p. XIV.
32. J.T.F. Jordens, *Dayanand Saraswati, Essay on His Life and Ideas,* Manohar Publication, New Delhi, 1998.
33. J.T.F. Jordens, *Swami Shraddhananda, His Life and Causes,* Oxford University Press, Delhi, 1981.

34. *Ibid,* Preface, p. vii.
35. Bhawanilal Bhartiya, *Navajagaran Ke Purodha : Dayanand Saraswati,* Vaidik Pustakalaya, Paropakarini Sabha, Dayanand Ashram, Ajmer, 1983.
36. Bhawanilal Bhartiya, *Navajagaran Ke Purodha : Dayanand Saraswati,* Vaidik Pustakalaya, Shri Ghudmal Prahladkumar Arya Dharmarth Nyas, Hindaun City (Rajasthan), 2009.
37. J.M. Sharma, *Swami Dayanad : A Biography,* UBS Publishers, New Delhi, 1998.
38. *Ibid,* Preface, p. III.
39. *Ibid,* Prologue, pp. 1-2.
40. Ganga Prasad Upadhyay, *The Origin, Scope and Mission of Arya Samaj,* Printed by J.K. Sharma at the Allahabad Law Journal Press, Arya Samaj Chowk, Allahabad, 1940.
41. *Ibid,* pp. 2-4.
42. Indra Vidyavachaspati, *Arya Samaj Ka Itihas,* Pratham Bhag Evam Dwitiya Bhag, Published by Sarvadeshik, Arya Pratinidhi Sabha, Delhi, 1957.
43. Radhey Shyam Pareek, *Contribution of Arya Samaj in the Making of Modern India 1875-1975,* Published by Saravdeshik Arya Pratinidhi Sabha, Delhi, 1973.
44. Dhanpati Pandey, *The Arya Samaj and Indian Nationalism (1875-1920),* S. Chand & Co., New Delhi, 1972.
45. *Ibid,* p. VII, Foreword.
46. *Ibid,* p. 13.
47. Kenneth W. Jones, *Arya Dharm : Hindu Consciousness in 19th Century Punjab,* Manohar Publishers, New Delhi, 1976, Reprinted 1989, 2006.
48. *Ibid,* p. IX, Preface.
49. Swami Satya Prakash Sarasvati (Ed.), *Dayanand Commemoration Volume, (Maharshi Dayanand Nirvanshati Smritigranth),* Paropkarini Sabha, Ajmer, 1983.

50. K.C. Yadav, K.S. Arya, Arya Samaj And The Freedom Movement, Volume One : 1875-1918, Manohar Publishers, New Delhi, 1988.
51. *Ibid*, pp. 204-9.
52. Satyaketu Vidyalankar (Chief Editor), Aryasamaj ka Itihas, Seven Volumes, Arya Swadhyay Kendra, Sarvadeshik Arya Pratinidhi Sabha, New Delhi, 1985-1988.
53. B.R. Nanda (Editor), *Collected Works of Lala Lajpat Rai,* 15 volume, Manohar Publishers, New Delhi, 2003-2010.
54. Sangeeta Sharma, *Women's Liberation : The Arya Samaj Movement in India*, Rawat Publication, Jaipur, 2010.
55. *Ibid*, pp. IX-X, Preface.
56. K.S. Saxena, *The Political Movements and Awakening in Rajasthan (1857-1947)*, S. Chand & Co., New Delhi, 1971.
57. Richard Sisson, *The Congress Party in Rajasthan,* Oxford University Press, Delhi, 1972.
58. Shaymalal, *Ambedkar and Dalit Movement,* Rawat Publications, Jaipur, 2008.
59. Brij Kishore Sharma, *Social, Economic and Political Contribution of Caste Association in Northern India (A case Study of All India Jat Mahasabha)*, HAR-ANAND Publication, New Delhi, 2008.
60. B.K. Sharma, *Mass Movement and Freedom Struggle in Rajasthan (1818-1949)*, Books Treasure, Jodhpur, 2013.
61. V.K. Vashishtha, *Arya Samaj Movement in Rajasthan during the Nineteenth Century*, Published in the volume, 'Dissent Protest and Reform in Indian Civilization', Edited by S.C. Malik, Indian Institute of Advanced Study, Simla, 1978.
62. Prithvi Singh Mehta, *Swatantrata Andolan : Mewar aur Arya Samaj*, Shodh Patrika, Udaipur, Varsha 37, Ank 3-4, July-December, 1986.
63. Tej Kumar Mathur and Meghna Sharma, *The efforts of Arya Samaj in Elevating the condition of women folk : In Light of*

its publication (1875-1950), Rajasthan History Congress Proceeding Volume XX, Udaipur Session, Jodhpur, 2005.

64. N.K. Sharma, *Shaikshnik Kshetra Mein Arya Samaj Ka Yogdan (1865 se 1945 tak),* Rajasthan History Congress, Proceeding Volume XX, Udaipur Session, Jodhpur, 2005.

65. Professor V.K. Vashishtha, *Bhartiya Swatantrata Andolan Mein Ajmer-Merwara Mein Arya Samaj ka Yogdan*, Rajasthan History Congress, Proceedings Volume XXVII, Ajmer, 2012.

2

Brief Life History of Swami Dayanand Saraswati and Foundation of Arya Samaj

It is very interesting to know that how a person born in conservative Brahaman family became the crusader against reactionary religious and social practices. Who began his journey in search of the truth and true way of salvation transformed into Martin Luther of India. He was Swami Dayanand Saraswati. A brief life history of Swamiji has been narrated in the future pages of this chapter. On the basis of facts of his life journey his personality and works has also been evaluated and analysed. The Arya Samaj did not come into existence abruptly, but it took long route. It is equally interesting to know that how it was founded with solid base. The history of its rise and growth has also been traced here.

Early Life (1824-1845)

Swami Dayanand Saraswati in his autobiography has mentioned that : I was horn in an Audichya Brahmana family in the State of Morvi in Majokatha region of Kathiawad, South Gujarat, in VS 1881 (= AD 1824). I refrain from mentioning the name of the town of my birth, for if my father, mother, or any other relative happen to be alive at the moment, they might come to me and create obstructions in the work of reform I have undertaken. I do not want that any part of my energies, resources, etc., should be used up in moving with or attending to the needs of my parents or relatives.[1] Thus for a long time the people were ingnoratnt about personal details of Swamiji. Later on his biographers could collect some personal and family details of him. His original name was Mool Shankar, and his father's Karsanji Trivedi. He was the head of an eminent Brahman family of the village and was rich, prosperous and influential. Karsanji was in service, holding the position of *Jamadar,* which office was hereditary in his family. The post of *Jamadar* was one of great responsibility, being much like a Tehsildarship, and the principal duty of its incumbent was the realization of State revenue. Karsanji had under him a number of sepoys to assist him in the discharge of his duties. The family over which he presided had lands of its own, and the income from these was largely supplemented by the interest on sums regularly lent to the neighbours in need of money.[2] Obviously, he was born in an affluent family in all respect. The Arya Samaj and the biographers of the Swami have come to a now generally accepted conclusion that within the State of Morvi the town of Tankara had the honour of being Dayanand's birthplace.[3]

At the age of five (A.D. 1828), he began to study the *Devanagari* characters and when he was eight (A.D. 1831), he was invested with the *Yagopavita,* given practical lessons of the *Gayatri Sandhya* and taught the Yajurveda Samthita starting first from the Rudradhyaya.[4] Though his mother tongue was Gujarati, he was first taught the Devanagari script, which was used for Sanskrit. Instead of Regveda and Samveda he was first taught the Yajurveda. The Yajurveda is held in special reverence by Shaivites, to which sect his family belonged. The reason attributed was that the Yajurveda contained a chapter on Rudra, who was indentified, though erroneously with Lord Shiva.[5] Thus, the beginning of early education of Moolshankar was as per family tradition, but since the initiation there existed an anomaly which led him in search of proper and logical end.

Karshanji Trivedi was keen that his son grow up as an ardent Shiva devotee. Therefore, since the beginning Moolshankar was trained in the Shaivite rituals. But at the age of 14 one incident related to the ritual of Shiva worship proved turning point in his life. Swami Dayanand Saraswati at this tender age learnt by heart the whole of the Yajurveda, some parts of other Vedas and grammar work such as *Shabdarupawali.* He has himself narrated the whole story as follows : "In that year 1838 - my father, unmindful of my mother's remonstrance, ordered that I should begin practicing *Parthiva Pujanam.* Accordingly, when the great day of fasting called *Shivaratri* came, my father after reciting the sacred legend on the Magha Badi 13 (Jan-Feb 1838), commanded to observe a fast and to participate in the night long vigil in the temple of Shiva. I obeyed him and went to the temple where the rich people of the town were going with their children. The *Shivaratri* vigil was divided into four *praharas* of three hours each. After the first two *praharas* I saw that the *pujaris* and some lay devotees had left the temple and lay asleep outside it. Having been taught for years that by sleeping on that particular night, the worshipper lost all charm of his devotion. I tried to avoid sleep by washing my eyes now and then with cold water. My father was however, less fortunate in this respect. He fell asleep, leaving me to watch alone a miracle which happened just then : a mice came out of its hide-out and began to wander around the idol of Shiva. Not only that, it even climbed on the idol and ate away the *akshat* (offerings) too.

Now thought upon thought and question upon question crowded upon and disturbed my mind. It is possible, I asked myself, that he was the same Mahadeva, the semblance of man, the idol of a personal god that I see bestriding him before me, and who, according to religious accounts, walks about, eats, sleeps, and drinks, and who holds a trident in his hand, beats *dumroo* and pronounces curse upon men? Is he the one who is invoked as the Lord of Kailash, the supreme being and the divine hero of all the stories we read of him in the *"Puranas"*.[6]

The incident of Shivaratri was a turning point in the life of Moolshankar. He began to lose his faith in idol worship as he found no logic in it. The spontaneous thoughts made him uneasy and he could not resist a number of questions in his mind. He awoke his father and asked him to tell whether the hideous emblem of Shiva in the temple was identical with the Mahadeva of the scriptures. Moolshankar felt that it is impossible to reconcile to the idea of an omnipotent, living god, with this idol which allowed the mice to run over his body and thus suffers his image to be polluted without the slightest protest.[7]

Perturbed with this incident Moolshankar left the temple and returned to home with the formal consent of his father. Though his father allowed him to go to home but he reiterated not to break the fast. But against his father's instruction Moolshankar given up fast. He had narrated the story as follows : In the morning, when my father returned home and learnt that I had broken my fast, he was very angry. He tried to impress me with enormity of my sin. But I could not make myself believe that the idol and Mahadeva were one and the same god, and, therefore, could not comprehend why I should be made to fast for it and worship it. I had, however, to conceal my lack of faith, and bring forward as an excuse for abstaining from regular worship my study, which really left me little or no time for anything else. In this I was strongly supported by my mother and my uncle, who pleaded my case so well that my father had to yield. I was allowed to devote my whole attention to my studies. My academic sweep was now extended to

Nighantu, Nirukta, Purvamimansa and other *Shastras* as also to the rituals.[8] Thus, at the age of fourteen Moolshankar set aside the authority of his father and took his own way to pursue his studies as per his choice. The Arya samajists celebrate the night of *Shivaratri* as the anniversary of Dayanand's enlightenment, but actually it was the night of doubt which lead him to enlightenment.

In addition to the above there were certain other incidents which diverted him from worldly life to spiritualism. When he was 16 his 14 year old sister expired. He has narrated that : It was my first bereavement, and the shock I received was indeed great. Friends and relatives were sobbing and lamenting around me. I stood like one petrified plunged in revery. It resulted in a series of long and sad mediations upon the instability of human life. Not one of the beings that lived in this world could escape the cold hand of death, I thought. I too may be snatched away anytime. Now I asked myself : What should I do to alleviate this human misery? Where shall I find the assurance for and means of attaining salvation? I came to decision then that I would strike to find an answer to these questions, cost whatever it might, so that I could save myself from the untold miseries of the dying moment.[9] Another tragic incident was death of his beloved uncle after three years. Both these deaths changed his perception towards worldly life. Moolshankar expressed his feeling as follows : His death left me in a state of utter dejection, and with a still profounder conviction I settled in my mind that there was nothing stable, nothing worth living for in this world.[10]

Moolshankar moved around distracted, asking his friends and the learned *Pandits* of his acquaintance if they could inform him how death could be overcome. The reply was that *Yogabhyas* (contemplation or communion) was the way to secure it. Dayanand thought over the answer, and reached the conclusion that in order to learn yoga he must leave home.[11]

Still Moolshankar was not satisfied with the knowledge which he acquired through education and practical experiences. Therefore, he insisted upon going to Banaras for his educational pursuits. He wanted to complete his knowledge of Sanskrit grammar, astronomy and medicine science. But his parents declined to send him Banaras, rather they planned to put him in the bandage of wedlock. However, he could manage avoidance of wedlock for two years. When he attained the age 21 his parents finalized his betrothal. He was surprised to know that everything had been prepared for his marriage ceremony. He fully realized that he would not be allowed to avoid marriage any more, therefore, on one fine evening in VS 1903 (A.D. 1845) he fled from his home and set on his journey in search of truth and salvation. Lajpat Rai has rightly analyzed the incident as follow : This was his final separation from home and all that the word implies. It was casting himself adrift from worldly ties. He felt filial sorrow for his mother, who loved him devotedly, but he had to fulfil a mission; and even as early as 1903 *Vikram* (about 1845 or 1846) he could visualize it, though faintly, in his mind's eye. He was leaving home to make all India his abode. He was forsaking his kindred to succour humanity and the cause of truth. From whatever we know of him he never did regret the step he had taken : a step which alone enabled him to serve his people, his country and his God as greatly as he did. It was the logical conclusion of the step taken seven years ago when he revolted against his father's misuse of parental authority in attempting to dictate on matters affecting his innermost beliefs.[12]

Attainment of Knowledge and Enlightenment

At the age of 21 Moolshankar fled from his home to satisfy his thirst for true knowledge and enlightenment. After leaving home he reached a place Sayale the residence of a learned scholar, named Lala Bhagat of whom he had heard much from wandering *Sanyasis* and *Vairagis.* There Mookshankar became his disciple and he gave him name *Shudhhachaitanya* (pure minded). He was also given the outfit of *Sadhu.* Following in the footsteps of the *Sadhus* he began to practice austerities.[13] From there Shuddha Chaitanay moved to Sidhapur to visit the *Kartika* fair to be held there during October-November 1846.[14] By that time his father reached there with sepoys and put him under the strict vigilance, but he eloped from there again. This time he went to Baroda and settled for some time at the Chetnamath where he took long lesson on *Vedanta.* From Baroda he moved to Chanod Kanyali on the bank of Narmada, where he became *Sannyasi* of *Dandi* order. The ritual was administered by one of *dandi Swami* of Shringerimath named Purnanand Saraswati and he gave him the name Dayanand Sarasvati.[15]

Dayanand Saraswati did not stay at a place for long and remained wandering from one place to other. From Chanod he went to Vyasashram where he took lesson in the theory and practical modes of the science of Yoga from a *Sannyasi* named Yoganand. From Vyasashram he proceeded to Chhinaur, where under the guidance of Krishna Shastri he perfected in Sanskrit grammar.[16] Still he was wandering within the areas of Gujarat. In 1952 he visited Mount Abu in search of great yogis and stayed there for about two years.[17] Before coming to Mount Abu he was taking lesson on Yoga from two Dashanami monks, Jawalananda Puri and Shivanand giri.[18] He has narrated that : Later I was told that there were many far higher and more learned yogis than those I had hitherto met on the peaks of the mountain of Abu in Rajputana. I visited all the noted places such as the Arbada Bhawani etc. and met yogis like Bhawani Giri whom I so eagerly sought. I learned from them various systems and modes of Yoga.[19] In 1854-55 Dayanand Saraswati went to Haridwar to attend Kumbha *Mela.*

In V.S. 1912 (A.D. 1855) he visited for the first time, the Kumbha fair at Haridwar. Here he met to so many sages and individual philosophers. He interacted with a lot of people and could know about the various sects of broader Hindu religion. Here he could also visualize the deficiency of his knowledge. Thus, the Kumbha fair opened various vistas for more search and knowledge. From Haridwar he went to Rishikesh, where he had interviews with many yogis and mahatmas and learned more of practical Yoga from them.[20] From Rishikesh he entered into the well known religious places of Himalayas and also in the remote interiors of it. He visited Tehri, Shrinagar, Kedarghat, Rudraprayag, Devprayag, Shivpuri, Kedarnath, Guptakashi, Triyugirnarayan, Ukhimath, Gourikund, Bhim Ganga, Tunganath Hill, Joshi Math, Badrinarayan, Alaknanda's origination place, Sadapat Tirath, Vasudhara, Kashipur, Daronasagar etc.

During his visits of the above places of Himalayas he came into contact of various shades of sects and *Sadhus.* During the visit of Tehri he came into contact of *Vam Marg* and *Tantraism.* One of the *Rajya-Pandita* (Royal Priest) invited Dayanand on dinner, but when he went there he found that they were meat eaters. When Dayanand asked the same *pandita* as to what books and manuscripts be procured at that place. Dayanand writes that : He (*pandita*) mentioned some work on Sanskrit grammar, classic, lexicography, astrology and tantras. The latter (i.e. tantras) were the only ones unknown to me and I asked him to procure the same. The learned man brought to me several works on the subject. But no sooner had I opened them than my eyes fell on such an amount of incredible obscenities, mistranslation of the ancient texts and absurdities, that I felt horrified. In these tantras I found that incest was permitted even with mothers, daughters, sisters and low-born maids of the outcastes. They recommend worship of gods in a perfectly nude state, spirituous liquors, fish and all kinds of animal food are allowed for all, right from a Brahmana down to a *Manga.* And it was explicitly stated that these five things whose names commenced with letter 'm' : *Madya* (intoxicating liquor), Meena (fish), Mans (flesh), Mudra (naked worshipping) and maithuna (sexual intercourse) were means of attaining salvation. By actually reading the whole contents of the *tantras* I was fully convinced of the craft and viciousness of the authors of this disgusting literature which is regarded as religious.[21]

From Daronsagar Dayanand went to Moradabad via Sambhal and then crossing Garhmuktashwar. Then he took route to Farukhabad, Kanpur, Allahabad, Mirzapur and Banaras alosngwith Ganga. After this adventure from Banaras, on 26 March , 1857 he set out on journey to the hills, where the Narmada takes its rise.[22] He kept wandering for three years on the bank of the Narmada and enjoyed the learned company of the *mahantas* and yogis.[23]

The account of Dayanand Saraswati's wandring life for three years on the bank of Narmda and in the jungle and mountains of Vindhyas has been depicted by some authors in mythical and conjectural manner. A myth has been created that Dayanand Saraswati himself was involved in the revolt of 1857 during these three years from mid 1857 to 1860. It has been convincingly analysed by a recent author as follows : Dayanand's three-year seclusion has, of late, led some Aryas (members of the Arya Samaj) to link it with the army revolt of 1857. One theory claims that during this period Dayanand wandered incognito in the countryside, mobilising people against the British. However, the evidence available does not support this theory. In May 1857 when the revolt flared up all of a sudden at Meerut (a town in present day Uttar Pradesh, near Delhi), Dayanand was far away in the thick forests of the Vindhyas. He could not have learnt of the revolt by any means. Even otherwise, there was no reason for him to abandon his mission, which had totally absorbed his mind. There is not even circumstantial evidence to show his involvement in the 1857 revolt, there was no reason for him to hide it. His autobiographical account in the Theosophist appeared in late 1879 and early 1880. He had earlier delivered an autobiographical lecture in 1875 at Poona (now spelt Pune). By then the 1857 revolt had become a part of history. He did not have even tactical reasons not to divulge his alleged involvement. Neither Pandit Lekh Ram nor Debendranath Mukhopadhyaya, two writers who painstakingly collected material for Dayanand's biography, even remotely suggests any such involvement.[24]

Dayanand's note in his own hand at the end of the fourteenth chapter in the manuscript of the first edition of his book Satyarth Praskash (now in the custody of the descendants of Raja Jaiksihan Das) clearly discloses where he was in the 1857-60 period and what he was doing. "I studied the six Darshanas on the banks of the Narmada," sates this note. Dayanand occupies a prominent place in history even without his participation in the revolt.[25]

Still Dayanand's search for a Guru was not completed. Though, he heared of a great scholar of Sanskrit grammar and scriptures Swami Virjanand Saraswati but he could not meet him. Pandit Lekhram in his Urdu biography of Dayanand says that Swami Dayanand reached Mathura on *Kartik Sud* second S. 1917, the 14th of November, 1860. Pandit Lekhram says that he heared of Virjanand from somebody while he was living on the banks of the Narbada.[26] While Devendranath Mukhopadhyaya in his biography of Swami Dayanand Saraswati says that Swami Dayanand told late Pt. Mohanlal Vishnulal Pandya the Secretary of the Paropkarini Sabha, Ajmer that "I first went to Haridwar to Poornashram Swami for study but by that time he became very old and he was observing connivance (maun vrat), therefore, he did not agree to teach me. When I requested him more then he wrote on a paper that if you study from Virjanand at Mathura your wishes will be fulfilled.[27]

Dayanand Saraswati himself has mentioned that : I kept wandering for three years on the banks of the Narmada... from there I returned to Mathura in order to pursue higher studies. Here I met a true *Sannayasi,* aged 81, whom I accepted as my *guru.* His name was Vrijanand. Earlier he used to live at Alwar. He had acquired mastery over the *Vedas,* shastras and the ancient literature composed by the sages and seers. He was blind and suffered from acute stomach trouble. He did not think high of the modern Sanskrit grammar works, such as Kaumudi, Shaikharabodha, etc.; and denounced the Puranas, Bhagavat, etc. in irrevocable terms. He had great faith in the *arshagranthas* (books authored by ancient seers). When I presented myself to him he told me that grammar could be learnt in three year's time.[28]

In the first meeting Swami Virjanand told Dayanand that there is a vast difference between the true Aryan literature and the books composed by common mortals, and as for himself, he had absolutely no respect for the latter and never taught them. Dayanand could not disabuse his mind of the idea he had clung to for years, in a moment, but the argument of the Swami prevailed, and he eventually consented to have nothing to do with the works which had not the stamp of true science and true wisdom on them. He even went so far as to throw into the Yamuna his old stock, so that Virjanand might be pleased and admit him as his people. But, though all this was satisfactory enough, the fact could not be lost sight of that Dayanand was a Sannyasi, and Virjanand could not see how a Sannayasi could afford to carry on his studies with him. "I am not in the habit of teaching Sannyasis", said he, "but if I take you in as a pupil, how will you manage to live? Dayanand replied that he would find himself food somehow or other, no matter if it was the coarset possible : all that he cared for was knowledge, and that, he hoped, Virjanand would not refuse him. Finding him persistent in his entreaties, Virjanand at last granted Dayanand's prayer, and having raised a subscription of thirty one rupees got him a copy of the Mahabhashya to commence his studies with.[29]

J.T.F. Jorden has commented on the arrival of Dayanand at Mathura as follow : That is where Dayanand arrived in November 1860. He was then a mature man of thirty six. His whole adult life had been devoted to some study of Vendanta but mainly to that of Yoga. He had combed the holy land of Kumaon and the rugged peaks of the Vindhyas in search of the perfect *guru* who would show him the way to *moksha.* But so far this search had remained fruitless. One would like to know what happened to him in those last three years. What frustrations and new discoveries made him at that stage give up that search for *moksha,* and take the road to Mathura in order to study grammar under the guidance of Swami Virjananda Sarasvati, the famous blind *guru.*[30]

This may be analysed that the early efforts of Dayanand before coming to Mathura had not remained fruitless. As has also been mentioned that he was in search of true knowledge and his thirst for the same constantly kept him wandering. During his wandering life of fifteen years he could come to the conclusion that none of the yogi had conquered the death and this had been an ostensible idea and concept. He came across many sadhus and yogis who claimed to posses supernatural powers, but he found them to be impostors as they could not prove such powers. He had also found that superstition, mythical and vulgar practices being promoted in the name of religion. He could come to know about large number of evil practices had corrupted the religion and are pushing the people towards darkness and ignorance. Thus, his wandering had not gone waste. He had also convinced himself that true knowledge of religion and salvation is hidden in the ancient scriptures, which can only be understood with the help of proper Sanskrit grammar. Hence, his search for salvation brought him to great teacher of Sanskrit grammar Swami Virjanand.

The biographers tell us that he studied Panini's grammar, the *Ashtadhyayi* and its chief commentary, the *Mahabhashya* of Patanjali. These two were probably the only part of formal curriculum at the school of Swami Virjanand.[31] It is obvious that Virjanand must often have discussed the favourite ideas with his favorite student. The key idea is the judgment that the degeneration of Hindustan is fundamentally connected with the proliferation and influence of 'spurious' works of a sectarian nature giving rise to numerous sects, accompanied by a parallel neglect of the real source of Hinduism, the books of the rishis. The implication is that the regeneration of Hinduism can come only through a renewal of the study and influence of those books and the elimination of sectarian works and groups. This key idea was also an expression of a deep concern, a concern new to Dayananda : the concern for Hinduism and for the Hindus, as distinct from the narrow individualistic concern for personal *moksha.* This concern which his guru communicated to him was constantly being reinforced by his close experience of real Hinduism in the heart of Mathura. For the rest of his life Dayananda was to be preoccupied with that concern and the search for ways to reform a Hinduism torn asunder by the sects. He would also remain fascinated by the idea of the real sources of Hinduism, and he would soon begin that pilgrimage to the sources. But it would take many years before this vague idea would find its final formulation.[32]

In fact Dayanand got a skill and tool in the education of grammar by which he may test the authority of scriptures that which one belongs to the creation of rishis and which one is composition of ordinary authors. By the end of March 1863, Dayanand had been with his *guru* virjanand, when his guru told him that his education was over and that he had nothing more to teach him. In this context the depiction of Baba Chhajju Singh in very lucid and interesting which as follows : Dayanand read with Swami Virjanand for two years and a half, and during this period he had mastered Ashtadhyayi, Mahabhashya, the Vedanta Sutras, and many other works. And when his course of education was finished, and he thought it was time for him to leave, he in conformity with the usages of olden times, approached his *guru* and, laying half a seer of cloves before him, asked for permission to depart. Virjanand gave him his blessing and called upon him to produce, after the fashion of the students of yore, suitable *dakshina* (present) marking the termination of his course of education. Dayanand made answer that he had nothing that he could venture to offer to his most revered *guru.* "Do you think I would ask you for anything you have not got?" Was the rejoinder. Being silenced by the loving rebuke. Dayanand said : "Most holy Sir, I am ready to lay at your feet whatever you think I have really got in my possession." "Dear son, you have got it, and that is *true knowledge.* If you would pay me my *dakshina*, give this knowledge to thy mother-land. The Vedas have long ceased to be taught in Bhaartavarsha, go and teach them; teach the true Shastras, and dispel, by their light, the darkness which the false creeds have spread. Remember that while works by common men are utterly misleading as to the nature and attributes of the one true God, and slander the great Rishis and Munis, those by the ancient teachers are free from such a blemish. This is the test which will enable you to differentiate the true, ancient teaching from the writings of ordinary men.

Dayanand bowed his head in acquiescence, assuring his *guru* that he would do his best to accomplish the task assigned to him, upon which the guru once more gave him his blessing and permitted him to depart. How far Dayanand kept his word and how far he succeeded in redeeming that word, is known to the world. Few men have laboured as Dayanand did. His self-sacrifice and his patriotism were of the highest possible type, almost who can but say that they might once more prove the making of India? Verily, they will![33]

In April 1863 Dayanand left his *guru* and began his mission to refute the evil religious practices and propagation of Vedas.[34] During his stay at Agra he denounced the Bhagwata.[35] From Agra he went to Gwalior, Dholpur and Karauli in 1865. At Gwalior he denounced the Vaishnava sect. From Karauli he went to Kushalgarh (Now known as Gangapurcity) and from there moved to Jaipur in October 1865.[36] Throughout this period right from Agra Swami Dayanand gave public discourses and held *shastrarthas.* At Jaipur he finally gave up the Vaishnavism and tilted towards shaivism but denounced the idol and linga form of shaivism.[37] In March, 1866 Swami Dayanand left Jaipur for Pushkar.

Swami Dayanand had himself confessed that at Karauli he denounced the Vaishnavism sect and praised Shaivism. But from Pushkar-Ajmer he began to denounce Shaivism too. He had said that : About that time the Maharaja of Jaipur was going to Agra to meet the lieutenant Governor (of the North-Western Provinces). The maharaja summoned me with a view to taking me along with him for disputation, if need be, with the Vaishnava scholar Rangacharya of Brindaban. I reached Jaipur, but the Maharaja, on knowing that I had began to denounce Shaivism too, became displeased with me. I, therefore left Jaipur for Mathura where I discussed some difficult matters with Swamiji (Virjanand).[38]

From Mathura Dayanad moved to Haridwar where he participated in the Kumbha Mela in March, 1867. There he hoisted the flag of *Pakhandamardana* (down with religious hypocrisy) on his hut and debated religious issues with Panditas. But looking to the growing antagonism against him he took *maunvarta* but could not be kept for long because he was forced by the opponents to speak.

Swami Dayanand has revealed that : one day a man came and standing in front of my hut said : "The Vedas are nothing as compared with the Bhagavata. Rather they are much inferior to it." I could not bear with this and giving up my maunvrata began to denounce the Bhagvata. I decided at once that whatever little knowledge I have acquired by the grace of God should be transmitted to other for their good.[39] He began publicly to denounce idol worship, *avataras* (Incarnation of God), the Bhagwata, pilgrimages, painting faces, and tying *kanthis* round the neck, and similar other things.[40] He discarded the puranas and other works of *unarsha* category and accepted the authorities of Vedas and Vedangas and other compositions . During his stay at Haridwar he also refuted the translations and explanation of Vedas by traditional scholars. The well known Sanskrit scholar from Banaras was conducting a discourse in Haridwar on the origin of the four *varnas.* He cited the eleventh *mantra* of *Adhyay* 31 of the Yajur Veda to prove that the four *Varnas* had a divine origin and translated the *mantra* as follows : "Brahmins are born out of the mouth of Brahma, Kshtriyas out of his arms, Vaishas out of the stomach and Sudras out of Brahma's feet". Swamiji declared that it was wrong and that the meaning of the mantra was that Brahmins are like the head, the Kshtriyas like the arms, the Vaishas like the stomach and the Sudras like the feet.[41]

Har Bilas Sarda has lucidly narrated the facts about the experience of Dayanand as follows.[42] It was at this Haridwar

Kumbha fair that Dayanand saw clearly and fully how the world was compassed by ignorance. Those who knew Sanskrit were selfish and plundered the people in the name of religion. Those very people whose duty it was to instruct the householders in true religion were teaching them false doctrines and making then irreligious. The Sadhu communities were in a bad way, divided into innumerable factions and were worse than householders. There was no evil which they did not practice. Instead of preaching peace they themselves were torn asunder by discord and disunity. Religion was only a screen.

The deplorable condition of the people touched Swamiji's heart and the desire to help them and redeem them now possessed him more that ever. He thought that living and working like an ordinary sadhu would lead him nowhere. He realized that the occasion demanded that he should rise above the limitation set by social conditions, and fearlessly proclaims the truth and imparts to others the knowledge (*Jnana*) which he had acquired by the study of the Vedas.

Swamiji on Mission with Full Vigour

From Haridwar Dayanand took path towards farukhabad along the Banks of Ganga. He visited small towns and villages and preached the people Vedic religion. This time his mission met with enthusiastic response from the people who came into contact with him. He taught the devotees chanting Gayatri Mantra and the rituals of *Sandhya* and *Agnihotra*. People began to leave the idol worship and various other superstitious and evil religious practices and gave *yajnopavit* to the twice born (dwij) in large numbers. A number of Brahmins, Kshatriya and Vaishyas became disciple and follower of Swami Dayanand Saraswati. Overwhelmed with the public response Swami Dayanand performed a Yajna on a grand scale at Karnavas assisted by some forty pandits from Anupshahar, Danpur,

Karnavas, Ahmednagar, Ramgarh, Jahangirabad etc. .[43] Baba Chhajju Singh has given a lucid description of this event as follows : So well was everything managed and so faithfully the ancient ritual followed, that function produced the happiest effect on the mind of the population in the neighbour hood. A desire to tread once more in the footsteps of the sages of yore was aroused in the mind of the twice-born classes, and Brahmans , Kshatriyas and Vaishyas thronged around the Swami from all sides, with a prayer to be invested with the "sacred thread." Nothing could give him greater pleasure than to comply with such a prayer. But at the same time he did positive work, he took care that the negative was not left undone. The preaching of the *Gurumantra* and the investiture with the sacred thread and similar other things were uniformly followed (provided the Swami's leisure permitted) with a merciless exposure of the Puranas, and of the Tantras, Vammargism, polytheism, and so on. "Whatever makes you forget virtue in the most comprehensive sense of the word, he would say, addressing the people, in the course of his observation, "whatever makes you take to drinking, to adultery, to stealing, to lying, and so on, the same is the destroyer of the soul, and must be shunned.[44]

At Anupshahar discussion on idol worship took place with Shastri Hira Vallabh who accepted the view of Swami Dayanand. Shastri told that worship of stocks and stone was false and he submerged the idols into the Ganges. Thus, this incident brought clear impact on the minds of people. But this alarmed the conservative and sanatani Hindus. Therefore, various attempts were made on the life of Swamiji.[45] During this period Dayanand adopted a new means of propagating his ideas by the foundation of Sanskrit schools. The influence of his guru Virjananda was obviously still at work. He founded four schools between early 1869 and the end of 1870, at Farrukhabad, Kasgan, Mirzapur, and Chalesar. The reason for this venture is obvious : The proper knowledge of Sanskrit was essential for the reform he envisaged. He himself acquired this knowledge through Virjanand, and he occasionally sent promising aspirants to his *guru* for training. However, Virjananda died on 14 Septemeber 1868. Dayananda never aspired to a role similar to his *guru's,* but he knew from personal experience how necessary a proper language training was for the task of reformation. The traditional Sanskrit schools produced the traditional pandits, whose knowledge was inadequate and who wasted their time on vluesless, unauthoritative works. There was a need, and the only way to provide for it was for Dayananda to start his own schools.[46] The fifth school (Pathshala) was opened at Banaras in the Sambat 1930 (1873 A.D.).[47]

From the banks of Ganges Swami Dayanand took the extensive journey into the interiors of doab of Ganga and Yamuna. Swamiji reached Garhya Ghat from vicinity of Anupshahar and from their he moved to the town of Swaron (Soron) in March 1869 which was a strong hold of sanatani Brahmins. Soron shares with Pushkar the distiction of having a temple of *Varah* (Boar incarnation). It is considered as a great centre of Hindu pilgrimage. His presence in Soron created sensation in the town and under his influence many *pandits, sadhus, gosains* and common people denounced the idol worship and pauranik sects and accepted Vedic religion. But all it did not happened uninterruptedly as Swamiji also faced severe opposition and threats on his life.[48]

The Swami styed in the vicinity of Soron for about six months and by teaching and preaching reclaimed people from superstitions. His shastrarth of Farrukhabad of May 1869 is known when Pandit Shri Gopal a native of Meerut was called upon by the orthodox Hindus to take up the cause of idolatry against the Swamiji. The discussion remained indecisive, therefore another scholar Pandit Haldhar Ojha was summoned from Kanpur and on 19 June 1869 another shastrarth was held. But he too failed in counteracting the Swamiji. Therefore, the infuriated orthodox and conservative fanatics issued threats to Dayanand.[49]

Moving on, Dayanand arrived at Kanpur in July 1869. Here also, he continued his efforts against idolatry. He has already established that the Vedas did not sanction idol worship, hence he limited his discussion only on the Vedic sources. On 31 July, 1969 a debate ensued and Pandit Haldhar Ojha pitted against Swami Dayanand. But the pandit could not prove their point in support of idol worship on the basis of Vedic sources. One of the *madhyastha* (mediator) Lakshman Shastri supported the view of Ojha which was based on non-Vedic sources and Dayanand insisted on Vedic evidences only.[50]

From Kanpur Dayanand moved to Banaras on 22 or 23 October, 1869.[51] In the background of Dayanand's visit to Banaras Prof. Jorden has written that[52] : Looking back over that lustrum on the banks of the Ganga, a clear development can be seen in Dayanand's life, thought, and action. After his disappointment at Hardwar and a time of retreat and reflection, he initiated a new kind of reform work concentrating on the leading castes and the pandits in a basically rural area where they were present in great numbers. His negative denunciation of contemporary Hinduism was to a greater and greater degree counterbalanced by a positive instruction in Vedic ritual and moral life. At the same time his fame as a challenging and successful debater spread further and the local pandits, defeated by the Swami, imported more eminent pandits from bigger centres. The key issue in all these debates was idol worship, and more specifically : was idol worship sanctioned by the scriptures? This process of challenge, success, and fame, finally brought the Swami to Banaras.

Kashi (Banaras) has been the seat of learning in India since ages and centuries. It has been also a centre of religious influences. Baba Chhajju Singh has said that : No European city, ancient or modern, not even Rome has ever been or is so powerful with the student or with the religious inquirer as Kashi in this continental country.[53] No doubt Banaras was the great citadel of idol worships, where temple were as plenty as blackberries and where idols were more numerous that the swarming population. There the many sects of Hinduism thrived, but they were all only varieties of idoltary under different guises. Banaras was also the capital of the India of the Hindoo, the head-quarter of Hindoo orthodoxy, enjoying and exercising the metropolitan authority throughout Brahmindom, that Rome once did throughout Christendom.[54]

Before his arrival at Banaras Dayanand stayed at Ramnagar on the opposite bank of Ganga which was the seat of Maharaja of Banaras. From there he moved to Varanasi and made his residence in Anandbagh alongwith the famous Durgakund owned by the Raja of Amethi. News of Dayanand's arrival spread everywhere and hundreds of people began to visit Swamiji. Finally on the 16 November, 1869 the famous Kashi Shastrarth was held in the presence of the Kashi Naresh Maharaja Ishvariprasad Narayan Singh.[55] But when the pandits and scholars could not succeed in defending the idol worship then the pandits got up shouting 'defeated, defeated', clapped hands and departed. The goondas threw stones and lumps of earth on Swamiji. He could be saved by the police under the Kotwal. A notice was posted on the behalf of pandits that Dayanand had been defeated. A counter notice was issued saying that Dayanand had not been defeated and that he was willing to continue the shastrarth. The pandits of Banaras knew in their heart of that Dayanand was right and there was no authority in the Vedas for idol worship but for fear of losing their livelihood, they were not prepared openly to say so. Even the state pandit told privately that what Dayanand had said was quite true and the teachings of the puranas were not acceptable, but that he was in the service of the Maharaja of Banaras and in order to please him, he had to do what he did. He would otherwise lose his job.[56]

On the Kashi Shastrarth Dayanand himself has said as follows : I agreed to have a debate with the orthodox *panditas* from Kashi. The subject chosen for the debate was whether or not the word *pratima* (idol) was there in the Vedas. I told them the word *pratima* was there but it meant 'measuring'. So far I have visited this place four times. Whenever, I went there I advertised that if anybody had been able to find idol worship in the Vedas, he should show that to me. No one came to me.[57]

The Kashi Shastrarth brought many changes in the thought and action. He reached on the conclusion that he can succeed in his mission only by organised efforts, otherwise his individualistic works will not yield required results. During this shastrarth he came into contact of a number of modern social reformers belonging to Prathana Samaj and Brahmo Samaj. Thus, his proximity with these reformers enlightened him regarding social, political, economic, and national issues. Therefore, in addition to theological discourses he began to cover the other issues confronted by the nation. By this time he finalised his list of readings of scriptures. The first of the three forms the foundation of his whole reform. The only writings which he acknowledges as Shastras are the following twenty-one : I-4, the four *Vedas;* 5-8, the four *Upavedas;* 9-14, the six *Vedangas;* 15, twelve *Upanishads;* 16, the *Sarirakasutras;* 17, the *Katyayanasutras,* etc.; 18, the *Yogabhashya;* 19, The *Vakovakya;* 20, the *Manusmriti;* and 21 the *Mahabharata.* The four *Vedas* are the *Rigveda, the Yajurveda, the Samaveda, and Atharvarveda, including their respective Brahmanas.* The four

Upavedas are the *Ayurveda* on medical science, including two books; the Dhanurveda, military science; the Gandharvaveda on musical science; and the Arthaveda on mechanical science; the six Vedangas are the Siksha on pronunciation; the Kalpa on ceremonial; the Vyakarana or Grammar of Panini; the Commentary of Patanjali (Mahabhashya); the *Nirukta* or etymological vocabulary ; the Chhanda on prosody; and the Juotisha on astronomy and astrology, including only one book; the *Bhrigu Sanhita*. The twelve *Upnishads are : Isa, Kena, Katha, Prasna, Mundaka, Mandukya, Taitareya, Aitereya, Chhandogya, Brihadaranyaka, Svetasvatara, and Kaivalya.* There exist many more *Upanishads* which are acknowledged by orthodox pandits; but they are all rejected by Dayanand. The *Mahabharata* is not acknowledged by him in its entirety; but many portions are declared by him spurious, among others, if I mistake not, the famous *Bhagavadgita.* This list of shastras here given may be relied upon as correct, as the reformer wrote them down for me on a paper with his owns hand.[58]

After Kashi shastrarth Swami Dayanand finally rejected the idolatry and mythology. He further rejected polytheism and accepted monotheism. He stressed upon acquisition of true knowledge of God and observance of the moral laws as the will of God. He suggested the worship of God by *Agnihotra.* During the Kanpur (31 July, 1969) shastrarth the Assistant collector Mr. W. Thaine asked from Dayanand whether *agnihotra* was not the worship of fire. Dayanand replied in negative. He said fire sacrifice was a means to purify the air by burning ghee and aromatic herbs.[59] Dayanand also rejected the theory of incarnation or *avataras.* In his view it was the wrong notion and myth created by Puranas.

Swami Dayanand also rejected the theory of Devine origin of *Varnas* and castes. He considered the caste a political institution made by the rulers for the common good of society, and not a natural or religious distinction. It was not based on birth rather was based on profession. Even before Kashi shastrarth he subscribed this view and not observed any distinction and discrimination on the basis of caste, as on the way from Haridwar Swamiji accepted the half roti from a *manjhi* (boatman). During his stay at Farrukhabad Dayanand had an especially close relationship with *Sadh* community. When he was criticized by the Hindus for accepting food from a *Sadh*, whom they considered low in ritual status, Dayanand retorted that food can only be spoilt by dirt or by the tainted money that procures it.[60]

Lajpat Rai has concluded that : From this date (Kashi Shastrarth) may be reckoned the effective beginning of Dayanand's mission for a refromed Hindu church, free from cant, superstition, and popular error.[61]

From Banaras Dayanand arrived at Allahbad on 5 February, 1870 to attend the Kumbha fair where he stayed for about a month and kept his mission continued to preach the people as per his ideas. Than went to Mirzapur and from there returned to Banaras. In between Dayanand took visits to Soron, Kasgunj, Chhalesar, Anupshahr and Ramghat and Farrukhabad. In addition of his usual discourse he delivered lecture against *shraddha* for deads and advocated for the shame only to the elders who are alive. He also included the issue of cow protection in his discourses.[62] Dayanand again went to Banaras and on the invitation of barrister Chandrashekar Sen, a leading figure of the Brahmo Samaj and pandit Satyavrat Samashrami of the Bengal Asiatic Society preceded to Calcutta from Banaras on 16 April, 1872.[63] Both of these persons came into contact with Swamiji at Banaras during the Kashi shastrarth (1870) and they published a detialed account of the Banaras shastrarth. An invitation was also made by Devendrababu Thakur (alias Devendranath Tagore) the main leader of Adi Brahmo Samaj when they met at Allahabad in Kumbha fair.[64]

The details of the Calcutta visit has been precisely summed up by Prof Jorden that[65] :

In April 1872 Dayanand left Banaras and started his unhurried journey eastwards : it took him eight months with only six stops on the way to reach Calcutta. Obviously he continued the pattern of study and reflection that had regulated his life after the Banaras disputation, staying for long periods in the same place. He only spent a fortnight in Mughal Sarai and Monghyr, but one month each in Arrah and Patna, two months in Bhagalpur, and nearly four in Dumraon. The biographers mention very few public performances by the Swami in those eight months. He held a *Shāstrārth* on idol worship at Arrah, and another at Patna, which soon broke up when the pundits started to quarrel among themselves. At Arrah he gave two lectures on Vedic *dharma,* and at Bhagalpur one on the duties of man. Apart from this there is mentions of a few discussions with various individuals. At Mughal Sarai he had an exchange of views on sin and its forgiveness with the Reverend Lalbihari De, and at Dumraon a discussion on Vedānta with the famous Shaivite pandit Durgadatta. A conversation with the District Magistrate, H.W. Alexander, mainly about caste, took place at Arrah. On his last stop before Calcutta, at Bhagalpur, Dayanand debated the nature of God with European and Indian clergymen, and interlining with the local Brahmos.[66]

Swami Dayanand arrived in Calcutta on 16 December 1872. The Indian Mirror, noticing his arrival spoke of him as an iconoclast of a superior type, as a man of unbounded learning who had proved himself a name in Northern India. During his stay in Calcutta he met the galaxy of scholars, theologists, social workers, political activists and educationists. One of the prominent preacher of the Adi Brahmo Samaj Hemchandra Chakravarti became pupil of Swamiji. Maharishi

Debendranath Tagore and Rajnarrayan Bose invited Dayanand as Chief Guest in the Magha festival being celebrated on 21 January 1873 as anniversary of Adi Brahmo Samaj. Swamiji learnt a lot from the company of Debendranath Tagore and Adi Brahmo Samaj which reflects in the Satyarth Prakash.[67] Keshab Chandra Sen the leader of the Sadharan Brahmo Samaj also met Swamiji. During their meeting Keshab Chandra Sen said that there were three great religions, Christianity, Islam and the Vedic, and asked which of them should be taken as the true religion. Swamiji gave six reasons for the acceptance of the Vedic religion, one of which was that both the Bible and the Quran contained stories and disputes but there were no such things in the Vedas.[68]

Keshab Chandra Sen gave the swami two useful advices which he readily accepted. The first was the suggestion that he cover his nakedness and Dayanand adopted this suggestion immediately. Second suggestion was that Swami should lecture not in Sanskrit, but in Hindi.[69] Swamiji also inspired from the works of Indian Reform Association founded by Keshab Chandra Sen.[70] Swami Dayanand's many meetings with Ishwarchandra Vidyasagar shaped the views on education and women's emancipation. After serving as Head Pandit of the Bengali Department of Fort William College and Principal of Sanskrit College he had established twenty model schools and about thirty five girl's schools. Against the fierce opposition of the great majority of Hindus, he had successfully carried out a campaign in the fifties to have the Widow Remarriage Bill passed, and was currently fighting his frustrating battle against the polygamy of *kulinism.* As early as 1847 he had established his own Sanskrit Press; by now he had published no less than twenty books, mostly educational textbooks, and edited ten Sanskrit texts. His conversations with Dayanand focused on the problems of women and of education. Dayanand found in Vidyasagar a man after his own heart, steeped in the tradition, and basing all his projects for reform soundly on the teachings of the *Shāstras.* It was with Vidyasagar that for the first time he talked about his own concept of *niyog,* which was to become his own ideal solution to the problem of widows.[71]

Dayanand also visited the Bengal Asiatic Society accompanied by Pandit Rajkumar Vidyaratna, later famous under the name of Ramanand Bharati.[72] Swamiji also discussed ancient history with R.C. Dutt, the civil servant and a renowned historian.[73] His conversations with Rajendra Lal Mitra about ancient Indian history must have been more instructive. This historian hppens to be the Vice-President of the Bengal Asiatic Society and who became first Indian President in 1885.[74] Conversation with these historians, and others like Rajnikanta Gupa and A.K. Datta, opened Dayanand's eyes to a world of historical scholarship of which he had been hitherto little aware.[75] Thus the Calcutta visit helped the Swamiji in shaping his ideology and programme. Swamiji who was concentrating on the religious issues untell the Calcutta visit but there he could understand the importance of social and political reforms. His idea of establishing an organisation got matured and at the same time he could understand the importance of publication and printing.

On 1 April 1873 Dayanand left Calcutta and set on back journey and reached Bhagalpur on 16 April 1873. He took the same route. He extensively visited the areas of U.P. to consolidate his work as preacher. Charged with new ideas Dayanand began to plan his future course of action and after a year his plan of action came into being in the form of the famous work Satyarth Prakash. It is a detailed discourse of Swami Dayanand Saraswati which became an organ of the establishment of Arya Samaj.

Satyarth Prakash

Swami Dayanand Saraswati presented a complete blueprint of an ideal society and religion. In the first part of this he has explained that how and on what lines an ideal society may be oragnised and in the second part Swamiji has examined the prevailing religions and on that basis he conclusively told that only the Vedic religion is true to follow.

Before talking and commenting on the other religions Swamji has made a detailed discourse on the religions of the Aryas, i.e. the prople who lived in Aryavarta (India).[76] In the opening remarks the Satyarth Prakash explain the deplorable conditions as follows[77] : When the Brahmans become destitute of knowledge, there could be not talk of ignorance of the Khsatriyas, Vaishyas and Shudras. Even the ancient practice of the study of Vedas and other Shastras with their meanings died away. The Brahmans only learnt the Vedas by rote - just enough to enable them to earn their livelihood. Even that much they did not teach to the Kshatriyas and others. As the ignorant became the teachers of the people, deceitfulness, fraud, hypocrisy and irreligion began to increase among them. The Brahmans thought that they should make some arrangements for their livelihood. They held a council among themselves and agreed to preach to the Kshatriyas and others : "We alone are the object of worship to you. You could never enter Heaven or obtain salvation except by serving us. Should you not serve us, you shall fall into an awful Hell."

The Vedas, and the Shastras written by the Vedic sages and seers have declared men of learning and righteousness as Brahmans and worthy of respect; but here they, who were ignorant, lascivious, deceitful, licentious, lazy and irreligious, declared themselves as Brahmans and worthy of homage. But how could the sterling virtues of the righteous, learned, and truth-loving Brahmans be found in them. When the Kshatriyas, and others became absolutely destitute of Sanskrit learning, whatever cock and bull stories the Brahmans concocted, the simpletons believed. These nominal Brahmans then became bolder still. They ensnared all in their net of hypocrisy, brought them under thorough control and began to teach - "Whatever a Brahman declares is an infallible as words falling from Divine lips."

It has been clearly mentioned that one doesn't become a Brahman or a sadhu by being the offspring of Brahman parents or a disciple of a Sadhu. A man becomes a Brahman or a holy man by bearing a good character, by doing righteous deeds and by possessing such good virtues as altruism.[78] In the Satyarth Prakash Swamiji has condemned the evil practices of Brahmans and Sadhus. They have been compared with the popes and also condemned their popish practices which used to ensure heaven for people after death in lieu of money. It has been revealed that the popish practices lasted in Europe, but in India popery appeared in a thousand different forms, and cast its net of hypocrisy and fraud; in other words, the Indian popes have kept the rulers and the ruled from acquiring learning and associating with the good.[79]

Swamiji has written in the Satyarth Prakash that : When the preaching of truth died away, ignorance spreads all over India and its people began to quarrel and fight among themselves, for it is said, "Righteousness, wealth, gratification of legitimate desires and salvtation are attainable only when teachers of the highest type are found in a country, but in the absence of good teachers and good disciples dense ignorance prevails. Whenever good teachers are born who preach the truth, ignorance is dispelled and light of truth begins to shine forth."[80]

Then the popes got the laity to worship them and their feet, and began to say that in that alone consisted their future happiness. When the people were completely brought under subjection, the popes became entirely negligent of their duty, and extremely immersed in sensuality. As they were like shepherds, and the people like their sheep-ignorant dupes, knowledge, intellectual power, strength, courage, bravery and valour and all other good qualities were gradually lost. When they became licentious, they began to use meat and drink wine secretly. Then a sect sprung up among them whose followers wrote books called the *Tantras* in which various statements were introduced with the words Shiva said, Parvati said, Bhairawa said. In these book such curious things are written as follows :

"Wine (Madya), meat (Mansa), fish (Meena), cakes (Mudra), Copulation (Maithuna), all these five beginning with the letter M lead to salvation in all ages",Kalitantra. "While in the circle of *Bhairwa* persons of all classes are regarded as twice-born, but after leaving the *Bhairavi* circle the all revert to their respective classes" - *Kularnava Tantra.* "He, who drinks and drinks till he falls to the ground, gets up and again drinks shall never be born again - "*Mahanirmama Tantra."*

"Excepting his mother let a man have sexual intercourse with all women. The Vedas and the Shastras and other ancient books are like harlots. But the Shambhavi Mudra is like a lady of high birth who lives in privacy."[81]

Swamiji has vehemently condemned the *Tantraism* and *Vam Margis* for their heinous and immoral rituals of lower level. He has given a detailed discourse on these aspects as follows[82] : "Now look at the trickery of these stupid popes that whatever is considered to be highly sinful and opposed to the Veda is regarded as virtuous by the *Vam Margis.* The use of meat, wine, fish, delicious eatables, such as various kinds of cakes, and copulation are considered as means of attaining salvation. Believing all men to be incarnations of Shiva and all women incarnations of Paravti they mutter the absurd couplet,

"I am *Shiva* and thou art Parvati, let us then cohabit" and they cohabit - no matter who the man and the women be, and see no harm in it. The low women whose very touch is considered to be polluting are regarded extremely pure by them. As for instance the Shastras forbid the touch of a woman when she is menstruating, but the *Vama Margis* believe her to be very clean. Reader! Mark, now meaningless is that verse of theirs which says : - "Sexual intercourse with a woman in menses is like having a bath in the sacred Tank at Pushkar, with an outcast woman a pilgrimage to Kashi, with a woman working in leather like a bath in the Ganges at Pragaya and with a washer-woman like a pilgrimage to Mathura, and with a prostitute like a pilgrimage to *Ayodhya."* They call wine pilgrimage, meat purity and flower, fish No. 3 and water-cucumber, copulation No. 4 and a cake, No. 5. They have employed such names to meat, etc., so that others may not understand them. They call themselves lotus-like, kind hearted, brave, merciful, mighty (like lean animals). They say that in a social gathering of the Vama Margis all persons, whether Brahmans or outcasts, become Dwija (i.e. twice-born), but as soon as they leave that meeting, they revert to their respective Classes.

In a Bhairavi circle, they mark of draw a triangle, a square, or a circle on the earth or on a piece of board, on which they place a pitcher full of wine, worship it and read this mantra : "O Winel Thou ar free from the curse of Brahma." In a sequestered place, where none but the Vama Margis can go, men and women meet together; the men strip a woman naked and worship her, while the women strip a man naked and worship him. Then any man can get hold of any woman, be she own wife, daughter, mother, sister or daughter-in-law or anyone else's and co-habit with her.

They fill a cup wine and place meat and sweets on a plate. Then the officiating priest takes that cup in his hand and saying,

"I am Bhairava (the Indian Bacchus) or I am Shiva" drinks it up. Thereupon the rest of the company drinks out of the same cup. Having stripped naked someone's wife or a prostitute, or a man, they give a sword in her or his hand, call her a goddess (Devi) or him a great god (Mahadeva).

They worship her or his private organs and make that goddess or god drink a cup of wine and themselves drink of the same cup turn by turn. They go on drinking till they get completely drunk. Anyone of the men can then co-habit with any woman, be she his own sister, mother or daughter, he likes. Sometimes when extremely intoxicated they fight among themselves with their shoes or fists, pull each other's hair, or kick one another. If anyone vomits there, he who has attained the highest stage of perfection, i.e., is an Aghori (an omnivorous person) or an adept would even eat up the vomited matter. The following are the qualifications of an adept among them : - "He that drinks away bottle after bottle in a public house, sleeps in a brothel in order to misconduct himself, and commits similar other sins without compunction or shame, is like a great Sovereign Emperor of the whole earth among the Vama Margis." In short, the greatest sinner among them is called Great, whilst he who is virtuous and afraid of committing evil deeds is called Small, for it is recorded in one of their scriptures, "He that is restrained from the commission of sinful deeds by the fear of public opinion, of disobedience to the dictates of the scriptures, of tarnishing the family name and of being looked down upon by the country at large is human, whilst one who commits wicked deeds without any shame is Divine (Eternal Shiva)" - *Jnana Sankalani Tantra.*

The *Uddisa Tantra* describes a ceremonial thus. Let bottles filled with wine be placed in niches in all four walls of a room. They let a man drink a bottle of wine from one of the niches and go to the next, and have another bottle, thence go to the third niches, and have still another bottle and then go to the fourth and go on dinking till he falls down on the earth like a log. When he comes round a bit let him again drink in the same way till he falls a second time, let him repeat it a third time, and when he gets up a fourth time, he shall never be born again. But the fact is that it is extremely difficult for such men to be born again as men. They shall, on the contrary, enter the bodies of very low creatures and remain there for a long time to come. The law has been laid down in the *Tantra books of Vama Margis* that a man can have sexual intercourse with all women (except his mother) even if they be his daughters, sisters or other near relations. There are ten kinds of higher knowledge known among them. One of them is Matangi knowledge, one who is versed in this believes that even a mother should not be spared, that is, a man can have sexual intercourse even with his mother. These people mutter some intercourse incantations while having sexual intercourse in the hope acquiring occult power. Very few people indeed are there in this worlds who are so insane and as idiotic as these *Vama Margis*!!!

He who would advocate untruth must revile the truth. Mark what the Vama Magis say : - "The Vedas and the Shastras and other ancient books are like common harlots, but the *Shambhavi Mudra* is like a lady of high birth and of great chastity."

No wonder! These Vama Margis being so low and degraded in their morals founded a religion so entirely opposed to the Veda.

Now the word *Sura,* that does not mean wine, has been translated as wine in one of the above quotations. The word *Sura* really means the juice of creeper called Soma. These *Vama Margis,* who have started such wicked practices as killing animals in a sacrifice, should be asked if, as they hold, it to be true that a slaughter ceases to be as such in a Vedic sacrifice, what harm will there be if a Vama Margi and his family members be slaughtered and then offered in a sacrifice?

It is childish to say that there is no sin in eating meat, drinking wine and committing adultery, for meat cannot be had without killing animals, and it can never be right to hurt or kill animals without an offence. With regard to drinking wine, it is interdicted everywhere, and nowhere except in the books of Vama Margis has it been allowed, on the other hand, its use has been forbidden in all sacred books.

Sexual intercourse with a woman excepting one's wedded wife is undoubtedly sinful. He who declares it permissible is indeed himself a great sinner.

They interpolated these and similar other verses into the works of the seers, and also wrote books in the name of many great sages and savants, and thus introduced such sacrifices as *Gomedha* - a sacrifice in which cows were slaughtered - and *Ashwamedha* - one in which horses were killed. They as a sacrifice both - the animals sacrificed and the Yajamana - went to Heaven. This evil practice seems to have originated on account of their ignorance of the true meaning of such words aa *Ashwamedha, Gomedha,* and *Narmedha* that occur in the Brahmans, for had they understood them they would not have committed such blunders"

In Satyarth Prakash Swamiji refuted various evil religioous practices unhesitatingly. He has also explained various wrong notions regarding concepts and meanings. For instance he has explained the *Ashwamedha*, *Gomedha*, and *Narmehda* as follows :

"Wherever in the authentic books of the sages the sanction of such a sacrifice is found, it should be understood that the verse or the passage has been interpolated by the Vama Margis. Now mark! What the *Shatapatha Brahmana* sayas on the subject : - "A king governs his people justly and righteously.

This is called *Ashwamedha."* "A learned man gives a free gift of knowledge to the people. This is also called *Ashwamedha."* Again, "The burning of clarified buter and odoriferous and nutritious substances in the fire in order to purify the air is also called *Ashwamedha*." "To keep the food pure or to keep the senses under control, or to make good use of the rays of the sun or keep the earth free from impurities is called *Gomedha."* "The cremation of the body of a dead person in accordance with the principles laid down in the Vedas is called *Naramedha."*[83]

In theological discourses Swamiji explained that God is formless and being omnipresent he cannot be separated from anything in the whole universe. He has opposed the Shaktas, Vam Margis and Shaivites. He refuted the wrong notions related to besmearing ashes on body and wearing of rosaries. He has written that the Shaktas share this belief. Later on the Vama Margis and the Shavites combined together and introduced the worship of male and female reproductive organs which are termed *Jaladhari* and *Linga.* These unblushing wretches did not feel slightest shame in following these idiotic practices. They began to look upon the worship of stalks and stones and of the reproductive organs as the sole means of attaining righteous ends, wealth, the fulfillment of legitimate desires and even salvation.[84]

Swamiji has also written about the futility of Puranas and *Pauranic* religious practices. He has also revealed the fact that Vyas composed 4,400 verses of the *Mahabharat* which reached to 30,000 by adding the verses by his pupils. These puranas based on superstition deprived the people from the benefits of the Vedic religion, thus world sank deep in degradation. The puranic popes under the influence of Jainism concocted the theory of incarnations and created a number of mythological deities. The Puranic popes wrote out 18 puranas and sub-puranas. The shavites had the Shiva Purana, and the

Shaktas their Devi Bhagwat Purana wrote so the Vaishnavites their Vishnu Purana. The authors did not publish these books in their own names, but instead fathered their publications on sages and seers like Vyasa.[85]

By refuting the idol worship and mythical foundations of different sects in the Satyarth Prakash it has been narrated that : Vaishnava idols symbolized gods having by their sides goddess, who were dressed out in fine style and excited lascivious thoughts by their lewd charms and licentious looks. The Jainees never blow conch-shell, nor ring bells (at the time of worship), while the Vaishavites and other make a tremendous noise (by blowing conch-shell and beating drums, etc.). It was thus that the disciples of the Vaishnavites and the like vily popes escaped from the clutches of the Jainees and were ensnared into the nets spread out by these people. They also composed many books, which are replete with incredibly absurd stories, in the name of the great seers like *Vyasa.* They named them Purana (ancient books) and began to read out select portions from them. They then began to practice wonderful frauds and trickery.

One of these popes would take an idol made of stone, conceal it in a mountain cave or a secret recess in a jungle or bury it in the ground. After this was done, he would proclaim to his disciples that Mahadeva, Parvati, Radha, Krishna, Sita, Ram, Lakshmi, Narayana, Bhairava, Hanuman, or some other god or goddess had visited him in his dreams and informed him that he or she was in Such and Such place, commanded him to get him or her (out of that place), install in a temple and become his or her priest. If these demands were complied with he or she would grant him his heart's desires. The ignorant people who had more money than brains' would hear such stories and believe them to be true; they would enquire of him as to the exact site where the god or goddess was to be found. At this the pope would answer "The idol can be found in this mountain or that jungle, should you desire it I could lead you to the place." There-upon those fools would accompany that scoundrel to the place, find the idol and being struck with astonishment, fall at the feet of the pope and exclaim : "The god is indeed very gracious unto you. Take the idol home and we will build him a temple wherein the idol may be installed, you shall be his priest and we shall also gain our hearts' desires by paying our adoration to him." When the trick played by one of the popes was successful, the others followed his example, had recourse to jugglery and imposture and installed idols with a view to earn their livelihood.[86] Swamiji in Satyarth Prakash has not let a single stone unturned which teaches the idol worship and superstition. In the question- answer form Swamiji has explained as under[87] :

Q - God being Formless cannot be contemplated. Idols are, therefore, absolutely needed. Where is the harm if we stand before an idol with folded palms, think of God and recite His name?

A - God being Formless and Omnipresent cannot have an image. If the sight of an idol puts God in one's mind why cannot this wonderful creation which comprehends the earth, water, fire, air, and vegetation and a hundred and one other things? Cannot one think of God when he looks at the earth and the mountains which are wonderfully constructed, and out of which human beings fashion idols? It is altogether wrong to say that the sight of an idol makes one think of God. This would mean that when the idol is out of sight, the devotee would not think of God, and consequently when all alone, may succumb to the temptation of committing theft, adultery and the like sins - believing as he does that there is no one to witness his actions, he would not scruple to commit the most degrading sins. These are some of the evils that result from the worship of idols. Now mark the difference! He, who has no faith in idols and believes that the Omnipresent, Omniscient and Just God pervades the whole Universe, cannot even harbour evil thoughts in his mind - leave alone committing sins, because he knows that God witnesses all actions - good and bad - and that He is never away from Him even for one moment. He is fully aware of the fact that if he committed a sin - in word, deed or thought - he connot but he punished by a just Providence.

Merely taking the name of God is of no use, even as the repetition of the word Sugar does not give a sweet taste to the mouth, nor does the repetition of the word Neem (*Melia azadiracts*) imparts a bitter taste to the palate. The sensations of sweetness and bitterness are produced only when sweet and bitter substances are brought in contact with the tongue.

Some questions and answers related to the refutation of idol worship, importance of the Vedas and their philosophy and righteous religious practices are of worthy to reproduce here are as follows[88] :

O - Mark! The Vedas are eternal. The practice of Idol worship could not have existed in remote antiquity. At that time the gods were visible. This practice originated with the authors of the Tantras and Puranas. When the knowledge and mental capacity of men suffered diminution, they found a bit hard to contemplate the Deity. Such men can of course fix their minds on idols only, hence idol-worship is meant for the ignorant, even as a man can get to the top of a house only if he uses all the staircases in the house. Should he try to do without the staircases, he could never succeed in his object. Idol-worship is therefore the first step. When after worshipping images for a length of time, the devotee will gain in divine knowledge and in purity of heart, he will then be fitted for divine meditation. Just as a marksman acquires skill in his art by shooting at the target and by continued practice learns to hit smaller objects, in like manner, one who worships the visible symbols of the

Deity will, in course of time, attain to the realization of the abstract Deity. Little girls play with dolls only so long as they do not actually get married. For these reasons idol-worship is not an evil practice.

A. - When it is held that only those acts are righteous that are sanctioned by the Vedas, while those that have been interdicted by them are sinful, idol-worship is a sin even from your standpoint. Whoever accepts as authoritative books whose teachings are opposed to the Vedas may not inappropriately be termed a Nihilist. "Whatever, books have been written by low, despicable people who are opposed to the Vedas drag down the world to the lowest depths of misery and are therefore useless and false. They further envelop the world in dark ignorance and are the cause of great misery in this world as well as the next." All books whose teachings are opposed to the Vedas gain publication and enjoy an ephemeral existence as they do not inculcate eternal principles. It is useless and wrong to believe in them." All the sages from Brahma down to Jaimini have held that righteous conduct consists solely in rejecting all that is opposed to the Vedas and practicing whatever has been enjoined by them, the reason being that the Vedas expound truth and nothing but truth, while all books like the Tantras and Puranas that are replete with anti-Vedic teachings are false and, therefore, the worship of idols which they inculcate is likewise a sin. People never gain knowledge by the worship of material objects; on the contrary, they forget even what they have previously acquired. Knowledge is increased by serving the learned and by associating with them - not by image worship. Can God ever the contemplated thought the worship of stalks and stones? Certainly not. Idol worship cannot be compared with a staircase. It may more appropriately be looked upon as a deep ditch, whoever falls into it is hacked into pieces, can never come out of it and even dies there. Undoubtedly the acquisition of true knowledge and cultivation of habits of truthfulness and like virtues by association with pious and learned men of the ordinary stamps as well as with learned Yogis of the highest order constitutes steps that lead to the realization of the Great God, even as a ladder takes one to the upper storey of a house. No one has yet become a learned man through the worship of idols, on the contrary, most of the idol-worshippers have remained in ignorance and wasted their precious lives and died in despair. Moreover, all those who worship idols now and will do so in future will die without enjoying the fruits of human life which are the practice of righteousness, acquisition of wealth, realization of legitimate desires and attainment of salvation. Idol worship cannot be likened to target-shooting. Association with pious and learned men and a study of the laws of nature constitute the real target, by practicing at which one can reach God by gradual steps. Nor is the worship of images like playing with dolls. The learning of the alphabet and good habits may fitly be compared to playing with dolls and is, therefore, the first step towards the realization of God. Bear in mind that whoever receives the right sort of training and culture will also, in due course of time, reach God, his true Master.

O. - Mind can be concentrated on a material object, but it is difficult to rivet it on an immaterial one, hence the worship of idols is justifiable.

A. - No, the concentration of mind on a material object is impossible, for it can grasp it at once and after mastering all the details wanders over fresh objects. On the other hand, in the case of Immaterial, infinite God, do what it will, the mind will never be able to comprehend Him. God being Indivisible the mind cannot wander, it contemplates His nature, attributes, characteristics, and being beatified is perfectly focused. Had it been possible to concentrate the mind on a material object, all the people of the world would have been able to concentrate their minds, because it remains engrossed in worldly objects such as other minds, one's wife, children and friends and wealth, but no one can concentrate his mind except on an abstract Being because He is Indivisible. Hence, idol-worship is a sin. (This is the first argument against idol-worship).

1. Millions of rupees are spent in constructing temples for idol-worship. This leads to poverty and indolence.
2. Free and promiscuous mixing together of the sexes in the temples leads to adultery, internecine quarrels, and the spread of disease (contagious).
3. The idol-worshipers regard this mode of worship as the sole means of the practice of righteousness, the acquisition of wealth, the fulfilment of legitimate desires the attainment of salvation. They therefore, give up all active work and waste away their precious lives.
4. Since the people worship idols with different names, forms and characteristics, they have no unity of faith and their mutually antagonistic beliefs and practices create bad blood in the county and lead it to its ruin.
5. They depend upon the idols for the defeat of their enemies and the triumph of their arms, and, therefore, do not exert themselves. The result is that they are defeated and the government of the country, independence and wealth with its attendant pleasures, fall to the lot of their enemies. They are themselves robbed of their independence and reduced to the condition of a subject race, suffer in a hundred different ways like the pony of an innkeeper and the donkey of the potter.
6. If someone were to say to another person that he would put a stone in his name or place, he will feel angry and

will most likely abuse him or hit him back. In like manner the ignorant people who take a stone to be the symbol of the Deity and worship idols in place of God will surely have the Divine wrath visited upon them.

7. Labouring under mistaken notions, they peregrinate from temple to temple and from one country to another, endure untold misery, lay axe at the root of their worldly and spiritual welfare, suffer at the hand of thieves and are duped by thugs.
8. Money is given away to wicked priests who spend it on debauchery and the gratification of the bestial appetites of flesh and wine and in fomenting quarrels and in promoting litigation. Thereby the donor forfeits its happiness and is pained beyond measure.
9. These people lay themselves open to the charge of ingratitude by not showing due respect to their parents and other persons worthy of esteem and worshipping idols instead.
10. When these idols are stolen by thieves or are dashed into pieces (by some iconoclast) they set up loud lamentation.
11. The priestesses and priests are corrupted on account of illicit intercourse with other men and women and thus forfeit their connubial felicity.
12. The servants do not properly obey their masters and they turn against each other and are thereby ruined.
13. The souls by constant contemplation of dead and inert matter lose the power of sound judgment, because the material properties of the object contemplated (such as a stone) are transmitted to the soul through the Manas.

14. God has created fragrant substances like the flowers to purify air and water and to prevent disease. If the priests were not to pluck the flowers, the purificatory process would go on for an indefinitely long period, air and water would be purified and the flowers would continue shedding fragrance till the time of their natural decay. They cut off their useful career in the prime of their life. The flowers get mixed with mud, are decomposed, and emit stench instead of sweet odour. Has God created flowers and other odoriferous substance for making an offering of them to the idols?
15. Sandalwood, un-husked grain and the like offering get mixed with water and mud, and are then thrown into a drain or a cistern where they rot and give off such offensive odours as issue from human ex-crement. Thousands of tiny creatures are constantly produced and die and cause it to stink still more.

These are a few evils caused by the worship of idols. It should, therefore, be given up by all righteous men. Who ever worshipped idols, worship it, or will do so in future could not have, nor can he now or will in future escape, from the effects of these evils.

O. - Is no form of idol worship permissible? What is then meant by the expression worship of the five gods which has been in common use since time immemorial? Does it not imply the worship of the gods called Shiva, Vishnu, Ambika, Ganesha and Suryas?

A. - No from of idol-worship is permissible, but the worship of the five living gods is our duty. This expression Pancha Yajna or the worship of the five gods - has a very good meaning, but the ignorant fools have degraded it and construed it to mean something altogether different from what was originally intended. The worship of Shiva and the like gods has already been condemned. But we shall now explain what is meant by the worship of the five gods which is sanctioned by the Vedas. This may be termed worship of gods that are truly worthy of reverence. The first object of worship is the mother. It is the duty of her sons and daughters to serve this goddess with all their heart and all their soul, and keep her happy. Let her never be treated harshly. "The second object of worship is father. This god should also be served like the mother." The third object of worship is the teacher who bestows knowledge (upon his pupils). This god should also be served with utmost devotion." The fourth object of worship is the altruistic teacher of humanity who is learned, deeply preaching the truth and thereby making the people happy." "The fifth object of worship is the husband for the wife and the wife for the husband." These are the five living gods who bring a man into being and bring him up, and it is through them that he gains true knowledge, sound culture and is instructed into the righteous principles of conduct. It is the worship of these that leads one to God. Whoever does not worship them and worship idols instead is a transgressor of Vedic principles.

Dayanand Saraswati repeatedly stressed upon the fact that true happiness consists solely in giving up altogether the worship of idols and in serving the mother and other living gods. The hypocrite priests have created superstition for their personal ends. Under a righteous government these lovers of idols (priests) would have been compelled to earn their living by breaking stones, making bricks and carrying materials for building purposes or doing like work. It is evil practices like idol worship that are responsible for the existence of millions of idle, lazy, indolent, and beggarly priest in India, who are mainly answered for this widespread ignorance, fraud and mendacity in the country.[89] He also refuted the miracles of various deities, temples, and idols. Swamiji refuting the practice of *Shraddha* criticised the priests of Gaya as follows : Hundred and Thousands rupees are given away in charity to the priests for the good and happiness of manes; these priests of Gaya waste all this money in prostitution and other sinful practices. If this be the merit of offering cakes to the manes of Gaya, why can Gaya not be freed from sins like prostitution.[90] He has also exposed the futility of pilgrimage of holy places. He also clarified the difference betwen astronomy and astrology and also refuted the astrological misbelief developed or created by the astrologers to fulfill their materialistic greed and lust.[91] He has made mockery of *gaudan* at the time of death and condemned the *Garud Puran* written by priests and pandits to make their good living for generations.[92] Refutation of the theories of Heaven and hell created by priests and fruitlessness of fasting (*Vrata*) has been extensively deliberated in the Satyarth Prakash.[93]

Swamiji has wrote about the status of Brahmacharis and Sanyasis of his time as follows : The two orders are good in principle, but there is a great deal of hypocrisy rampant even among them now-a-days. There are many among them who assume the name of Brahmachari, grow long matted hair, pretend to possess wonderful powers, but are engrossed in muttering the name of some deity and rituals. They never even take the name of studying. They do not at all exert themselves for the study of that Brahma-Veda-which gives them the name of Brahmachari. All these Brahmacharis are as useless as the teats (loose flesh) hanging from the neck of a goat. There are also any number of Sanyasis who are destitute of knowledge, and carry staffs and water-gourds symbols of their Order-with them, but do nothing to further cause of the Vedic religion. Such men generally enter into Sanyas when they are quite young, leave off their stuides and wander about begging from place to place. Such Brahmacharis and Sanyasis waste their time in visiting sacred places (such as rivers, hills, temples, etc.), and stone images, and paying homage to them, do not hypocrisy and false practices rampant in the land, eat and drink and live in ease (not caring a brass farthing for their country). They are engrossed in their little jealousies and feuds, revile each other, and conduct themselves improperly (in various other ways). It is thus that they pass their time.

They seems to think that they have done their duty simply by wearing ochre-coloured garments and carrying their staffs and water-gourds, believe themselves to be superior to all, never do any good works. Such Sanyasis live useless lives in this world. Of course, those among them who are engaged in altruistic works are alright.[94]

In the last Para of chpater II of Satyarth Prakash entitled "On An Examination of the different Religions prevailing in India" Dayanand has refuted the activities of hypocrite *Sadhus, Siddhas, Yogis, Mahantas.* The same is worthy to reproduced here in verbatim as follows[95] :

> "O- Are the giris, the Puris and the Bharatis and other Gosaeens good? They go about in groups, help thousands of Sadhus to enjoy themselves, preach Vedanta (pantheism) wherever they go, and read and teach a little, therefore, they must be very good people, indeed.

A. - All these ten names such as Giri, Puri, etc., are not ancient but of recent origin. They form themselves into groups for the sake of getting good food. There are plenty of Sadhus who join these companies for food only. They practice a great deal of hypocrisy as well. For instance, they make one of their company their Mahant (religious superior) who is also their headman. Every evening he sits on the raised cushioned seat, all the Sadhus and Brahmans stand up before him with flowers in their hands, read such couplets as "Unto Narayana, Padamabha, Vasishtha Shakti, his son Parashar, Vyasas, Shuka, and the great

Gaurpada", and then shout Hara Hara (God, God), shower flowers on him and prostrate themselves before him. Whosoever does not want to do it, finds it hard even to live among them. They practice all this hypocrisy for mere show so that they may get a name for holiness in the world, and thereby obtain plenty of money to enjoy themselves. There are any numbers of abbots, (heads of convents or sacred places) who, though married, pride themselves on being Sanyasis. They do nothing useful. They never perform the duties of sanyasis (Vide Chapter V) and simply waste their time. They even oppose one who gives them good advice. Mostly these people smear their bodies with ashes and wear Rudraksha. Some of them are proud of belonging to the Shaiv sect. In religious discussions they advocate Shaivism as taught by Shankracharya and refute Chakrankitism. They never engage in advocating the Vedic religion nor in refuting false faiths. These Sanyasis hold that they have nothing to do with the advocacy of truth or the refutation of untruth, because they are great souls. Such people are a mere burden to the community. No wonder then that religions and sects opposed to the Vedas, such as the *Vama Marg*, Christianity and Mohammedanism have multiplied and are still on the increase while they (i.e., the followers of the Vedic religion) themselves are being decimated and yet their eyes won't open, but how is it possible when there is no zeal in their hearts for promoting public good and doing their duties. These people set a higher value on their dinner than on anything else, are very much afraid of the censure of the world. Sanyasis are enjoined to abjure live of public applause, love of wealth and sensual enjoyments and love of kith an kin and disciples. How can they be called Sanyasis when they have not been able to renounce these passions? It is the paramount duty of a Sanyasi to devote himself day and night to the promotion of the good and happiness of the world by impartial preaching of the Vedic religion. It is useless for them to call themselves Sanyasis as long as they do not duties obligatory on their Order. It is only when the Sanyasis devote themselves to the promotion of public good more earnestly than do the householders, actuate by self-interest, to their own affairs, that all Orders remain progressive. Mark you, false faiths are increasing before your very eyes, the people are even turning Christians and Mohammedans, you do not make the least effort to protect your own people and convert others to your faith (i.e., the Vedic religion)? You could do it only if you had a mind to do it. As long as you Sanyasis do not improve yourselves, the inhabitants of Aryavarta and other countries will not make any real progress. A county makes genuine progress only when the causes of advancement such as the study and teaching of the Vedas and other true Shastras, the keeping of Brahmacharya and other Orders in good condition, and the preaching of truth, are in operation. Bear you Sanyasis in mind, there are many false and hypocritical practices in vogue which you really know to be such. For instance, a Sadhu with trading propensities declares himself to be a saint (Siddha). He claims to possess miraculous powers such as making the childless women bear children. On hearing this many women go to him and, with folded palms, pray for sons. The fraud of a saint blesses them all saying, "You shall bear sons." Whosoever among them bears a son, attributes this happy event to the blessing of our Saint Poor women! What answer will she make if she were asked : "By whose blessing did pigs, donkeys, bitches and hens get their little ones? There are others who declare that they can bring the dead to life. The ignorant believe it to be true. Now, why should these people themselves die if they possessed the power they pretend to. There are other rascals, again, who invent such cunning devices to deceive the cleverest. Take, for instance, the thugs of Dhanasari. They go to distant places in parties of five or seven. Whoever among them looks robust and is of a taking appearance is appointed their ring-leader. Henceforth, he is a Sidhha. They place him in a sequestered place outside a rich town or village and themselves go into the town and ask everyone who comes across their way if he has seen or heard of such and such Mahatma. They are asked, "Who and of what kind is that Mahatma?" They answer, "He is great Saint. He can tell what passes in your mind. Whatever he says comes to pass. He is the king of yogis, we have left our hearths and homes in his quest. We heard from some one that he had come this way." The householder rejoins : "When you happen to meet that Saint, please do not fail to inform me also of it. I shall also have the pleasure of seeing him and questioning him about my heart's desires." All day long they repeat the same story to anyone who meets them. At night they all assemble together at the rendezvous, eat and drink together and sleep in the same place. They get up in the morning and all the four accomplices of our Saint again go into the town and repeat the same story. This goes on for two or three days. Then they go to a rich man and tell him that they have found a Saint and if he has a desire to see him they could take him to him. When he is about to accompany them, they ask him what they wants to inquire (from the Saint). He says, that he wants to have a son or wealth or to be cured of some disease or to overcome his enemy. They then take him to our Saint and seat him according to the understanding arrived at between the Saint and his accomplices. Thus if the visitor be desirous of getting wealth, they seat him on the right of our Saint, if of a son in front of him, if of getting cured of some disease on his left, if of overcoming his enemy, they bring him from behind and seat him among those who are in front. The instant the visitor salutes him, our Saint, proud of his powers, cries out with a loud voice, "Do I keep sons in store here that thou hast come with the desire of getting a son," or "Do I keep bags full of gold here that thou hast come with the desire of getting wealth. Mendicant never have wealth," or "Am I a doctor that thou hast come with the desire of getting cured. I am not a doctor that I should cure thee. Go thou to a doctor." These rogues have also certain signs by means of which they indicate to the Saint what relation the sick man bears to the visitor; for instance, if it be his father, one of the accomplices raises his thumb, it his mother, index finger, if his brother, middle finger, if his wife, ring-finger, if his daughter, little finger; and therefore our Saint can at once tell if his father, mother, brother, wife or daughter is ill. The visitor is quite captivated by these answers. The scoundrels say to him, "Is not he what we told you?" The visitor replies, "Yes, he is the same as you told me, you have done me a great favour. I am, indeed, very lucky to have had the pleasure of seeing him." Thereupon the rogues say, "Look here, brother, this Saint is his own master. He is not likely to stay here for long. If you want to have his blessing, serve him with all your heart and soul and wealth because it is said, 'It is service that bears fruit.' Should he get pleased with anyone, who knows what blessing he may give him as the old proverb says : Most inscrutable are the ways of Saints!" The visitor having heard such soft and soapy words, is highly pleased and wends his way back home praising the Saint. The swindlers also go with him, lest anyone should expose their fraud. He also praises our Saint before his friends or other people who happen to meet him on the way. By and by, the news spreads all over the town and then there is a great hullabloo. Everyone is heard to say, "A great Saint has come and put up at such and such a place, let us go to see him." When people go there and put questions to the Saint as to what their heart-felt desires are, all order being lost he does not answer any question and remains quite silent except that he says, "Pray don't tease me."

Thereupon all his accomplices begin to say, "If you tease him any more, he will go away." Sometimes a very rich man in the crowd takes one of the accomplices to one side and says, "Let the Saint tell me what passes in my mind and I shall believe him to be a true one." The swindler asks him what it is, the rich man tells him what his desire is, and the swindler then takes him and seats him according to the above understanding. The Saint at once tells him what his desire is. The whole crowd hears his answer; it is in the mouth of everyone that he is indeed a very great Saint. Everyone brings an offering according to his position, such as sweets, copper, silver, gold, cloth and flour, etc. The swindlers fleece them as long as the presents keep pouring in Sometimes our Saint can come across one or two such men as have 'more money than brains', who pay him a thousand rupees or so in return for which he gives them a pinch of ashes and his blessing for a son in the following words : "If thy devotion be true, thou shalt get a son". There are many such thugs who can only be found out by men of intelligence and enlightenment. The study of the Vedas and association with the good and the learned enables one to escape the clutches of such swindlers since the true visual organ of man is knowledge. Without education and culture, there can be no enlightenment. They alone are entitled to be called men and scholars who receive good education and training in early life, whilst those who live in bad company, become wicked and sinful, remain most foolish and thereby suffer terribly. Hence, it is declared that knowledge is the highest thing in the world. Whosoever knows believes.

It is said : "Whosoever does not know the merits or the properties of an object always runs it down just as a Bhil rejects the beautifully fragrant Gunja flowers and, instead, wear a garland of Gajamuktas. In like manner, he alone, who is learned, wise, and virtuous and associates with the good, is Yogi, is studious, energetic, possesses self-control and is gentle, reaps the fourfold fruit of human life, viz., practice of righteousness, acquisition of wealth, gratification of legitimate desires, and attainment of salvation and thereby lives in happiness here in this world as well as in the life to come."

In the end Dayanand has said that we have thus briefly discussed the religion of the people of Aryavarta. Thus, Swamiji has refuted the ill and evil religious practices prevailing in the so called Hinduism, whom Swamiji called the Aryans.

In addition of the foregoing Swami Dayanand had also critically examined the Jainism, Buddhism and Charbak whom he considered atheists. In the same manner he has also examined the Christianity and Mohammedanism. Through his study of Vedas and shastras Swami Dayanand proved the superiority of Vedic religion.

As has been already said that Swami Dayanand Saraswati has devised a complete system of ideal society along with social and political system in the Styarth Prakash. Thus, to implement his model and propagation of his ideas he felt urgent need of an organisation, which can play the role of an instrument of implementation .

Foundation of Arya Samaj

Though the Calcutta visit had deep impact on Swami Dayanand from where his idea of founding an organisation became matured. But before this visit the idea of founding an organisation was already stirring in his mind. When Swamiji began his journey to Calcutta then he also stayed at Arrah on the way for about fifteen days.[96] Here Swamiji also founded a *sabha* with the objective of promoting the *Arya Dharma* and its *Riti-Niti* (mode policy). It could not live long and after one or two meetings it became defunct after departure of Swamiji after few days.[97] Again second attempt of establishing the

Aryasabha was made at Banaras in June 1874. The same was founded for the good management of Kashi *Arya Vidyalaya.* It was also decided that the *sabha* will publish a monthly paper entitled '*Arya-Prakash*'. Thus, it was conceived that these three enterprises will help in the advancement of *Aryavarta Desh*[98] But all such efforts could not yield required results and within a period of one year all such activities seized to be exist.[99]

All above developments did not disheartened Swamiji and his thirst and efforts for foundation of organisation remained continued. Thus, these initial efforts proved as successful experiments. In December, 1874 Dayanand visited Ahmedabad where he had proposed the setting up of an Arya Samaj and Vedic school, but his proposal could not receive any response. All Dayanand did at this time was to plant the seed in the hope that it might germinate.[100] On 31 December, 1873 Swamiji arrived at Rajkot from Ahmedabad at the invitation of Hargovinddas Dwarkadas, the Secretary, Prarthana Samaj, Rajkot. The branch of the Prarthana Samaj, Rajkot came into being two years back i.e. 1873. In January, 1874 the proposal of Swami Dayanand the members of the Prarthana Samaj agreed to establish Aryasamaj by converting the Prarthana Samaj into it. Manishankar and in his absence Uttamram Nirbhayaram were appointed the *Pradhan* and Hargovinddas Dwarkadas and Nagindas Brajbhushan were appointed the *Mantri* of newly constituted Arya Samaj, Rajkot. Swamiji himself framed the rules of Arya Samaj, which were printed in multiple copies for distribution. Swamiji was of the view that the main headquarter of Aryasamaj remain in Ahemdabad and Bombay. It was also decided that on Sunday the weekly sessions of the Araysamaj will be held.[101]

The first Aryasamaj of Rajkot was short lived and within five-six moth it was disbanded on account of political trouble.[102] On his way back to Bombay from Rajkot Swamiji again tried to establish Aryasamaj at Ahmedabad but could not succeed. The efforts, however, continued and an Aryasamaj came into being at Ahmedabad but not before its foundation in Bombay.

Swami Dayanand returned to Bombay on 29 January, 1875 and he revived his efforts for setting up an Aryasamaj. Two of his followers and supporters Lachhmandas Khemji and Rajkrishan Maharaj enthusiastically initiated the membership drive. By 17 February hundred people agreed to become its members as on the same date some hundred people held an open meeting in Girgaon and formed a committee under the chairmanship of Rao Bahadur Dadoba Pandurang to consider rules and regulations. But due to some obstacles created by Rajkrishan Maharaj the task of drafting was entrusted to Panachand Anandji Parekh. Parekh drafted the rulers of Arya Samaj and Swamiji made necessary amendments in them.

On 10 April 1875 (Saturday, Chaitra Shukla 5, V.S. 1932) the Bombay Arya Samaj was formally established during a meeting held at the garden of a Parsi resident of the city, Dr. Manekji Aderji, living in a locality called Girgaon near Prarthana Samaj Hall. Girdharilal Dayaldas Kothari and Panachand Anandji Parekh were elected president and secretary, respectively. Weekly meetings were held on Saturday, but later Sundays were found to be more convenient, being government holidays. The initial membership amounted to 100. Dayanand was requested to be the president or at a least a patron, but he refused. He said that he would not like to start 'gurudom' in the Arya Samaj. He, however, agreed to be an ordinary member. In the list of members, given in alphabetical order, Dayanand's name figured at number 31. His *Varna* was mentioned as Brahmin, his profession as Sannyasi, and his education as having a knowledge of Sanskrit and Vedic Sanskrit.[103]

Thus, the Arya Samaj at Bombay came into being. In real sense it was the first Arya Samaj and now these days the foundation day is celebrated on the date of the foundation of the Bombay Arya Samaj. At the time of the foundation of the same twenty eight principles and rules were approved by the hundred founder members. These rules are as follows[104] :

1. The Establishment of Arya Samajes in the interests of Society is absolutely necessary.
2. The (Arya) Samaj shall regard the Vedas alone as independently and absolutely authoritative. For purposes of testimony and for understanding of the Vedas, as also for historical purposes, all the four Brahmanas-Shathpatha, etc., the six Vedangas, the four Upavedas, the six Darshanas, and 1,127 Shakshas or expositions of the Vedas, shall, by virtue of their being ancient and recognized works of Rishis, he also regarded as secondarily authoritative, in so far only as their teaching is in accord with that of the Vedas.
3. There shall be a *principal* Arya Samaj in each province, and the other Arya Samajes shall be its branches, all connected with one another.
4. The Branch Samajes shall conform to and follow as model the Principal Samaj.
5. The Principal Samaj shall possess various Vedic works in Sanskrit and Aryabhasha (Hindi) for the dissemination of true knowledge, and it shall issue a weekly paper under the name of "*Arya Prakash*", also an exponent of the Vedic teaching. The paper and the books shall be patronized by all Samajes.
6. Every Samaj shall have a President and a Secretary. Other men and women shall be the members thereof.

7. The President shall be responsible for the maintenance of the integrity and for the promotion of the prosperity of the Samaj, while the Secretary shall reply to all letters, and shall keep a record of the names, state, etc., of all the members of the Samaj.
8. The members of the Samaj shall be men of truth, of up-right policy and principles, of pure character, and of philanthropic impulses.
9. Whatever leisure a member gets from house-hold work, he shall devote the same to the good of the Samaj, with more than the earnestness displayed in the discharge of household duties. Those that have no family to care for, should, in particular, be always striving to promote the well-being of the body. In no other way should they behave.
10. Every eighth day the President, the Secretary and other members of the Samaj shall come together in the Samaj Mandir, giving precedence to punctual attendance over everything else.
11. Having assembled together, they should be calm and composed in their minds, and in a spirit of love, and free from bias, they may ask questions and obtain answers from each other. This done, they shall sing the hymns of the Sama Veda in praise of God, and songs bearing on the true Dharma, the right principles and the right teaching, to the accompaniment of musical instruments. And the *mantras* shall be commented upon and explained and the lectures delivered on similar (Vedic) themes. After this there shall be music again, to be followed by interpretation of mantras and speeches as before, and so on in succession.
12. Every member shall cheerfully contribute a hundredth part of the money he has earned honestly and with

the sweat of his brow, towards the funds of the Samaj, the Araya Vidyala and the *Arya Prakash* paper. If he contributes more, the greater shall be his reward. The money thus contributed shall be used for the purposes specified and in no other way.

13. The more an individual bestirs himself in bringing income to the Samaj for the purpose specified, and for the diffusion of a knowledge of the teachings of the Arya Samaj, the more honour shall he receive for his energy and zeal.
14. The Samaj shall do, *stuti, prarthana* and *upasana* (i.d. shall glorify, pray to and hold communion with the one only God), in the manner commended by the Vedas. To speak of God as the Being who is formless, almighty, just, infinite, immutable, eternal, incomparable, merciful, the father of all, the mother of the entire universe, all-supporting, the lord of all, possessing the attributes of truth, intelligence, happiness, and so on : as all-pervading and the knower of all hearts, indestructible, deathless, everlasting, pure, and conscious; as inherently in a state of salvation, endless, the bestower of happiness, the giver of righteousness, wealth, comfort and salvation; to speak of Him as endowed with such and similar other qualities and attributes, is to do His *stuti* (i.e. to glorify and praise Him). Asking His help in all righteous undertakings, is identical with *prarthana* (i.e. praying to Him), and to become absorbed in the contemplation of His to become absorbed in the contemplation of His Essence, which is absolute Happiness, is termed *upasana* (i.e., holding communion with Him). The aforesaid Being, possessing the attributes of *incorporeity* etc., shall alone be adored, and naught besides.

15. The Samaj shall perform Vedic *Sanskars,* such as *Anteshti,* etc.
16. The Vedas and the ancient Arsha Granths shall be studied and taught in the Arya Vidyala, and true and right training, calculated to improve males and females, alone shall be imparted, on Vedic lines.
17. In the interest of the country, two kinds of reform shall receive thorough attention in the Samaj, spiritual and worldly. There shall be uplifting in these two directions, for the promotion of purity; indeed, reform conducive to the welfare of entire mankind shall be undertaken by the Samaj.
18. The Samaj shall believe in what is right and just only, i.e., in the true Vedic Dharma, destitute of all element of partiality and standing the crucial test of all the *pramanas* occular demonstration and so forth. It shall never have faith in anything else, if it can help it.
19. The Samaj shall send learned men, of approved character, everywhere to preach truth.
20. In the interests of the education of both males and females, separate schools shall be established, if possible, in all places. In the seminaries for females the work of teaching and that of serving the students shall be carried on by *females only,* and in the schools for males, the responsibility of doing the same shall lie with *males.* Never shall this rule be infringed.
21. The schools shall be looked after and maintained as the President of the Samaj shall direct.
22. The President and the other members of the Samaj shall, for the maintenance of mutual good-will, keep their minds wholly divested of all feelings of pride, of willfulness, hate, anger, etc., and, with such vices shut

out, They shall, being free of enmity and pure of heart, love on another, even as each loves his own self.

23. When deliberating on a subject, that which has been, as the fruit of this deliberation, been ascertained to be in thorough accord with the principles of justice and universal benevolence, and absolutely true, the same shall be made known to the members and believed in by them. Acting thus is termed rising above bias or prejudices.
24. He who conforms his conduct to the principles specified, and is righteous and endowed with true virtues, the same shall be admitted to the superior portion of the Samaj, while he who is otherwise than this, shall belong to the ordinary portion of the Samaj. But the individual who openly appears to be utterly depraved and debased, he shall be expelled from the Samaj. Such a step, however, shall not be dictated by prejudice; on the contrary, both the things specified shall be done after due deliberation by the exalted members be done after due deliberation by the exalted members of the Samaj, and not otherwise.
25. The President and other *Sabhasads* of the Samaj shall ever strive, to the utmost of their power, to look after and improve the Arya Samaj, the Arya Vidyala, the *Arya Prakash* paper, and the finance of the Samaj.
26. So long as an Arya Samajist can get a brother Arya Samajist to employ or to serve him, so long he should not employ or get anyone else to serve him. The relations in existence between these two should be the relations that ought to subsist between master and servant.
27. Whenever an occasion for making a donation arises, as, for instance, in connection with a marriage, the birth

of a son, the realization of a fortune, or a death in the family, and so on, the Arya Samajist concerned shall be expected to make a donation on such an occasion. No act is more meritorious, and the members shall always bear this fact in mind.

28. Whenever an addition is made to the principles or rules above laid down, or whenever any of these is altered or amended, such an addition, alteration or amendment, shall invariably be the result of thorough deliberation on the subject by the exalted *Sabhasads* of the Samaj, and the nature of the same shall be previously made known to all the members.

Since the beginning the Arya Samaj organisations were based on democratic values. Every Arya Samaj was autonomous in nature as no paramount body as central authority was established. Swami Dayanand suggested certain rules and principal which were adopted by the general body of Bombay Arya Samaj. It was envisaged that all the Arya Samajs in India and abroad may adopt these principles and rules alongwith some amendments as per specific requirement and situations. The Bombay Arya Samaj came into being as a model because it was an outcome of Swami Dayanand's knowledge, experience and wisdom which was aquired by him during thirty years. Moreover, it was the first Arya Samaj which was founded by Swamiji himself. It may be concluded that an instrument of implementation of the ideas and thoughts of Swami Dayanand Saraswati came into being in the shape of the Bombay Arya Samaj.

From the study of twenty eight principles and rules the nature of the Arya Samaj organisation is very clear that it was a broad based organisation. It aimed to bring together all Hindus who agreed on the revival of Vedic religion. Looking to the moral degradation of Hindus the Arya Samaj aimed at moral upliftment of them. In totality it wished the religious, social and national advancement of the country. Basically, Arya Samaj wanted to reform the religion, society and polity. The same is clear from an important speech of Swamiji as follows : If you are able to achieve something for the good of mankind by Samaj, then establish a Samaj; I will not stand in your way. But if you do not organize it properly, there will be a lot of trouble in the future. As for me, I will only instruct you in the same way as I teach others, and this much you should keep clearly in mind : my beliefs are not unique, and I am not omniscient. Therefore, if in the future any error of mine should be discovered after rational examination, then set it right. If you do not act that way, then this Samaj too will later on become just a sect. That is the way by which so many sectarian divisions have become prevalent in India : by making the *guru's* word the touchstone of truth and thus fostering deep-seated prejudices which make people religion-blind, cause quarrels and destroy all right knowledge. That is the way India arrived at her sorry contemporary state, and that is the way this Samaj too would grow to be just another sect. This is my firm opinion : even if there be many different sectarian beliefs prevalent in india, if only they all acknowledge the *Vedas,* then all those small rivers will re-unite in the ocean of Vedic wisdom, and the unity of *dharma* will come about. From that unity of *dharma* there will result social and economic reform, arts and crafts and other human endeavors will improve as desired, and man's life will find fulfilment : because by the power of that *dharma* all values will become accessible to him, economic values as well as psychological ones, and also the supreme value of *moksha.* Thus, it may be said that the Arya Samaj organisation was broad based organisation free from sectarian and selfish interests for the betterment of human kind and humanity. But at the same time it promoted the national consciousness.

NOTES

1. *The Autobiography of Dayanand Saraswati* (Ed. by K.C. Yadav), p. 29, Baba Chhajju Singh has translated the V.S. 1881 into 1825 A.D.
2. Baba Chhajju Singh, Part I, *op.cit.*, p. 1.
3. J.T.F. Jorden, *Dayanand Sarasvati : His Life and Ideas, op.cit.*, p. 3.
4. The Autobiography of Dayanand Saraswati, *op.cit.*, p. 29.
5. J.M. Sahrma *op.cit.*, p. 4.
6. The Autobiography of Dayanand Saraswati, *op.cit.*, p. 30.
7. *Ibid,* p. 31.
8. *Ibid.*
9. *Ibid,* p. 32.
10. *Ibid.*
11. Lajpat Rai, *A History of the Arya Samaj,* (first published in 1914 from London), Orient Longman Ltd., New Delhi, Indian edition, 1967, p. 13.
12. *Ibid,* p. 15.
13. Baba Chhajju Singh, Part I, *op.cit.*, p. 11.
14. *The Autobiography of Dayanand Saraswati*, *op.cit.*, pp. 36-37.
15. *Ibid*, p. 39 and J.T.F. Jorden, op.cit., p. 20.
16. *The Autobiography of Dayanand Saraswati*, *op.cit.*, pp. 39-40.
17. *Ibid*, p. 96.
18. Harbilas Sarda, *op.cit.*, p. 13.
19. The Autobiography of Dayanand Saraswati, *op.cit.*, p. 40.
20. Baba Chhajju Singh, Part I, *op.cit.*, p. 16.
21. The Autobiography of Dayanand Saraswati, *op.cit.*, p. 41.
22. *Amar Kantak.*
23. The Autobiography of Dayanand Saraswati, *op.cit.*, p. 49.
24. J.M. Sahrma *op.cit.*, pp. 22-23.

25. *Ibid*, p. 23.
26. Lekhram's Jiwancharitra of Dayanand, p. 25, referred by Harbilas Sarda, *op.cit.*, p. 23.
27. Devendranath Mukhopadhyaya, *op.cit.*, p. 83.
28. *The Autobiography of Dayanand Saraswati*, *op.cit.*, p. 49. At Swaron Swami Virjanand came into contact with Maharaja Vinay Singh of Alwar and on his humble request he came to Alwar on the condition that the Maharaja should read with the Swami for three hours daily. He taught the Maharaja for three years. From Alwar Swami Virjanand moved to Bhartpur and at the request of Maharaja Balwant Singh he stayed there for six months. In the year V.S. 1893 (A.D. 1836) Swami Virjanand arrived at Mathura and he permanently settled there. (Baba Chhajju Singh, *op.cit.*, part I, pp. 29-27).
29. Baba Chhajju Singh, *op.cit.*, part I, p. 32.
30. J.T.F. Jorden, *Dayanand Saraswati : His life and Ideas, op.cit.*, p. 32.
31. Around in 1845 Swami Virjanand settled in Mathura and opened the school of grammar financially supported by the rulers of Alwar, Bharatpur and Jaipur states.
32. J.T.F. Jorden, *Dayanand Saraswati : His life and Ideas, op.cit.*, p. 38.
33. Baba Chhajju Singh, *op.cit.*, part I, p. 34. According to Harbilas Sarda Virjanand said; "I demand from you something else as *dakshina*. Take a vow before me that so long as you will live, you shall work incessantly to spread Arsha literature and a true knowledge of the Vedas, and condemn works which teach false doctrines and tenets, and that you shall even give up your life, if necessary, in re-establishing the Vedic religion. This is my *dakshina*". (Harbilas Sarda, *op.cit.*, p. 41) also see *The Autobiography of Dayanand Saraswati*, *op.cit.*, p. 57).
34. Harbilas Sarda has written that it was early in Vaisakh V.S. 1921 (May A.D. 1864) that Swami Dayanand Arrived at Agra (*op. cit.*, p. 43).

35. Harbilas Sarda, *op.cit.,* p. 44.
36. *Ibid,* p. 45.
37. Baba Chhajju Singh, *op.cit.,* part I, p. 37.
38. The Autobiography of Dayanand Saraswati, *op.cit.*, pp. 58-59.
39. *Ibid,* p. 59.
40. Harbilas Sarda, *op.cit.,* p. 51.
41. *Ibid,* p. 52.
42. *Ibid.*
43. Baba Chhajju Singh, *op.cit.,* part I, p. 44.
44. *Ibid,* pp. 44-45.
45. *Ibid,* pp. 46-50.
46. J.T.F. Jorden, *Dayanand Sarasvati : His Life and Ideas*, *op.cit.*, p. 65.
47. Baba Chhajju Singh, *op.cit.,* part I, p. 52.
48. *Ibid,* pp. 53-55.
49. J.M. Sharma, *op.cit.,* p. 47.
50. Baba Chhajju Singh, *op.cit.,* part I, pp. 59-65, Harbilas Sarda, *op.cit.,* p. 66 and J.M. Sharma, *op.cit.,* pp. 48-49
51. Baba Chhajju Singh, *op.cit.,* part I, p. 67.
52. J.T.F. Jorden, *Dayanand Sarasvati : His Life and Ideas*, *op.cit.*, p. 67.
53. Baba Chhajju Singh, *op.cit.,* part I, p. 66.
54. J.T.F. Jorden, *Dayanand Sarasvati : His Life and Ideas*, *op.cit.*, footnote 52, p. 67.
55. J.M. Sharma, *op.cit.,* p 52.
56. Harbilas Sarda, *op.cit.,* p. 71.
57. The Autobiography, *op.cit.,* p. 60.
58. Lajpat Rai, *op.cit.,* pp 32-33.
59. J.M. Sharma, *op.cit.,* p. 49.

60. J.T.F. Jorden, *Dayanand Sarasvati : His Life and Ideas*, *op.cit.*, p. 74.
61. Lajpat Rai, *op.cit.*, p. 38.
62. Harbilas Sarda, *op.cit.*, pp. 84.
63. Bhawanilal Bharatiya (Ed.) *Dayanand Shastrarth Sangraha*, Sonipat, 1969, pp. 218-38 and Y. Mimamshak (Ed.) *Rishi Dayanand Saraswati ke Patra aur Vijnapanon ke Parishisht*, Amritsar, 1958, p. 51.
64. Devendranath Mukhopadhyaya, *op.cit.*, p. 197.
65. J.T.F. Jorden, *op.cit.*, pp. 75-76.
66. For more details see, Devendranath Mukhopadhayay, *op.cit.*, pp. 217-28 and also Harbilas Sarda, *op.cit.*, pp. 84-87.
67. In the Satyarth Prakash Dayanand gave over forty quotations from the Upanishads, nearly half of which are to be found in the Brahnmo Dharma. As for Manu, Dayanand used forty two percent of the verses used by Debendranath Tagore. Thier ideas were identical on the theological, moral and ethical issues.
68. Harbilas Sarda, *op.cit.*, p. 89.
69. J.T.F. Jorden, *op.cit.*, p. 82. Later on in Kanpur, he himself gave as the reason for covering his body that his contacts with all kinds of people, and especially the presence of ladies at meetings and lectures and during visits to homes. At Kanpur in November 1873 he began to speak in Hindi. In May-June 1874, at Banaras Dayanand gave his first lecture in Hindi.
70. The efforts of Keshab Chandra Sen succeeded in getting the 1872 Marriage Act, which legalized the Brahmo marriages.
71. J.T.F. Jorden, *op.cit.*, p. 84.
72. Devendranath Mukhopadyaya, *op.cit.*, p. 235.
73. Y. Mimamshak (Ed.), *op.cit.*, p. 53.
74. Before 1885 All the Presidents of the Asiatic Society of Bengal were Europeans.
75. J.T.F. Jorden, *op.cit.*, p. 85.

76. Swami Dayanand has mostly used the word Aryans instead of Hindu.
77. Satyarth Prakash, *op.cit.*, p. 337.
78. *Ibid*, p. 338.
79. *Ibid*, *p*p. 338-39.
80. *Ibid*, p. 341.
81. *Ibid.*
82. *Ibid*, pp. 342-45.
83. *Ibid*, p. 346.
84. *Ibid*, pp. 363-64.
85. *Ibid*, pp. 365-366. It is said in the Satyarth Prakash that the founder of Vaishnava sect Shathakopa was the son of a professional prostitute. His successor was munivahana, the son of a scavenger. He was succeeded by Yavanacharya who was born in a Mohammedan family. The fourth was Ramanuja, a Brahman by birth, who propagated this creed.
86. *Ibid*, p. 374.
87. *Ibid*, pp. 374-75.
88. *Ibid*, pp. 380-85.
89. *Ibid*, pp. 386-87.
90. *Ibid*, p. 388.
91. *Ibid*, pp. 418-421.
92. *Ibid*, pp. 422-29.
93. *Ibid*, pp. 429-31.
94. *Ibid*, pp. 486-87.
95. *Ibid*, pp. 487-92.
96. Harbilas Sarda, *op.cit.*, p. 85.
97. Devendranath Mukhopadhyaya, *op.cit.*, p. 221.
98. *Ibid*, pp. 272-73.

99. *Ibid,* p. 273, The composition of Satyarth Prakash began on 12th June, 1874 at Banaras. Therefore, probably Swamiji could not devote much time in other activities.

100. *Ibid,* pp. 312-13.

101. *Ibid,* pp. 314-15. Through a letter of 16 January, 1875 the *Mantri* informed Gopalrav Hari Deshmukh at Ahmedabad that Aryasamaj at Rajkot has been established.

102. *Ibid,* p. 316.

103. Devendranath Mukhopadhyaya, *op.cit.,* pp. 324-28, Harbilas Sarda, *op.cit.,* p. 137 and J.M. Sharma, *op.cit.,* p. 111

104. Baba Chhajju Singh, *op.cit.,* Part I, pp. 103-6

3

Swami Dayanand in Rajasthan

The arrival of Swami Dayanand Saraswati in Rajasthan has great significance because he brought a ray of hope in the arch reactionary feudal atmosphere. When he stepped out for the first time from the territories of Gujarat he arrived at Mount Abu in Rajasthan in the year 1852. He was attracted with the popularity of *Yogis* of that place. He remained for about two years in the vicinity of Mount Abu. The facts show that since the beginning of his *Sanyas* he was a sincere learner of Yoga. In search of yoga he reached in Rajasthan and visited all the noted places there in the peaks of Aravalis. It has been revealed by the swamiji himself that from there he moved to Haridwar to attend the Kumbha Fair in 1855.[1]

There were many-fold reasons behind Swami Dayanand's inclination towards Rajasthan. He himself was born in the princely state of Morvi in the Kathiawar area of Saurashtra-Gujarat. For the first twentyone years of his life he knew no other than princely rule. While in Rajasthan there were about twentyone princely states as except the Ajmer-Merwara whole of the Rajasthan was under the control of princely order. He always considered his mission to embrace the whole of Aryavarta, and it was only natural that his interest should turn to the princely states, that other half of the country generally bypassed by the reformers.[2] Moreover, in the early stage of his public preaching his eyes had been turned towards the Rajas by his teacher Swami Virajanand. Swami Virjanand, who had been a teacher of princes and had enjoyed their patronage in establishing his school.[3] Virjanand had also dreamt of a great council of Hinduism, wherein these princes would take into their hands the protection and the propagation of the work of the *Rishis.*

In November 1859, after the suppression of the Indian Rebellion, Lord canning, the Governor General of India held a Durbar at Agra in which he invited all the Maharaja's the Rulling Princes of Rajputana. Swami Virjanand also went there with the hope to seek support of the Hindu rulers to protect and promote the *Arhsa* literature the works of *Rishis* and sages.[4] Virjanand approached Maharaja Ramsingh of Jaipur and asked him to convene a *Sarvabhom Sabha,* a universal council of Hinduism to protect the works of *Rishis.* The main point he makes is about the degeneratioin of Hinduism, and the remedy for its renaissance. There are two types of *gurus* he says : the ancient *guru* whoes wisdom became recorded in the books of the *rishis;* and the later *guru* whose teaching should be restricted to the oral interpretation of these works. The curse of Hinduism has been the multiplication of writings by all kinds of teachers. This has led to the multiplication of sects and to the practical oblivioun of the *rishis'* works. A proof of the strength of his conviction lies in the fact that Virjananda had two manuscript books on grammar composed by him thrown into the river by his disciples. The function of the *sarvabhauma Sabha* would have been to find means to halt the the proliferation and propagation of secondary sectarian writings, and to support proper language study through which to renew the study of the books of the *rishis.* It is important to note that the one work to be twice mentioned in this document as an example of these untruthful, worthless sectarian works, is none other thatn the *Bhagavata Purana.*[5]

Virjanand said to the Maharaja Ramsingh of Jaipur State that : "Maharaja, there is great scarcity of true Kshtriyas and Dharma cannot be protected except by Kshtriyas. Hence the country is without true Dharma, and the Brahmins are without (ignorant of) the Vedas. Sastras on sastras have come into existence but they are all false. You Maharaja, possess some qualities of true Kshtriyas and you hold a foremost position. I have come to you to ask you to convene an all India Assembly, and to invite all the learned *pundits* of India to attend it and yourself become convener or patron of the Assembly and send invitations to the various Rulers of Indian States. I will come there and place before the gathering the merits of the various books. I will expose the errors of the *Kaumudi* and other books on grammar and prove only Panini's *Ashtadhyayi* and Patanjali's *Mahabhashya* are authorities on grammar, that the Puranas and the Tantras are false and have no authority. I will then establish fully that the Vedic Dharama is the only true faith so that whatever Sastras are proved in that Assembly as true, may be taught in future and the untrue Sastras be rejected everywhere, and a proclamation be sent to every place in India to this effect. With this aim, an All India Assembly should be convened."[6]

Maharaja Ramsingh admitted that all that the Swamiji had said was true, but added that it was neither possible nor profitable to convene such an Assembly at once. He promised to convene it on his return to Jaipur.

Harbilas Sarda has narrated the episode as follows : The Maharaja offered rich presents to Virjanand but he declined to accept them and said that he did not care for money and had not gone to the Maharaja for it. He added that if the Maharaja undertook to convene an All India Assembly, he would become famous like Vikramaditya, but that otherwise no one would remember him after his death, just as men and animals die every day and no one cares for them. The Maharaja failed to keep his promise to convene the Assembly, for his court Pandits strongly opposed the idea. This caused great sorrow and pain to Swami Virjanand, who then addressed himself to Maharaja Ranvir Singh of Kashmir, and later, Maharaja Jiyaji Rao Gwalior, but found them all unresponsive. Swamiji was thus at his wits end and did not know what to do. The more and more he came to know and understand the social plight of the Hindus, he became more and more convinced of the importance of his mission.[7]

Blaming the court *Pandits* for opposing the idea of holding the Assembly seems not true. The *Pandits* do not have such authority and influence on the Maharaja that they might stop him from holding the religious assembly of Hindu scholars. In fact the position of the princely rulers was gravely pitiable as their very existence was based on the mercy of British Imperial rulers. The princely rulers were breathing under servitude subordination of the British. Thus, they were highly demoralised under the British rule and they were not in a position to act independently. Though, the British could retain their power with the support of princely states in 1857, but their loyalties were being looked upon suspicious by the British. Therefore, in 1859 the Governor General did not hold the *Darbar* at Agra to greet the princely rulers for their support but to ensure their loyalties towards the British empire.

Irrespective of all above the hope of Virjanand remained live till his death on 14 September, 1868. Even before the establishment of Arya Samaj Swami Dayanand in November, 1874 suggested that some sort of *Sabha* be convened to decide the issues of disagreement among the various sects of Hindus. On 16 November 1874 Swami Purnanand, on Dayanand's behalf, published in the papers answers to twenty four questions that had been anonymously sent to the Swami, probably by the Vallabhacharyas. The last answer contains the following sentences : If we, the Aryans, dicuss with love and without prejudice the Vedic *dharama,* then all kinds of benefits will arise; that is what I wish. For that purpose there should exist a perpetual Sabha. It would be a wonderful thing if that could come about. That means, by which the manyfold sects may be destroyed, that is the means all should adopt. This Sabha, however, was not the Arya Samaj, but rather a super sectarian Hindu Council, an idea conceived by his *guru* Virjananda, to which Dayananda periodically came back.[8]

Thus, Swami Dayanand kept the hope alive and when Lord Lytton the Governor of India organized a *Durbar* in Delhi on 1 January 1877 to celebrate the assumption by Queen Victoria of the title of 'Empress of India', he went to Delhi to present his cause before the rulers of princely states. The same story was repeated which happened with Swami Virjanand at the Agra *Durbar* organized by Lord Canning. Except few insignificant talukadars of Oudh and thakurs from doab only and Maharaja Tukojirao Holkar of Indore came to Swamiji.[9]

The failure at Delhi Darbar did not disheartened Swami Dayanand and he kept his effort alive of pursuing them towards the service of *Dharama.* The Swami knew from experience the power of the princes in their domains, and he too had sometimes contemplated the idea of a great Council of Hinduism in which they would play an important role. Dayanand's intense focus on Rajasthan is explained by Colonel (Sir) Pratap Singh, the prime minister of Jodhpur, in his autobiography as follows : "If you reform one man, you reform one individual. If you reform a ruler you reform a whole state. Dayanand had pinned high hopes on Rajasthan. That is why he spent his last years in Rajasthan.[10]

The drift of Dayanand's early preaching had brought him to British India, and it was in the urban centres there that he had finally found response and success. He always believed that those in political power could and should exert their influence for the sake of *dharma,* as all his dissertations on statecraft amply demonstrate. On several occasions he had tried to convince the administrators of the British Raj that they sould take some steps for the sake of the protection of *dharma,* specially by protecting the cow, promoting the study of the sacred language, and legislating to protect widows. But none of these attempts had been blessed with success.

Eventually Dayanand began to look towards princely states. In his opinion the princes might well be persuaded to exert their considerable power in the service of *dharama.* He asserted that the full prospertity of India depended on the unity of *dharma,* language, and aims, and he continued, 'That is why I wish that the rajas of our country bring about in their own territory that threefold unity'. In his agitation against cow-slaughter he worked on two fronts : influencing the British to legislate against it, and urging the princes to ban it. He complained about the fact that in Jaipur so many churches were being built, and that the missionaries were conducting intensive propaganda. 'The pundits and the rajas have not made any effort to remove them.' These statements, his pronouncements on statecraft in his *Satyarth Prakash,* and also his directives to the princes that will be analysed later, indicate clearly that Dayananda was of the opinion that the princes could well apply their considerable power and influence to help in the reconstruction of Aryavarta in a way in which the British were not prepared to do in British India.[11]

Rajasthan was the strong hold of princely states whom Swami Dayanand considered the Hindu states. Moreover, in his opinion the rulers of Rajasthan were the heirs of Vedic Kshatriyas. Therefore, his enormous expectations from the rulers of princely states of Rajasthan were obvious and justified. Thus, his attraction and inclination towards princely states of

Rajasthan remained live till his death. But by and large the rulers of Rajasthan remained unresponsive to the calls of Swami Virjanand, Swami Dayanand Saraswati and Arya Samaj for protection of Vedic religion and its reforms. Here it may be said that Swami Dayanand's understanding of these rulers was erroneous, because they were not the sovereign rulers of their so called states.

Swami Dayanand visited Rajasthan four times after completion of his studies at Mathura under Swami Virjanand.

Swami Dayanand's First Visit to Rajasthan (1865-66)

During his first visit Swami Dayanand's ideas were in a state of flux. He had not as yet broken with Pauranic belief and practices completely. It has been already mentioned that after completion of his studies under Swami Virjanand he went to Agra where he stayed for about two years. At Agra he denounced the Bhagwata. In January, 1865 Swami Dayanand arrived at Dholpur in search of Vedas.[12] From Dholpur he went to Karauli via Gwalior in June, 1865. He stayed in the garden of Gopalsingh on the Bank of Bhadravati river. Maharaja Madanpal of Karauli made the arrangements for Swamiji's food etc. . Looking to the knowledge and scholarship of Swamiji none of the pandit dared for *Sastrarth.* The court Pandit Maniram also escape *Sastrarth.* One day Pandit Maniram mispronounced a word while giving *Sankalp* to the Maharaja, Swamiji pointed out the mistake and told to the Maharaja that your pundits are foolish and your assembly is foolish assembly, then who will do the Sastrarth? After saying it Swamiji left this assembly.[13] On account of one more reason Maharaja Madanpal became dissatisfied and annoyed from Swamiji. In the presence of Swamiji one Pandit blessed the Maharaja and called him *annadata.* Then Swamiji abruptly reacted that the *annadata* is *parmeshwar,* how man can be *annadata.*[14]

One memorable incident of Karauli was the meeting of a Kabir Panthi Sadhu. In his autobiographical note Swamiji had mentioned as follows : From Gwalior I went to Karauli, where I met a Kabirpanthi who used to give a strange derivation of the word Kabira - Kabira = of a warrior. He told me that there was a *Kabiropnishad* too.[15]

From Karauli Swami Dayanand went to Khushalgarh, now known as Gangapurcity and stayed there for two days. There the Brahmins treated him with respect. But due to their unawareness of *Shastras* no shastric discourse or *shastrarth* could take place. From Khushalgarh Swamiji moved to Jaipur.[16] He put up at Bhawanilal Bohras garden and later shifted to the temple of Dhuleshwar Mahadev.[17] Three or four Shastrarthas were held here, on a minor scale. One of the discussion held in the presence of Vyas Bakshi Ram in a State temple. The Raj Pandits went so far as to deny that the *Mahabhashya* was an authoritative grammar. When the Swamiji called upon them to put the same in writing, they looked foolish and said nothing. They also felt ashamed. Bakshiram Vyas (probably chief Pandit) requested Swamiji to end discussion due to fear of over exposer of the pandits ignorance.[18]

A Jain monk named Shri Jatiji teacher of Oswal Vaishyas also wished to talk with Swami Dayanand for which Swamiji consented and ask Jatiji to come. But due to fear of loosing his reputation among his followers could not come to Swamiji. Then Swamiji sent 15 questions to Jatiji on grammar, shastras and theology. Jatiji did not reply to these questions rather he sent 8 questions relating to Jainism to Swamiji. Swamiji replied all 8 questions and put 8 new questions before Jatiji on Jaina sect, then without any reply Jatiji went in connivance.[19]

Thakur Ranjit singh of Achrol was fond of visiting sannyasis who came to Jaipur. Having heard about Swami Dayanand he invited Swamiji to take food at his residence. The thakur was so impressed with Swamiji that he requested Swamiji to stay in his garden situated outside the Gangapol in Badanpura. Thakur Ranjit Singh and his son Lakshman Singh took lessons from Swamiji and became his disciples. The Swami's discourse produced the desired effect on the Thakur's mind. He gave up idolatry and began to attend the Swamiji's lesson regularly. The expositions of Swamiji were so clear and convincing that the listeners could not fail to be influenced for the better. If they were addicted to drinking, it was that noble individual whose comments on the words of the Rishis weaned them from their evil habits. If they were loose in morals and were wont to set the dictates of virtue at defiance, it was he who taught them to behave better. And so on. Every man who had occasion to come in contact with the Swami, felt all the better for having been in his company.[20] Many elite people accepted the teachings of Swamiji and became his disciple alongwith Thakur Ranjit Singh and Thakur Indrajit Singh of Dudu was main among them. Even Hiralal Kayastha, Kamdar of Thakur Achrol gave up drinking and meat eating under the influence of Swamiji.[21]

During the Jaipur visit Swami Dayanand could not meet the Jaipur Maharaja Ram Singh. The foregoing account of Swamiji's Jaipur visit is based on the authentic and authoritative biographical works. In his autobiography Swamiji has given a very brief account of his Jaipur visit as follows : From Karauli I proceeded to Jaipur. There I met a learned scholar, Harish Chandra. I denounced there, for a first time, the Vaisanava sect and praised Shaivism. The Maharaja of Jaipur, Swai Ram Singh, was a follower of Shaivism. The sect became very popular and I gave thousands of *rudraksh malas* to the people with my own hands. The people in their over-enthusiasm bedecked their elephants and horses with rosaries.[22]

Swami Dayanand has himself confessed that he denounced the Vaishnavism and praised the Shaivism at Jaipur. The fact has also been mentioned by his biographers but it has been refuted by Harbilas Sarda. During Swamiji's visit in Jaipur there was a sharp confrontation between Maharaja Ram Singh and Vaishnavite Mahantas, Sadhus, Acharyas Brahmcharis, priests and Mathadishas. These Vaishnavite have acquired immense power and they became a challenge to the authority of Maharaja. The Maharaja denounced the Vaishnavism and promoted the Shaivism.[23] Swami Dayanand kept himself aloof from Shaiv-Vaishnav controversy of Jaipur. Even When he was asked by the supporter of Shaivism and Maharaja to support them in communal shastrarth then he declined because he was not ready to speak as per the dictation of Maharaja party. It is also hard fact that at the age of 14 Swami Dayanand had lost faith in idol worship and after meeting Swami Virjanand he finally discarded it. Thus, his Shaivism was of different kind which did not resemble with the traditional form of Shaivism. This was quite a new departure as Swamiji used to indicate the unmanifest Lord (*Nirankar Paramatma*) by the name of Shiva. He did not mention Shiva the husband of Parvati. When later in Pushkar he was asked what the name of the Lord was, because some call Him Brahma and others Vishnu, etc., he answered, '*Saccidananda* is the name to repeat, no other'. At that time, says Lekhram, he did not venerate Vishnu or Shiva, but only *Parameshvar*. In Pushkar too he declared that he only recognized *saccidananda* or *parameshvar*, and, when asked about the name 'Shiva', he answered, 'We do recognize Shiva, but the name Shiva means "the auspicious one". The other Shiva who is the husband of Parvati, him we do not recognize.[24]

This is clear from the above description that Swami Dayanand's Vaishnavism was different from the traditional one. It is also a fact that the rulers of Jaipur were Vaishnavites but due to various reasons Maharaja Ram Singh became Shaivite. Though, with the support of Maharaja the Shaivites won and

Vaishnavites lost the battle, but Swamiji without being involved in the controversy left for Pushkar.

On 6 March 1866 Swami Dayanand left Jaipur for Pushkar after a stay of four and half months.[25] The Thakur of Achrol made the arrangements for conveyances and sent three Brahmins with Swamiji to serve him. He also sent his *Kamdar* Rupram to take Swamiji to Pushkar and bring him back. On the way Swamiji stayed for two days in Bagru and two days in Dudu the village of Thakur Indra Singh who became the disciple of Swamiji at Jaipur.[26]

From Dudu Swamiji went to Kishangarh, where he stayed in a temple on the Sukhsagar well. Maharaja Prithvisingh the ruler of Kishangarh made arrangements of food etc. for Swamiji's comfortable stay. When, however the Rajpandits Devidutt and Vitthaldas, whom the Maharaja had sent to Swamiji, told the Maharaja that Swamiji denounced Bhagwata and Vaishnavism, the Maharaja became angry and ordered Swamiji to leave Kishangarh. Swami Dayanand ignored the orders of the Maharaja and stayed there for six days. He left for Ajmer, where he stayed in Daulatram's garden for four days and from there departed to Pushkar.[27]

Swami Dayanand arrived at Pushkar on 23 March, 1866 and took up residence in Brahmaji temple and began to denounce idol worship and the Vaishnava faith. This offended the Brahmins of Pushkar. Many Brahmins took up the challenge, but were invariably worsted in the struggle. In the condition of despair the Brahmins took help of a learned man named Baikunth Shastri (Venkat Shastri) but he could not succeed in defending the Bhagwat and Vaishnavism. As a last resource, the Shastri took Swamiji to his guru, who on hearing the arguments of both parties, gave his verdict in the favour of Swamiji. Baikunth Shastri bowed to his master's superior judgment, and had the frankness to acknowledge in public that

Dayanand was in the right. At Pushkar Swamiji had ceased to be even a nominal adherent of Shaivism.[28] Irrespective of his best efforts Swamiji could not create a group of his followers there because it was a strong centre for Pauranic conservatism. Thousands of people of Pushkar were getting their livelihood out of traditional Pauranic religious establishments. It seems that due to dull response from the Brahmins Swamiji got irritated and he began to tease the *Pujaris* and *Gusain* of Brahma temple where he took abode. One of the Pujaris named Shivadayalu gave up his job of Pujari. Gusain Manpuri got annoyed from Swamiji on calling the idol of Brahma a stone.[29] It has been mentioned by Harbilas Sarda and Mukhopadhyay that many of the Vaishnavites gave up their *Kanthis.*[30]

Swami Dayanand kept his efforts continued to refute the Pauranic misconceptions at Pushkar. Swamiji used to say that the *stotras* composed on the name of *Acharyas* were not their creation but the ordinary people composed these and popularized them under the name of *Acharyas.* He told to a Pandit Gangaram Brahmin a reciter of Bhagwat *Katha* that the Bhagwata had been composed by Bopadeva not by Vyas.[31] Apart from disputation and refutation Swamiji could not create goodwill of himself and his ideas.

After staying for about two months Swamiji left Pushkar for Ajmer. Being directly governed by the British the place Ajmer has significantly a very different social and cultural environment. Swamiji reached Ajmer on 30 May, 1866. There he stayed at the garden of Rai Bansilal.[32] Here two important Shastrarthas were held between Swamiji and theologists of Islam and Christianity. Maulvi Murad Ali discussed various religious issues and after becoming answerless he returned to his place.[33] Swamiji had a discussion with three Christian Padris (Fathers) viz. Revs. Gray, Robson and Shoolbred on God, Soul, Laws of Nature (creation) and the Vedas.[34] The discussion lasted for full three days. Swamiji profuoundly presented the Vedic explanation on the subject and impressed the opponents. Rev. Robinson (Robson) gave him a certificate, stating that the Swamiji was profoundly versed in the Vedas, and that he had never seen so learned a man in his entire life. Such individuals, wrote the Padri, were rare in the world, and their company could not but be productive of good to all. The document enjoined upon all who wished to see the Swami to treat him with all possible respect. The Swami also called upon Mr. Davidson, Deputy Commissioner of Ajmere, and, in the course of conversation, said to him : "People of false creeds are plundering your subjects. The King being like a father, it behoves the representatives of Government to take steps to remedy the evil." The Deputy Commissioner's answer to this was, that the policy of Government was perfect neutrality in matters of religion.

The Agent to the Governor-General in Council was another European gentleman with whom Swami Dayanand had an interview at this place. The Swami talked to him on the necessity of protecting the cows, setting forth, in detail, the benefits which Government and the people would derive from the adoption of the measure recommended. The Agent admitted the force of the Swami's arguments but said he was sorry he could do nothing in the matter. This worthy gentleman gave the Swami a letter, saying that it would secure him an introduction to whom so ever it was shown. He further sent a letter to Raja Ram Singh of Jeypur, in which he expressed regret at His Highness having given but an indifferent reception to a man of the Swami's stamp. It was a rule with Swami Dayanand to never allow a woman to come into his presence. At Ajmere, a large number of ladies, hearing of his fame, came to receive *updesh* from him, but they had to go away disappointed. The Swami had them informed that he never preached to women, and that if they must receive *updesh* from him, they should send their husbands to him who might hear what he had to say and communicate the same to them.[35]

When Swamiji was in Ajmer, a Mahanta of the Ramsanehi sect was also staying in Ajmer. One day passing by the Mahanta's abode, Swamiji saw a number of women going in and coming out. Swamiji sent a message to the Mahanta inviting on Shastrarth, but the Mahanta declined and during the night slipped away from Ajmer.[36] Swamiji also advertised his presence in Ajmer publicly and asked the people to have Shastrarth on idol worship, but no one could dare to take the challenge. Though, some Pandits tried to take the challenge but could not dare.[37]

As Swamiji denounced the Bhagwata and idol worship, the Brahmins of Ajmer were annoyed with him. Through a Patwari they got put some ten questions before the Swamiji. One of questions was that a Sannyasi Should not stay more than three days at a place. Swamiji replied that the fact regarding the stay at one place is true but where ignorance and darkness exist he may stay more than three days for preaching and enlightenment of the people.[38]

At Ajmer Swamiji also interacted with the followers of Jainism. One person named Babulal Jain discussed on religious issues and in the and he accepted the Swamiji's view. He also conversed with two another Jainis viz. Dhannalal and Amritsingh. Dhannalal put some questions before Swamiji. Swamiji made him understand but he remained adamant. Swamiji took his book and told him that you are atheist, you come again, I will make you understand properly, but he did not come again. He went to the Deputy Commissioner and told that his book has been snatched by Swamiji. *Sahab* told to Rai Daulatram who get the book returned from Swamiji. In Ajmer too, people discarded *Kanthis* on the persuation of

Swamiji. The Thakur of Sawar presented himself to Swamiji and after preaching he also gave up his *kanthi*.[39]

In June 1866 Swami Dayanand left Ajmer for Jaipur. He in his return journey again stayed in Kishangarh where one Thakur Gopal Singh with 30-40 men and 5-7 Rajpandits came to Swamiji to dishonour him but could not succeed as some of the Swamiji's supporters reached there. Behind this incident the signals and advise of Maharaja Prathvi Singh may not be ruled out.[40] After stayed for five days at Kishangarh Swamiji reached Dudu where stayed for three days. From Dudu he arrived at Bagaru for a night and from there reached Jaipur and put in the garden of Thakur Ranjit Singh of Achrol.[41]

Swami Dayanand stayed for about four months in Jaipur (June-October 1866) but he could not meet the Maharaja Ramsingh. Even after fixing the meeting Maharaja declined to meet the Swamiji. Swami Dayanand in his autobiography has said that ; I reached Jaipur, but the Maharaja on knowing that I had began to denounce Shaivism too, became displeased with me. I, therefore, left Jaipur for Mathura where I discussed some difficult matters with Swamiji (Virjanand).[42]

Irrespective of various reasons of avoidance of Mahraja Ram Singh to meet with the Swami Dayanand the main reason was the fear of British. Obviously, the Maharaja was not in a mood to take any risk as he could save his rule in Jaipur after the revolt of 1857, while his services were appreciated by the British. Even then he was not assured for stability of his power. Swamiji not only offended the *Sanatani* Hindus, but also the Christians too which was the religion of the British imperialists. Swamiji's thoughts were purely indigenous and against foreign influence. Thus, the activities of Swamiji since the inception were being considered suspiciously by the British in India.

During the first visit to Rajasthan (1865-66) Swami Dayanand received dull response from the masses, rulers and *jagirdars.* It was due to lack of education and political oppression. The intricate social structure with lot of evil rituals and social inequality were the factors not conducive for new ideas.

Second Visit to Rajasthan (1878, November-December)

Irrespective of dull response from the princely states Swami Dayanand's attraction towards them could not lessen and he kept his efforts continued to win over their favour for his mission. One of Swamiji's biographer has written as follows : Hearing that a grand Durbar was to be held at Agra (November, 1866), Swami Dayanand felt that he could not miss such a splendid opportunity for the determination of truth, and consequently left for the place in company with five vidyarthis. The Durbar came off, and was a magnificent affair, all the Native Rulers of the country with their followers being present on the occasion. The Swami commenced his *updesh,* publishing at the same time, in Sanskrit, an eight-page tract, showing the puerile character of the teaching of the Bhagwat. Thousands of copies of this publication were distributed free among the gathering to the real delight of all true inquires, particularly of those who could understand Sanskrit.[43]

Due to lack of enthusiasm Swami Dayanand did not visit Rajasthan for a long time. His extensive visits in United Provinces and Pubjab yielded required results, therefore Swamiji concentrated on these areas for the success of his mission. After a long gap of about 12 years Swamiji visited Rajasthan during November-December 1878. The native states had so far been little affected by the work of reform; they constituted the other half of India, where Dayanand's message scarcely penetrated.[44] But Swamiji did not left the hope. Though, this time Swami Dayanand was busy in preaching in Delhi and from there he has plans to take extensive tour of Western U.P., but his affection with Rajasthan tempted him to postpone his preconceived programme.

Swamiji got an invitation from Thakur Ranjit Singh, *Jagirdar* of Achrol in Jaipur State to hold a great Yajana under the supervision of Swamiji. He sent his *Kamdar* Rupram Joshi to bring the Swamiji with him to Jaipur, but Swamiji sent him back and promised him to reach Jaipur himself in the month of Kartik V.S. 1935. Another invitation to Swamiji was extended by certain gentlemen residents of Ajmer and the annual fair of Pushkar was one more attraction of Swamiji, thus he planned his Rajasthan visit. Swamiji left Delhi for Jaipur and when on 6 Novemeber, 1878 the train reached the Jaipur Railway Station, Jaipur he saw Joshi Rupram and other servants with shaved heads. On enquiry Swamiji came to know that the Thakur had died three days back. Then Swamiji told to Joshi Rupram that instead of stay at Jaipur he would go to Ajmer and would come to Jaipur on his return from Ajmer.[45]

Swami Dayanand reached at Ajmer on 7 November, 1878, where he was received by many gentlemen alongwith Munshi Samarthdan Cahran at the railway station.[46] Ajmer turned out to be highly receptive to Dayanand's mission in the Rajasthan region. Being under direct British administration, Ajmer was more exposed to Western ideas than the native states and therefore more receptive to reforms. Ajmer became a major Arya Samaj centre. Without making a halt at Ajmer, the Swami proceeded direct to Pushkar, a famous *tirtha* of the Hindus, situated at a few miles distance from Ajmer. The annual fair was taking place, and the work of *prachar* could not be neglected on an occasion like the present one. The Swami put up at the *ghat* of Maharaja Jodhpur, popularly known as the "Window of Nathji", and he stayed at Pushkar as long as the fair lasted. Notices were issued, inviting all true enquirers to come and hold religious conversations, but nobody came forward for the purpose. The *updesh,* however, was regularly given, and we may be sure that it did not fall on deaf ears. As soon as the fair was over, the Swami returned to Ajmer, and kept lecturing here till 1st December 1878. His lectures were attended by the gentry and nobility of the town, and by the local Officials, such as Rai Bhag Ram, Extra Judicial Assistant; Sardar Rai Bahadur Amin Chand, Judge; Sardar Bhagat Singh; Rao Sahib Masooda, etc.. The first named gentleman was long a member of the Ajmer Samaj.[47]

At Ajmer Dayanand delivered seven lectures. The topics covered a wide spectrum; the unity of god; the Vedas; the revealed word of god; the Vedas; the fountainhead of all knowledge; the Bible and the Koran; the transmigration of the soul; the custom of sati and other social evils, and the rise and fall of the Aryas. Rai Bahadur Shyam Sunder Lal, a founder member of the local Prarthana Samaj, frequently visited Dayanand's place of residence. He was the first individual in Ajmer to acquire a bachelor's degree and had held the position of minister in many princely states. One day he remarked that Dayanand's purpose would still be served if he was less severe in his criticism of idol worship. The Rai Bahadur also observed that many persons would like to agree with him but adopted an extreme position as they were annoyed by the severity of his attacks. Dayanand answered that if he toned down his criticism his followers might, in course of time, compromise with idolatry. Another point the Rai Bahadur raised was regarding the scientific knowledge contained in the Vedas. His opinion was that scientific knowledge became outdated as fresh discoveries were made. In that case, he felt that Dayanand's interpretations would become irrelevant and the Vedas' position would be compromised. Dayanand responded with the remark that he could not help highlighting the scientific laws if they were found in the Vedas.[48]

During his visit to Ajmer in November-December 1878 Dayanand had a formal debate with the Reverend Grey and Dr. Husband of the Scottish Presbyterian Mission, about some points in Genesis. One Muslim and two Hindu scribes took everything down in writing. The Swami opened with his usual type of attack, based on a native and literal interpretation of the text, and the missionaries gave their considered answer. The pace of the debate was excruciatingly slow, being little more than boring dictation from both sides. The first days's session produced only a few paltry pages of text, and the missionaries were completely exasperated, as was the chairman, Judge Amichand, who remarked, 'we will be here for six months!' The clergymen declined to continue the debate in the same way, and suggested that written communications and answers should replace the painful dictation sessions. However, Dayanand refused to alter the agreed method, and the debate was discontinued in such a manner that the Aryas interpreted it as another victory for their Swami.[49]

A detailed narration by a biographer Baba Chhajju Singh of the above episode is of worth mention as follows[50] :

One of the lectures the Swami delivered at Ajmer was on the teachings of the Bible. Mr. Rev. Grey, and some other Missionaries, were present at this lecture, and being anything but pleased with what was being said, they, finding their opportunity, intimated to the Swami that they were ready and willing to hold a discussion with him in connection with any objections he might being forward against the Biblical teachings *provided* that he had these objections handed over to them in advance for consideration. The Swami agreed to the condition, and getting some sixty-four out of the numerous objections he could raise against the dogmas of Christianity, had them sent to the Rev. gentleman, through Rai Bhag Ram. After the Rev. gentleman had considered them for full ten days the 28th of November, 1878, was fixed for the discussion. The public announcement that a discussion of such a character was going to take place between the Missionaries and Swami Dayanand attracted thousands of men to the place of meeting. Three reporters were in attendance. When the objections against the Bible were read out to the audience, Rev. Mr. Grey insisted that only two or three objections should be made the subject for discussion, and that no objection should be spoken upon, if possible, *more than once.* It was pointed out, in reply that the restriction imposd was unfair, and that, though it did not signify much what objections were disussed and what left out, it was material that the objections that were selected for discussion should be *discussed thoroughly.* The Rev. gentlemen would not listen to this, and so the discussion being nominal led to no definite result; the more so as the Missionary declined to resume it after the first day had closed. Whatever, however, was said by the parties, was published in the *Theosophist.*

The following extract will give the reader an idea of what was said :

Swami - "Genesis, Ch. I. verse 2, says :- 'The earth was without form and void.' Now, God is omniscient. His knowledge is perfect. That which he has made by his knowledge, cannot be imperfect or void and without form. Man's knowledge is limited his works are therefore without any form or order. But such can never be said of the works of God."

Missionary - "The pharase without form does not mean imperfect, it means uninhabited. As, for instance, the book of Ayub, Ch. ii, verse 24 : -'They shall have to wander in trackless wilderness.' The word which signifies wihtout form here means 'wilderness' there.

S. - "In the verse preceding it, it is said that 'in the beginning God created heaven and earth. And the earth was without form and void; and darkness was upon the face of the deep.' This passage shows that the words without form cannot mean 'uninhabited' ; for it says, it was void or uninhabited. If the pharse meant 'uninhabited', there was no necessity of using the word void or uninhabited again, if God alone created the world, could not he have created it by His knowledge from the beginning with some kind of form?'

M. - "All languages have synoymous words, generally coming one after another; as, *bood-o-bash* in Persian, the two words being synonymous : in like manner, it is right to say in Urdu that the earth was barren and a waste."

Obervation. - The Swami was going to say something more, but the Missionary said that only two questions and answers could be put and given on one point : or else the questions being many would not be finished that day. Upon this the Swami said that it was not necessary that all the questios should be disposed of in one day : some should be discussed that day, and others in two, three, or in as many days following, as it would take them to be discussed. The Missionaries did not consent to more than two questions being asked and two replies being given on a point. The Swami remonstrated against this, observing that so many men had come together in order that they might hear something, and that if nothing worth their trouble was said, they would go home disappointed ; but all was to no purpose. The Missionaries were obstinate.

S. - "Gen. i., verse 2. - 'And the spirit of God moved upon the face of the waters.' The first verse tells us that God created heaven and earth; but the creation of water was not mentioned. Whence, then, did water come to exist? Is God of the form of spirit, or is He corporeal like us? If he has a body, He can have no power to create heaven and earth; for the atoms are more delicate than the limbs of the body, and, consequently, it is impossible for limbs to hold and unite them, to create things with. Also, He cannot be omnipresent or all-pervading. When

His spirit was floating on the surface of the waters, where was His body?

M. - "When He created the earth, water was included in it. God is spirit, and so is He called in the Bible from beginning to end."

S. - "The account of God in the Old and the New Testament makes Him corporeal in many places; for, His coming down to Eden for Adam, His descending on the Mt. Senai, His talking with Moses, Abraham, and his wife Sera, his going into their tent, his wrestling with Jacob, and the like adventures of His show that He must possess some sort of body, or assume it on such occasions."

M. - "These things do not concern the verse, and are mentioned as the outcome of ignorane. Suffice it to say in reply the Jews, the Christians, and the Muhammandans, who accept the Bible, are all unanimous in declaring that God is spirit."

S. - "Gen. I, verse 26. - 'And God said, let us make man in our image, after our likeness.' This verse clearly proves that God is like Adam in form. God had body and soul like Adam according to this verse. How could He make Adam after His likeness, if He had no form?"

M. - "This verse makes no mention of body. God created Adam holy, intelligent, and happy. He is a holy, intelligent, and happy Himself, and made Adam like Himself. When Adam sinned, he fell from the likeness of God, as is manifest from the 24th and 30th questions of the First Catechism. Epistle to Corinthians iii : 9 and 10 : - 'Don't tell lies amongst you, for ye have cast off the old Adam with his works, and put on a new life, which is like your Creator's in knowledge. This shows that man was made like God in knowledge and holiness. We are made anew. Corinthians iii : 17 and 19 - 'God is spirit; God is spirit. Wherever the spirit of God is, there is peace. We distinctly see the glory of God, and change into His form from glory to glory by means of His spirit.' This shows that the faithful or believers are changed into the likeness of God, i.e., in knowledge, holiness, and happiness; for being endowed with certain qualities, man's body is never changed."

S. -"The creation of Adam after the image of God proves the corporeity of God. Had God made Adam holy and happy, how could he have broken the command of God? If he broke the law, it is evident that he was not wise or knowing. His statement that when he tasted of the fruit of the tree of knowledge, his eyes were opened, proves that he got knowledge afterwards. If he had knowledge before he tasted the fruit, it is unreasonable to say that he got knowledge after the commission of the act. God at first blessed Adam with prosperity. But when he broke the divine law by eating the forbidden fruit, he became endowed with knowledge and knew that he was naked. He covered his body with the leaves of *goolar.* Only reflect a little that if Adam was like God in knowledge, holiness and happiness, he should have been omniscient and ever-happy, and should have experienced no pain whatever : for, he was like God in the qualities above-mentioned. He could not have fallen from his state. If he fell, he could not be like God; for, God never falls off from His knowledge and the like divine attributes. Since Adam, being like God in those three qualities fell from them the believers will suffer the same fate, unless they have more knowledge than Adam, and consequently, than God! If they have equal knowledge with Adam, they will fall, as fell he who was like God in these respects."

M. - "The first answer will suffice most of the objections, As regards the disobedience of Adam, he was holy at first, but became sinful after he disobeyed God. It is incorrect to say that he acquired knowledge afterwards; because when he tasted the fruit of the forbidden fruit, he simply came to know of evil, of which he did not know before. That his eyes were opened and he knew that he was naked means that being sinful he became ashamed. As for the assertion, that had he been like God, he would not have fallen, I say that he was made after the image of God, but he was not equal to God. Had he been equal to God, he would not have fallen into sin. As for the question, if the believers were more holy than Adam, I say that the question is not one about more or less holiness, but about form or likeness, -as to whether the image of God was material or not. If the image in question was material, the believers, when regenerated by the grace of God, would change their corporeal frame.

S. - "Gen. ii., verse 3 : - 'And God blessed the seventh day, and sanctified it : because in it He had rested from all His work which God created and made.' God can experience no fatigue in creating the world, being almighty, all-pervading, truth, intelligence, and happiness. Then how can He have the necessity to rest on the seventh day? If He rested at all, he must have worked very hard during the previous six days. If He blessed the seventh day, what did He do with the foregoing days? We can't believe that it takes God more than a moment to create the world, or that He is ever fatigues.[51]

Colonel Olcott's opinion on the discussion at Ajmer is worth a perusal. It was given in the following words : "The account of discussion given above shows what policy the Missionaries pursue in India. As far as possible, they avoid discussions with Native Scholars, and confine there preaching to the low classes and ignorant. In the Missionaries Schools and Colleges also the teachers do not like answering the questions of intelligent youths on matters of religion in class : they would have student come to their houses if they would have the same answered. It is no secret to the impartial Europeans who have visited India that the Missionary propaganda here has had to face bitter disappointment. The gentlemen of philanthropic impulses who donate millions to the Padris are in reality wasting their charity. Many Anglo-Indians are in absolute sympathy with this view of ours. It is our intention to publish from time to time whatever evidence on the point is forthcoming.

The above was a crucial debate at Ajmer. All the parties were adamant on their stands. It is very interesting to note that after the episode of 28 November on 29 November the Padrees wrote to the Swamiji to convey that if the questions and answers are not reduced to writing he is ready to continue the debate. Swamiji did not agree to it, and the debate came to an end.[52]

Maulvi Murad Ali, editor of the 'Rajputana Gazette' (an Urdu weekly), of Ajmer visited Swamiji five times and was thoroughly satisfied with the answers given to the questions put by him.[53] In one of his lectures, Swamiji exposed the untruths of various religions. According to the bible, he said, God created the Sun on the fourth day. As it is only the Sun that causes day and night, and if the Sun was created on the fourth day, how could it be said that three days passed before the Sun was created. Listening to it one Muslim Mirza Sahab spoke that our Quran had landed from the Heaven, look how pure is that? Maharaj told that in your Quran is written that the men who offers five times *Namaj* will go to heaven and he will get 70 *Hoors* to enjoy. Wheter the women who offers five times *Namaj* will go to Heaven she will also get 70 man? A book with such tales can not be God created. Mirza Sahab became mute after listening this. In the meantime Swamiji's discussion took place with Peerji of Naugazewale.[54]

The arrival of Swamiji in Ajmer created an intensive movement or sensation. Thousands of people used to come in the lectures among them Ajmer's commissioner, Deputy Commissioner, European Padrees, respected Muslim personalities were included. Students came in large numbers to hear Swamiji, as the Principal of the Government College had given them permission to do so. Even women who assembled at the wells to carry water for home, talked of a Pandit who refuted all religions, and the Muslim women prayed *Khuda* to save Muslims.[55]

From Ajmer Swami Dayanand arrived at Masuda on 2nd December, 1878 on the invitation of Rao Bahadur Singh the Estate holder of Masuda and stayed there till 9 December. During his stay at Masuda he daily delivered lectures. Rao held long conversations with Swami Dayanand on religious matters and had his doubts cleared. On the 10 December, 1878 he visited the Nasirabad cantonment where he was invited by Pandit Sukhdevaprasad, a teacher in the Mission school at Nasirabad. The *Pandit* was inclined towards Christianity due to his contact with the missionaries but after listening to Swamiji's lectures he lost faith in the Christian tenets.[56]

On 15 December Swami Dayanand arrived at Jaipur from Nasirabad and took up residence in Sadasukh Daddha's garden outside the Sanganeri gate.[57] He stayed there for 9 days. Thakur Fateh Singh (of Jobner) etc. met with him there but not the Maharaja.[58] Mukhopadhyay has written that an upper level state official Shriprasad was disciple of Swami Dayanand. He was friend of Thakur Fateh Singh, the member of Jaipur State Council (minister). He requested Thakur Sahab to arrange conversation of Swamiji and Maharaja. Thakur requested the Maharaja for the same. Maharaja was annoyed with the Swamiji, so he declined and Maharaja told that if I have the power then I will get him (Swamiji) tear off by the dogs. Then Thakur conveyed the Swamiji through Shriprasad to leave Jaipur immediately. But Swamiji ignored it and stayed in Jaipur for about 9 days. Shriprasad was targeted by the Maharaja and on some pretext he was put in the Jail.[59] Swamiji left Jaipur for Rewari on 24 December, 1878 on the invitation of Rao Yudhishtrasingh the premier Zamindar of Rewari. There he delivered lectures and left Rewari for Delhi on a January, 1879.[60]

Dayanand's second visit to Rajasthan too could not get required response. At Pushkar Swamiji created sensation among the conservative *pundits* and *pandas* but could not convince them with his ideas and also could not change their ideas and practices. His image emerged of a rebellious *Sannyasi.* Thus, he antagonised them. In the same manner at Ajmer Swamiji came into open confrontation with Christian missionaries. The Muslims and Jains were also offended by him. During this visit even Arya Samaj could not be founded at a single place. The ruler of Jaipur State Maharaja Ram Singh got annoyed with Swamiji to the extent that Swamiji was ordered to leave the territories of Jaipur. But, he could successfully recorded his presence in Rajasthan and his ideas began to penetrate in the mind of people here.

Third visit to Rajasthan (1881, March-December)

As I have already mentioned that irrespective of dull response and nonresponsive attitude of the rulers and people of Rajasthan the attraction of Dayanand towards Rajasthan continued. Baba Chhajju Singh has written that :

Swami Dayanand had already been more than once to some of the States in Rajputana, but there had been no regular *prachar* during these visits in the States in question, and it was with the intention of doing systemic work, of preaching and disseminating the principles of the Vedic Religion in conformity with the methods followed in the Punjab and some other parts of India, that he determined to re-visit the tract immortalized by Tod in his Annals and Antiquities of Rajasthan. And in pursuance of his purpose, he left Agra on 10th March, 1881, for Bharatpur, where he stayed up to 28th of the month, lecturing and giving *updesh* during the period of his stay. On 29th he left for Jeypur, where more than a month was spent, and though the number of lectures delivered here was the reverse of 'large', yet the *updesh* being daily given at his quarters, an Arya Samaj was at last established in the place.[61]

The visits of Bharatpur and Jaipur remained insignificant and rulers of both the princely states just ignored and took no cognizance of Swami Dayanand Saraswati. But this noncognizance did not dishearten him and he left Jaipur for Ajmer on 4th May, 1881.

Dayanand arrived at Ajmer on 5th May, 1881 and took residence in the Kothi of Seth Fateh Mal. Baba Chhajju Singh has someup the Ajmer visit as follows : Leaving Jeypur, he reached Ajmere on 5th May, 1881, and stayed there for more than a month and-a-half. During this period no less than 37 lectures were delivered. Rai Bahadur Pandit Bhag Ram (sometime Member, Council Kashmere State), arranging for and taking the greatest interest in these lectures. There was talk of a shastrarth also, but the orthodox at last thought it best to keep in the back-ground, and to forego the pleasure of holding a discussion. The local Arya Samaj (established, February, 1881), was considerably strengthened by the Swami's lectures and presence.[62] Swamiji has himself written that : A small Arya Samaj has been established here. May god effect its growth.[63] Thus, it is not clear that the Branch of Arya Samaj at Ajmer was founded before the arrival of Swamiji or during his present visit is not clear because Swamiji has also not given any date of its' foundation.

No event of worth mention took place at Ajmer. It has been written by some biographers that meeting of Pandit Lekhram with Swamiji was of historical importance. P. Lekhram, a resident of Peshawar, who later became known as *Arya Musafir* (Arya Traverller) and wrote the first biography entitled "Maharshi Dayanand Saraswati ka Jivan Charitra" in

Urdu, was very anxious to have Swamiji's darshana.[64] During his interaction with Swamiji he put some basic questions on philosophy and religion, which Swamiji replied with clarity. Thus, Swamiji's theological discourse on the questions of Pt. Lekhram benefitted the audience of Ajmer.

Swamiji told Maulvi Imadad Husain at Ajmer that a man once came and stood behind him holding a naked sword, while Swamiji was attending a call of nature. Swamiji asked him to wait till he finished the call and then use his sword. The man agreed. But when Swamiji bent his head later for the blow, the man was so impressed by Swamiji's act that without uttering a word, he ran away.[65]

No doubt the Swamiji's visit to Ajmer indirectly brought many changes in the mind of people. Swamiji could achieve more refinement in his thoughts in Ajmer by interacting the people of all religions. Thus, his visit of Ajmer left positive energy. One Hindu youth inclined towards Christianity came to Swamiji for clarification of doubts, who after meeting the Swamiji abandoned his idea of conversion into Christianity.[66]

Harbilas Sarda has mentioned about an interesting incident at Ajmer as follows : One Sunday morning, when Swamiji and Mir Shafi Hussain, uncle of the Diwan of Durgah Khawaja Sahib, P. Salig Ram, Head Pandit of the Government college, Ajmer and some other pandits and muslims were present, and the merits and demerits of Hinduism and Muhammadanism were being discussed, the muslims pointing out the prejudices of the Hindus and the pandits the prejudices of the Muhammadans, Swamiji remarked pointing towards Mir Shafi Hussain, "I will catch you by the beared", and pointing towards the Pauranik pundits, he said, "And you by the *choti*, but I have neither the beared nor the *choti* and none of you can catch me".[67]

It was while the Swami was yet at Ajmere, that a terrible fire broke out outside the New Gate in Ganj. The fire caused considerable loss of property, and the Swami, moved by the sufferings of those who had been the victims of the catastrophe, appealed for a subscription on their behalf, and thus had them assisted.[68]

Rao Bahadur Singh of Masuda became Swamiji's devotee or disciple during Swamiji's visit of Pushkar in 1878 and later on Swamiji also visited Masuda during that visit. The Rao of Masuda was not a Raja of a state, but was a holder of a big estate within the British-administered territory of Ajmer-Merwara, only about thirty miles from Ajmer itself. Being under direct control of the British Masuda Rao had a different kind of bent up of mind. He could easily grasped the ideas of Swamiji in the first meeting.

During the Swamiji's visit of Ajmer in 1881, Rao of Masuda sent Pandit Virddhichandra there to invite him for a longer stay, and Swami Dayanand accepted immediately. In defence to the wishes of Rao Bahadur Singh of Masuda Swami Dayanand left Ajmer for Masuda on 23rd June, 1881, and stayed there till 17th August, 1881.[69] Swami Dayanand was guest of the Rao for about two months. He was accommodated in the pavillion in Rambagh and a guard was posted there. He delivered lectures in the palace in the fort, where the people of the town assembled to hear him. The Rao took intense interest in the work of Swamiji. He listened to his twenty-two lectures and tried to arrange some public debates. He invited Dr. Schoolbred for that purpose, but the latter declined a debate. The prince also put pressure on the Jains, who in fact invited Sadhu Siddhakaran to represent them, but the written debate that followed between him and the Swami was only short-lived.[70] Dayananda's preaching, with the wholehearted support of the Rao, was very successful, as was openly demonstrated at a public ceremony of investiture with the holy thread. It was a grand affair with all the pomp that could be mustered. A great

Vedic altar was prepared, and the oblations were offered first by the Rao and then by four Brahmins. Thirty-two people were initiated by the Swami himself while Vedic *mantras* were being chanted. Among the recipients of the sacrament were brhmins, kshatriyas, and kayasthas, but the most striking fact was that half of the initiates were Jains. Another similar ceremony was held a few days later in which a smaller group was initiated, more than half of whom were Jains. This quite extraordinary event was reported not only in Arya journals, but even in the *Bharat-Mitra* of Calcutta.[71]

In Masuda, some Muslims, converted from Hinduism during the Mughal period, had retained the custom of obtaining their brides from their former Hindu caste. When Dayananda heard of this, he berated the Hindus for this evil custom, and they agreed to terminate it.[72] His friendship with the Rao had become very close, and the latter tried to persuade him to settle down in Masuda, promising that he would subsidize the *Vedabhashya.* At his insistence the Swami prolonged his stay, but eventually he declared that his duty as a *sannyasi* was to roam the land and instruct elsewhere. At last the Rao let him take his leave, and donated another Rs. 400 for the *Bhashya.*[73] The Rao kept in correspondence with the Swami, supported his cow-protection movement, and tried to dissuade him from moving to Mount Abu at the time of his final illness.[74]

Thakur Harisingh of Raipur (Marwar) invited Swami Dayanand for preaching which he accepted. On the insistence of Rao Masuda to stay more at his place Swami said that he was a *sadhu* and should not live in any one place. Accordingly Swami Dayanand left Masuda for Raipur where he reached on the next day i.e. 19 August, 1881. From Masuda the Swami went, on the invitation of Thakur Hari Singh, to Raipur. Although a great *yajna* and a series of public lectures had been foreshadowed, nothing much resulted. The Raja did come to the Swami's discourses at his residence but the other matters kept being postponed. When a telegram arrived announcing the death of the Thakur's wife in Jaipur, the Swami asked leave to move on, and went to Beawar in the Ajmer-Merwara territory where he gave a series of lectures. From there he went back to Masuda, where this time he only gave instruction to the Rao.[75]

Raja Govindsingh of Banera (Mewar) who was the maternal uncle of Rao Bahadursingh of Masuda invited Swami Dayanand to Banera. Swami Dayanand left Masuda and reached Banera on 10 October, 1881 and stayed there for about two weeks.[76]

Bahadur Singh wanted Dayanad to meet his maternal uncle, Govind Singh, of Banera. He was well read and patronized scholars. On receiving an invitation, Dayanand went to Banera. Govind Singh welcomed him in Sanskrit. His library contained an impressive collection of Sanskrit manuscripts. Dayanand compared his copy of the Nighantu (Vedic Lexicon) with the manuscript in the library and carried out certain correction in his copy. One day Govind Singh's two sons demonstrated their Vedic recital skills. Their impeccable pronunciation pleased Dayanand and he gifted some of his books to them. Later on, Govind Singh and his pandit handed over Mahidhar's commentary on the Yajurveda to Dayanand, who retorted that Mahidhar knew nothing about the Vedas.[77]

On 26th October, Dayanand left for Chittor, where he reached next day. It was the result of persuation of Mohanlal Vishnulal Pandya and Kaviraj Shyamaldas.[78] Both of these higher officers were worried about the atheist leanings and they wished to arrange a meeting of Swami Dayanand with the Maharaja. But the great chance came when the Swami met Maharana Sajjan Singh of Udaipur, ruler of one of the great states of Rajputana, with a princely pedigree that outshone that of most rajas. The prince had taken up the reins of government only five years previously, at the age of seventeen.[79] The house of Mewar was Shaivite, but the young prince had difficulties with Hinduism as he saw it around him, and became inclined towards atheism. Two of his closest advisers were very concerned about this development. Both were very learned men, Pandit Mohanlal Vishnulal Pandya, the Secretary of the Udaipur State Council, and Kaviraj Shaymaldas, a member of that Council and a famous historian. They made efforts to interest the young king in Dayananda's works and ideas. They told him all they knew about the swami, and got him a copy of the *Satyarth Prakash* to read. The Maharana's interest was aroused, and the two councilors corresponded with the Swami in the hope of brining the two together. There was, however, a procedural obstacle : Sajjan Singh would not meet Dayananda outside his territory, and the Swami was reluctant to go to Udaipur without a formal invitation. However, by chance, an occasion for their meeting arose. A durbar was arranged at Chittor, where Lord Ripon was to come specially to invest the young price with the title of G.C.S.I.. When Dayananda heard about this, he decided to go there, and informed Kaviraj Shaymaldas about it.[80]

No place in India symbolizes more the splendor, valour, and virtues of Hindus princedom than Chittor. 'My heart beat high', wrote Tod, 'as I approached the ancient capital of the Sesodias, teeming with reminiscences of glory, which every stone of her giant-like battlements attested.[81] The Swami too was reminded of those glorious events as Maharana Sajjan Singh showed him around the historic monuments. They proclaimed the fight to death of the Rajputs and the self-immolation of their women at the conquest of Chittor by Ala-ud-din, and the similar rite performed when Akbar sacked the city. The 'Tower of Glory' recalled the victory of Rana Kumbha over the Sultan of Malwa; and the bards still sang the praises of the giant figure of Pratap Singh whose heroic fight against the Mughals lasted a quarter of a century.

When the durbar was over, the Maharana and the Swami had several meetings and soon great affection and admiration sprung up on both sides. The ruler invited the Swami to accompany him to Udaipur right away, but Dayananda excused himself : he had urgent work to do in Bombay. However, he promised that after his stay in Bombay he would contact the Maharana, and that, if the prince still so wished, he would then go to Udaipur. Many other princes met with the Swami and asked him to visit them in the near future.

These were the events that drew the Swami to Rajputana. He had made close contact with one of its most powerful rulers, a young king earnest and keen to learn more about *dharma* and his kingly duties, who could have substantial influence not only in his own state, but also on the other rajas of the area : Sajjan Singh was noted for his concern to bring the native states closer together. At Chittor Dayananda had also met the Raja of Shahpura, from the same illustrious Sesodia clan of Rajputs as the Maharana, and with him to a close bond had quickly developed. The meeting with these two men was to the Swami an unexpected revelation. He said to Sajjan Singh : It was my opinion that in contemporary India the great majority of kings were a rather lazy lot, but having met you, I have come to believe that you are a very worthy person. Pandit Mohanlal had written to me that you are a lion for work, and that your virtues match your name. That is how I found you to be.[82]

During Dayanand's stay at Chittor two disciples viz. Jeewangiri and Atmanandgiri of Swami Kailash Parvat were also staying there. Listening to the popularity of Dayanand, Jeevangiri expressed his wish before the Maharana to have Shastrarth with Dayanand. Maharana did not agree to this proposal because to him both are honorable. Jeevangiri became very much jealous of Dayanand.

Swamiji stayed at Chittor for about two months from 27th October to 14th December, 1881. On leaving Chittor the Maharana presented him rupees five hundred and other courtiers also presented rupees two hundred. The Maharana also offered rupees five hundred to Jeewangiri to appease him, but he was so enraged that he did not accept the money and left Chittor.[83]

Thus, the third visit of Swami Dayanand to Rajasthan came to a conclusion which began in March, 1881 and ended in December. Obviously, it was a wandering of nine moth in Rajasthan and it had mixed results. He could not get any attention from the rulers of Bharatpur and Jaipur. Though, under the influence of Dayanand some Aryan organization known as *Vedic Dharma Sabha* came into being in Jaipur but remained unnoticed by and large. The Arya Samaj was founded about three months before the visit of Swami Dayanand but it could be strengthened by his presence in May, 1881. Thus, the first Arya Samaj organization was founded in Ajmer. The success of Swamiji at Masuda was unparalleled as a number of people adopted Vedic religion and among them the Jains were in sizable number. Raipur and Beawar visits did no yield required results. But it is amazing to note that during this visit not a single organisation of Arya Samaj could be founded. One thing is worthy to mention that the ruler of Mewar became the first who whole heartedly appreciated the ideas and thoughts of Swami Dayanand. He was so impressed that he requested the Swami to accompany him to Udaipur. But, by not accepting the invitation of Maharaja Swamiji conveyed to Maharana that on his return from Bombay he would write to H.H. from Khandwa, and if the Maharana Sahib then felt inclined to meet him, he would go to Udaipur.[84]

Fourth Visit to Rajasthan and Last days of Swami Dayanand

As per his promise Swami Dayanand left Bombay on 24th June, 1882 and reached Udaipur on 11th August. He came through Chittor and halted there for some time. From Chittor he was accompanied by Swami Atmanand and Brahmachari Pandit Bheem Sen.[85]

The great success of his work at Masuda and the meeting with these two unusual princes were the deciding factors that took the Swami to Rajputana after his stay at Bombay : a new large sphere of influence called him, with the promise of reaching, through the goodwill and power of the princes, that ever beckoning wider community of Hinduism.[86]

During his six months in Udaipur, the Swami concentrated his energies on instructing the Maharana and some of his family and main advisers. His mornings and early afternoons were taken up by his writing and correspondence, and the evenings were devoted to serious instruction; as soon as the pupils were sufficiently familiar with the elements of Sanskrit, the teaching moved on to consider selected texts from the *Manusmriti,* the political and ethical treatises of the *Mahabharata,* and the six *darshana.* The Swami praised the application and regularity of his principal pupil in his letters to the Aryas. He did not give any public lectures, and he took part in only one public debate, the one with Maulvi Abdul Rahman. If in the early days of Dayananda's stay, his pupils did not know their teacher too well, they soon discovered his convictions. Some influential courtiers tried to convince the Swami that, if he dropped his criticism of idol worship, he would get many more people on his side. The answer was the usual one : truth must come first. When Kaviraj came up with the suggestion of erecting some 'memorial' to the Swami, he was rebuffed in plain language. Some businessmen tried to get the Swami involved in their judicial wrangles, no doubt to make use of his influence on the Maharana in their favour, but the Swami made it clear that was completely outside his province. One day Sajjan Singh proposed to Dayananda that if he agreed to become the Mahant of the great Shiva temple, he would command much influence over the religion of the state. The Swami reacted with indignation because he thought that the king was tempting him with prospects of wealth :'You can never force me to break the commandments of the *Vedas.* Therefore, control your tongue. Hundreds of thousands have put their trust in me. It is my firm intention to follow the path of truth always and in every possible way'.[87] Swami Dayanand told the Maharana in indignation that : you held out a temptation to me and want me to break the commands of the almighty God. This small state of yours with its temple, which I can traverse in one run can never persuade me to violate the commands of the *Vedas* and God. Please remember that never shall I give up truth or hide it. Please think well before you talk to me like this.[88]

Swami Dayanand prepared a routine for the Maharana which the Maharana began to follow. As the months went by Dayananda's instruction clearly started to influence the life of the Maharana. When the Swami gave him a suggested order of the day fit for a king, he accepted it and tried to implement the demanding schedule. He also seems to have accepted Dayananda's doctrine of strict monogamy even for kings, for it is reported that at that time he declined to go ahead with negotiations to take a second wife. In this routine or schedule Maharana was allowed six hours, sound sleep. According to this women should be excluded from the night apartments. One night a week or a fortnight to be passed in the Maharani's apartments.[89] Maharana abandoned his evil addiction of visiting prostitutes under the influence of Swami Dayanand. Even Swami criticized the performance of dances in the palace by prostitutes (dancing girls) and Maharana discouraged such dances on regular basis.[90]

Thus, Dayanand's personal influence on Sajjan Singh spilled over into the area of court life and of the administration of the state. After the celebration of a great *yajna* that lasted several days, the king ordered that a daily *havan* was to be held at the court. At the time of the Dashahara festival, which celebrates ritually slaughtered in Udaipur. The Swami held in the court a mock trial in which he played the role of the lawyer for the defence of the condemned animals. The ruler accepted the Swami's arguments, but pointed out that these customs could not be stopped overnight on account of their great popularity. He nevertheless promised that he would see to it that the slaughter was gradually reduced. The Swami also proposed that the work of the courts be done in the *devanagari* script, and he supplied for that purpose a list of translation of Arabic terms into Sanskrit. Such a proposal could not be implemented quickly, as it involved wide-ranging administrative changes. Another proposal was that a special school should be founded for the education of the sons of noble families where they would learn not only the military arts but also the *Shastras.* Sajjan Singh accepted the proposal and took immediate action : plans for the building were drawn up forthwith; but the later illness of the ruler stopped further advance in the project. The Maharana also accepted and ordered the implementation in the Government schools of the curriculum prepared by Dayananda, which included his own Sanskrit textbook.[91]

Swami Dayanand was lodged in the Navlakha Palace in the Sajjan Niwas garden (Nawlakha Bagh) where he revised his famous work Satyarth Prakash and accomplished the second edition. And most of the part of Vedabhashya was also written in Udaipur.

The question of idol worship was discussed repeatedly during the Udaipur visit. One day Swami was on his way to palaces with the Maharana in the morning. In the way there was a temple of Sheetlamata where some men and women were assembled for worship. Swami asked the Maharana how *Darbar* allowed this to happen, then Maharana told that I may stop it right now but it may cause agitation.[92] On moral discourse Swami Dayanand stressed upon the fact that the loss of semen (essence of life) is loss of life and that it should be very carefully conserved, that frequent sexual intercourse weakened and ruined life and that sexual intercourse should be had only for procreation. He condemned Swami Ganeshpuri, a very learned and cultured Sannyasi in Rajputana, who owing to his learning, ready wit and great poetic talent was a welcome guest in every State in Rajputana. He used to teach women and enjoy their company. According to Swamiji, however, a sadhu should never look at a woman.[93]

One day while giving lessons to the Maharana, Swamiji happened to say that only such orders of even one's master should be obeyed as are consistent with one's Dharma. On this, Manoharsingh, Thakur of Sardargarh, said that the Maharana is his master, and if he does not obey his orders he would be deprived of his *jagir.* Swami said, Don't care. If you lose your life and *jagir* in the cause of Dharma, you must not mind it. Living by beggary is better than eating the bread of unrighteousness.[94]

While Swami Dayanand was present, a passage from some religious book was read out one day to the Maharana which said that if anyone gives a Brahmis a pair of shoes for his feet, he earns the merit of having given the whole world in charity. To ridicule such stupid statements, Swamiji addressing the Maharana said, "If this is true, then you can resume the *Jagirs* worth lakhs given to the Brahmins and give a pair of shoes to a Brahmin. You shall then have earned the merit of having given the whole of the earth in charity."[95]

The Maharana once asked Swamiji if Sri Ramchandra was a perfect incarnation of God. Swamiji said, "If Ramchandraji was such an incarnation, you then are an incarnation of God's incarnation; for tradition says that the members of Udaipur royal family are descendants of Ramchandraji's son Lava". On this, the Maharana asked for Swamiji's authority. *Valmiki Ramayana,* was Swamiji's reply. The book was sent for and Swamiji, by anyalysing the passage which described Narada rishi's talk with Valmiki about Ram's life, showed to the Maharana that though rishi Valmiki held Sri Ramchandra to be a man, the commentators had made him out to be an Incarnation.[96]

Two Sahdus came one day to Swamiji and after some talk advised Swamiji to give *updesh* (religious instruction) only to those who were fit to receive it. Swamiji said that there was no question of fitness or unfitness in matters of religion, and that all were entitled to receive *updesh.* He said, "Thousands of people are leaving the Arya Dharma, and you Sadhus are foolishly arguing about fitness and unfitness. Save the people first and talk of fitness and unfitness later." This reply shows that Swamiji was fully alive to the grave religious situation in India and earnestly strove to save people from becoming perverts to other religions. He knew well how this doctrine of vf/kdkj (fitness) had barred the doors of education to women and the sudras in India, and strengthened the hands of mahants who had became sole contractors or purveyors of Dharma.[97]

One day Pandya Mohanlal Vishnulal, Secretary of the state Council, Udaipur, asked Swamiji "When will India be regenerated?" Swamiji replied, "Regeneration of India is difficult to achieve without having one language, one faith and one aim. I, therefore, wish that Indian Rulers should create a common national sentiment and a common faith in their States." Upon this, Pandya Mohanlal said, "Why do you then condemn the faiths of people; for, that create disunity." Swamiji said that want of care and thought and indolence on the part of the leaders and the acharyas of dharma and their prejudices had resulted in the degradation of the ideals, the conduct, and the modes of life of people and in loss of national sentiment; and that unless the question of its regeneration was seriously taken in hand, the nation was sure to die owing to the prejudices of the *acharyas* of dharma : crores of people had become Mussalmans or were being converted to Christianity. "Unless the nation is awakened by giving her *bitter* doses of truth and right advice, and unless evil customs and practices and evil ideals and policies are destroyed, there is little doubt that the race will die. I am not doing my work in my own interest. I sffer all kinds of troubles and insults, get abuse and submit to assaults, became a target for stones and bricks; have been poisoned several times, yet I undergo all these for the sake of reclaiming Dharma and securing the uplift of the race." P. Mohanlal was overcome with emotion when he heard this from Swamiji's lips and said in words dripping with true devotion that if three or four more preceptors of religion like Swamiji were to appear in India, the country would be saved.[98]

The foundation of the Paropkarini Sabha by Swami Dayanand Saraswati at Udaipur is worthy to mention as an extraordinary achievement of him. When he was in Meerut during July-September 1880, he made a will by which he appointed a society called the Paropkarini Sabha and frame its constitution and rules and got it registered. But during his stay at Udaipur he made another swikarpatra (will), cancelling the previous one. He got it registered in the office of the state Council according to law on 27th February, 1883.[99] The following order was passed by the Maharana, Udaipur : Order of the Mahadraj Sabha (State Council) No. 290. Today the execution of his Will was admitted in the presence of Shriman Sri 108 Sriji *dhjir vir chir pratapi virajman* Rajya Sri Mahadraj

Sabha (State Council) by Swamiji Shri Dayanand Saraswatiji in due form. Therefore it is ordered.

That the original Will be delivered to Swamiji Sri Dayanand Saraswati under the signature and the seal of Rajya Sri Mahadraj Sabha and that a copy be kept in the office of the same Sabha, and that it be printed at the State Press and one copy each be sent to the members of the Paropkarini Sabha mentioned in the said Will for their information and action in accordance with its provisions. Dated Samvat 1939, Phalgun Krishna 5th, Tuesday, corresponding to 27th February 1883 A.D.

MAHARANA SAJJAN SINGH
Shri Medhapateshwara of Mewar and President of the
Rajya Sri Mahadraj Sabha

1.

1. Rao Takht Singh of Bedla.
2. Rao Ratan Singh of Parsoli.
3. Maharaj Gaj Singh.
4. Mararaj Rai Singh.
5. Mama Bakhtwar Singh.
6. Ranawaat Udai Singh.
7. Thakur Manohar Singh.
8. Kaviraja Shyamal Das.
9. Sahiwala Arjun Singh.
10. Rai Pannalal.
11. Purohit Padma Nath.
12. T. Mukund Lal.
13. Mohanlal Pandya.
14. Members of the Mahadraj Sabha.

SWIKARAPATRA

I, Swami Dayanand Saraswati, do give authority over my entire property, i.e., clothing, books, money, press etc. to a Society of twenty three Aryan gentlemen in accordance with the rules given below and constituting the same Society as *adhishtatha* (Manager) for the purpose of applying the said property to works of public requires. This Society is designated *The Paropkarini Sabha,* of which the under-mentioned twenty three gentlemen are members Out of them, the President of this Sabha being.

(1) Shriman Maharaja Dhirja Mahi Mahenda Yavadarya Kul Divakar Maharanaji Shri 108 Shri Sajjan Singhji Varma, Dhir Vir, G.C.S.I., Maharana of Udaipur, Raj Mewar.

(2) Vice-President - Lala Mulraj, M.A., Extra Assist Commissioner, Vice President, Arya Samaj, Lahore, born at Ludhiana.

(3) Secretary - Shriyut Kavi Shyamal Dasji, Udaipur, Raj Mewar.

(4) Secretary - Lala Ramsaran Das, Rais, Vice-President, Arya Samaj, Meerut.

(5) Assistant Secretary - Pandya Mohanlal Vishnu Lalji, residing at Udaipur, born at Mathura.

MEMBERS

Name		Place
Shriman Raja Dhiraj Shri Nahar Singhji Varma of	:	Shahpura, Raj Mewar
Shrimat Rao Takht Singhji Varma of	:	Bedla, Raj Mewar
Shrimat Rana Shri Fateh Singhji Varma of	:	Delwara, Raj Mewar
Shrimat Rawat Arjun Singhji	:	Asind, Raj Mewar
Shrimat Maharaj Shri Gaj Singhji Varma of	:	Udaipur, Raj Mewar

Shrimat Rao Shri Bahadur Singhji Varma	: Masuda, Dist. Ajmer
Rao Bahadur P. Sundarlal, Superintendent, Postal Work-shop and Press	: Aligarh
Raja Jai Krishna Das, C.S.I., Deputy Collector Bijnor	: Moradabad
Babu Durga Prasad, rais and treasurer, Arya Samaj	: Farrukhabad
Lala Jagan Nath Prasad, rais of	: Farrukhabad
Seth Nirbhai Ram, President, Arya Samaj	: Farrukhabad
Lala Kalicharan Ramcharan, Secretary, Arya Samaj	: Farrukhabad
Babu Chhedilal, Commissariat Agent, Morar Cantonment	: Cawnpur
Lala Sain Das, Sevretary, Arya Samaj	: Lahore
Babu Madhav Das, Secretary, Arya Samaj	: Danapur (Behar)
Rao Bahadur P. Gopal Rao hari Desh Muksh, member of Coundil of the Governor of Bombay and President, Arya Samaj, Bombay	: Poona
Rao Bahadur Mahadeva Govind Ranade, Judge	: Poona
Pandit Shyamji Krishna Varma, Professor of Sanskrit, Oxford University, England	: Bombay

RULES

The aforesaid Sabha, as it at present and in time of difficulty does, according to the rules, take care of me and all my property and applies it of works of general good, so shall it continue to do after me, *viz.,* after my demise also, in like manner :

(a) In the dissemination of the Vedas, Vedangas and other like sastars, i.e., by fostering the commentary, study, teaching, hearing and publication of these.

(b) The teaching and preaching of Vedic Dharma, by organising a body of teachers and lecturers to work in India and other countries, so that truth may be accepted and falsehood rejected.

(c) The providing of means and institutions for the protection, maintenance and right training of the orphans and the destitutes of India.

This Sabha, as it is in my life-time making all arrangements, it shall after my death also, in like manner, depute one of its members every three or six months to examine and check the accounts of the Vedic Yantralaya. The said member shall, after examining all the items of receipt and expenditure and the stock, affix his signature thereto and shall inform by letter every member of the Sabha of his having done so. In case he notes any defects or improvements in the management he shall send information of the same to every member with any suggestion that he may have to make. On getting the information it would be proper for every member, to submit his own opinion in writing to the President of the Sabha. The President shall make the necessary arrangements, in accordance with the opinions of all the members. No member should in this matter give way to indolence or act improperly.

It is proper for this Sabha, nay, absolutely essential, that as this is a work of the highest merit and universal benefaction, it shall be performed with similar zeal, energy, gravity and broadmindedness.

This Sabha of the said twenty three Aryan gentlemen should, after my demise, be deemed to be my representative in every respect - to wit, the Sabha has and shall have the same right and control over all my property as I myself have. In case anyone of the said members, influenced by selfish motives and contrary to these rules, or any other person asserts any claim of his own, the same shall be considered to be altogether false.

Just as this Sabha has at present according to its capacity, the right to take care of my person, all my property and to improve the latter, in like manner shall it have the right to look to the proper disposal of my body when dead, in other words, when my life is extinct, the sabha shall not permit my body to be buried or thrown into the water or left exposed in the jungle. The Sabha shall make a pile entirely of sandal wood, but if this be not possible, it shall then take two maunds of sandal wood, four maunds of ghee, five seers of camphor, two seer and a half of agar tagar (aloe wood), and ten maunds of fuel, and having made a *vedi* (pile) in accordance with the directions of the Vedas as described in the Sanskar Vidhi, shall reduce my body to ashes chanting the hymns as given therein. No ceremony apart from this shall be performed in any way opposed to Vedic rites. If the members of the Sabha be not present at the time, anyone who is present may perform the ceremony as described above and recover the costs from the Sabha and the Sabha shall pay the same.

This Sabha, during my life time and after my death, can expel any member, if it considers such action proper and can appoint any other fit person who is a Samajist and an Arya in his place, provided that no member of the Sabha shall be removed from the Sabha unless and until impropriety of conduct is exhibited in his actions.

In my place, any action that may be taken by the Sabha in the following matters, viz., the construction of this Will or the observance of its objects and rules, or the removal of any member and the appointment of another in his place, or the adoption of mine shall be with the unanimous approval of all the members. In the event of there being difference of opinion amongst the members, the decision shall be in accordance with the opinion of the majority, the President of the Sabha always having two votes.

At no time shall it be within the power of the Sabha to dismiss more than three of the members after having judged of their misbehavior without first nominating substitutes for those three.

Should any of the members of the Sabha die or, having renounced the above rules and the Vedic Dharam, should act in opposition, it would be proper for the President of the Sabha to remove the said member with the opinion of all the members, and to appoint in his place, another Arya person who is fit and is an adherent of the Vedic Dharma. Until then, save the ordinary business (of the Sabha), no new business shall be taken in hand.

This Sabha has full power to take all steps and devise original plans, but in case the Sabha has not full confidence in its own deliberations and counsels, it may call for the opinions of all the Arya Samajes by letters, fixing a date for the purpose, and act in accordance with the opinion of the majority.

The President of the Sabha shall annually or half yearly, give information by printed letter, to all the members, of the changes in the management of the Press, the approval and disapproval of work done, the dismissal and appointment of any of the members, the examination and checking of receipts, disbursements and stock and other matters of weal and woe.

No disputes connected with this Will shall be taken to the law courts. This Sabha should decide them itself according to justice. In case, however, it is beyond its power to do so, it may get the matter settled by resort to the law courts.

If, in my lifetime, I decide to give pension to any deserving Arya person and get a deed executed and registered to this effect, the Sabha shall accept it and give effect to it.

If some especial profit or beneficial progress results therefrom or important considerations of philanthropy or public welfare demand, I, and after me the Sabha, shall be fully and at all times competent to add to or take out from the above mentioned rules.

The foundation of the Paropkarini Sabha in Udaipur was a great success of Swami Dayanand. The overwhelmed response of the Maharana, Council Members, officers, and employees towards Swami Dayanand inculcate mutual confidence. Swamiji considered the Maharana, Mewar most trustworthy ruler among all the Hindu princely rulers. But still it is an amazing fact that a premier organization of Arya Samaj like Paropkarini Sabha was founded and headquartered at Udaipur under the Maharana Mewar but no organization like Arya Samaj could be founded there.

On 1st March, 1883 Swami Dayanand left Udaipur for Shahpura. Swamiji has experessed his experience in brief as follows : Aryakula Diwakara the Maharana of Udaipur came and met me in respectful terms. He is a man of great qualities. …Many chiefs met me, but none became so intimate as the Maharana of Udaipur. …He gave 1200 rupees for the *Vedabhashya*, one shawl for me, 500 rupees for orphanage at Ferozepur, 100 rupees for the girls doing work there, 100 rupees and ordinary shawl to Ramanand Brahmachari.[100]

Maharana Sajjan Singh presented rupees two thousand to Swamiji on his departure; but Swamiji declined to accept the money. When His Highness said that he could not take the money back, Swamiji asked that the money be credited to the account of the Paropkarini Sabha. The Maharana told Swamiji when he was leaving Udaipur that if Swamiji writes a commentary on the six darsanas, the Maharana would contribute rupees twenty thousand towards the expenses. Swamiji replied that he had to do the Veda Bhashya first.

H. H. the Maharana presented the following Farewell Address to Swamiji and showed him every respect on his departure.

"Benefactor of all, Merciful, Paramhans, Parivrajakacharya Sri 5 Srimad Dayanand Saraswati, the great Yati, from Maharana Sajjansingh."

"Now my mind enjoyed great happiness during the seven months of your stay here, (Udaipur); for your teachings are noble and most beneficial; and by association with you we all undoubtedly derived great profit in matters of *Dharma* and in personal affairs; for the teachings and instructions of those noble persons are effective, whose conduct and acts correspond to their teachings. We found this fully in you. Now though we do want to be separated from you, but as you have to do good to large numbers of people, it is not proper to insist on your staying with us : still you will kindly do us the favour to come here again soon. V.S. 1939, Phalgun Krishna 5, (27th February, 1883 A.D.)."[101]

Apropos of his stay at Udaipur and the *Swikarpatra,* Swamiji wrote the following letter to M. Samarthdan, Manager, Vedic Yantralaya from Chitor on 4th March, 1883.[102]

"We left Udaipur on Phalgun Bad 7 (1st March 1883) about half an hour before dawn in a mail carriage drawn by four horses and reached *Nimbahera* at 5 P.M. and took train from there and arrived at *Chitor* at 9 P.M. We will stay here for three days." We now give you the news about Udaipur.

"We have been very happy since the day we reached Udaipur, and His Highness's regard increased day by day. He read with us the seventh, the eight and the ninth chapter of Manusmriti dealing with politics and fully understood them. In addition to these, he studied several parts of the Mahabharata, Vidur's political wisdom and the principal topics dealt with in the six Darsanas. He also read some grammar and *Anvaya.* We found His Highness Arya Kul Diwakar (Sun of the Aryan Race) true and steadfast, and a good judge of men : virtuous and sincere; and willing to admit faults as kings should always be. I have met several Rajas : but there is little possibility that the happy relations which have subsisted and will subsist in future between me and the Maharana Sahib, will subsist between me and any other Raja."

We now give you the information you have asked for. My *Vedang Prakash* and other books have been introduced in the State schools and the schools for the Charans. His Highness has already began to act on the advice given to him openly and in private, on politics, on Vedic dharma, personal welfare etc. and he has promised to remain steadfast.

"On last Tuesday the 5th of Phalgun at 7 P.M. a meeting of the Ministers and chief Sardars was convened and my *Swikarpatra* (Will) was registered. The Will which was registered at Meerut has been cancelled. The names of H.S. Olcott, H.P. Blavatsky and Munshi Indramani have been taken out and Dr. Beharilal is dead. Four names have been substituted for them : New members have been added making a total of twenty three. His Highness the Maharana Sahib is President of the Sabha.

The Advice mentioned in the above letter means the following Rules and Regulations drawn up by Swamiji for the guidance of His Highness Maharana Sajjansingh : -

Administration of Justice

He should enter the court room in a cheerful and merciful mood and spread happiness among all present there - the plaintiffs, the defendants, the state officials and the visitors. Raising his right hand, he should remove their apprehensions and fear. After taking the seat of justice, he should with eyes closed, pray, "Oh, Just, All knowing, Ever-present God, may You show us grace that we may never do injustice overcome by passion, anger, greed, partiality, fear of sorrow. May you be so kind." He must never forget that greed lies at the root of all passion (*kama*) and injustice. He should keep greed away from himself and not let it come near him. He should be neither an enemy nor a friend of anyone, but absolutely neutral. Just as God and the *apta* (perfect men) do, he should treat all in the same unvarying way, free from all partiality.

Every week, Thursdays should be allotted for the hearing of civil suits, and Sundays for criminal cases. He should give full consideration, uninfluenced by partiality, to what the plaintiff, the defendant and the witnesses say. He should put them on the strictest oaths. The witnesses must be kept separate from one another. Tutored witnesses should not be believed. He should make it known that those who tell lies, accept lies, and act falsely will receive neither respect nor happiness in this life, nor in the next. In this short life, the righteous, that is, those who speak the truth, think the truth and act truthfully, will as a result gain satisfaction of their desires, and salvation; and those who tell lies, think lies and act falsely, always become miserable. Therefore, no one should act against his own self and the almightily by telling lies. One must say what one has got in his heart. The judge should try to know what they have got in their hearts by studying their attitude and demeanor. He should listen attentively to and reduce to writing the statements of all, even of impudent or loquacious persons, as well as the questions put by a barrister or a vakil and their answers. He should clear up points by putting proper questions himself. If after all this, he is unable to arrive at the truth, he should examine the respectable and experienced men and women of the locality, where the untoward happening took place. If an enquiry is being made from a woman behind a pardah, he should make sure that no person other than the one wanted for the purpose is speaking. When she is before the judge, nobody should gaze at her or frighten her or joke with her. If, inspite of all these things, he is unable to arrive at the truth, he should try to know it through righteous emissaries. Having known the truth he should give his judgment against the wrong doer and inflict on him punishment which he deserves, and should show respect to and decide the case in favour of the innocent. The defeated party should not be insulted but should be told that what he had done was not expected of him, and that having been born in such and such family and to such and such a person, he had done such an unworthy act which was a matter to be regretted, and that if he had not committed such an act he would not have got such punishment. If a rogue or a person wronged utters any improper word, it should be calmly borne. One must always protect one's person in every way possible, and should try to know other people's inost wishes as well as their outward intentions. However much a man may entreat or may give crores of rupees, one should never do an injustice. By acting in this way, a ruler's prestige, reputation, resources and authority will be enhanced. He should decide with perfect justice all disputes about land, money, trusts or boundaries whether oral or documentary, as well as cases in which injuries have been caused by the use of physical violence or abuse. He must organize the judicial department on the lines laid down in the eighth and the ninth chapters of the Manusmriti which prescribe eighteen ways of doing justice.

All this judicial work should be finished by 4 p.m. Then after taking rest for fifteen minutes, he should deliberate on State affairs with proper persons upto 5.15 p.m. and should give audience to the public. If he had taken his morning meals at 10 a.m., he should after attending to other necessities, take his dinner by 6 p.m. in summer, and for a walk to a place where fresh air can be had. If he is unable to walk, he should go in some conveyance. In winter, however, he should take his dinner after prayers. In other words, during summer it is proper to go for a walk and say prayers after 8 p.m. having taken food. In winter, he should have his walk and say his prayers between 5 to 7 p.m. and then take his dinner by 7.30 pm. After this, he should observe silence for fifteen minutes, but wash his hands and rinse his mouth and take a pan (betel) and walk one hundred paces and then lie down both on his right and left sides and then get up. Then from 7.45 to 9 p.m. he must hear from his representatives, report about his own and foreign territories with which he keeps relations, and give suitable instructions to serve his purposes. From 9 to 10 p.m. he should listen to a statement of income and expenditure and make appointments for the following day. Then in half an hour he should bid cheerful farewell to his ministers and friends, and go to bed at 10.30 p.m. in a quiet place. In summer he should retire at 10 p.m.. He must thank the Almighty at that time, praying that the next day and night may pass as happily as the preceding one.

On Tuesdays, he should hear complaints against the high handedness of State official, from which the public or state servants have suffered. On three days, viz., Wednesday, Fridays and Saturdays he should by himself or in consultation with loyal and right-minded ministers, who are well-wishers of the country, think of and devise ways and means for the progress of the State and the physical wellbeing of the people.

SPECIAL INSTRUCTIONS

1. When husband and wife meet, they must say Namaste to (greet) each other and behave in such a way as would promote mutual love. They should do nothing to the contrary.
2. Shortly after sexual intercourse, they should have a bath and then drink mildly boiled milk made fragrant with saffron and *salab misri* Salep, (or orchislatifolia) after it is cooled, in such quantity as they like, and wash their mouths and go to sleep in separate beds.
3. Both should make utmost efforts by their minds, bodies and resources to acquire knowledge, practice dharma, and achieve public welfare.

4. They must not entangle themselves in any religious dispute which is against the Vedas or Reason, but should themselves follow and guide others to follow Vedic Dharam.
5. In their own country as well as in other countries so far as possible, they must not allow anyone to be enticed or entangled into any faith which is against the Vedas. If, however, anyone does not listen to reason and persuasion and wants to fall in a well (ruin), it should be looked upon as his misfortune.
6. When the bad people do not give up their evil-doing, why should the good people give up their good actions.
7. Relying always on the policy taught by the Vedas and Sastras and enunciated by the Aryan statesmen, he should always work for their welfare in evey way mentally, physically, and by the employment of all his resources. He himself should not do anything to promote any language other than that of the sastras, nor make anyone else do so. But in foreign relations, when the others do not understand our language and where those others are politically more powerful, their language must be learnt.
8. No orders should be passed without fully considering the smatter or prematurely. All orders should be in writing. And then he must see that orders have been carried out within the time fixed for the purpose.
9. Those who carry out the orders with diligence within the specified time should be suitably rewarded and given promotion; and those who fail to do so should be degraded and punished.
10. No appointment, high or low, should be given to anyone without testing his ability, or when he does not possess necessary qualifications. Work should be got done under

the supervision of those who are righteous and competent. The indigent and the greedy should not be given a higher appointment in the beginning : nor should relations or friends be appointed in the same department.

11. The followers of the Vedic religion should not be placed under the authority of the followers of other religions. Leaving, however, the department of justice and such others as afford opportunities for bribery, if the followers of Vedic religion are not able to do any work, then that work should be got done by others.

12. Those who serve the State faithfully and diligently for thirty years should be given life pension equivalent to half their salary. If a man is killed in war, his widow and sons should also get such pensions so long as the latter do not attain majority. And when they do attain majority, they should be given suitable appointments according to their capacities. But the widow should be given maintenance for her life. If the deceased was getting only Rs. 5/- the widow should be given the full amount. But after the sons have attained majority, the widow should be given half the amount.

13. All children should be educated and made to observe celibacy (Brahmcharya).

14. No person should be allowed to marry before he is twenty five, and she is sixteen. The marriage should be in *Swayamvara* form, i.e. when the bride chooses the bridegroom.

15. He should take care that his prestige and authority increases day by day. It should never be allowed to diminish.

16. He should never give up what is due to him, but must not covet what is due to others.

17. He should take one sixteenth part of the plunder obtained from the enemy by his soldiers. But of the resources and property which victory brings he should distribute one sixteenth part, however large it may be, among his army and retain the fifteen sixteenths for the State.
18. An enemy wounded in the battle should be protected and medically attended to. One should never use weapons against women, children, the old, the distressed, the cowards, or those who come and seek protection.
19. The enemy, after he is defeated, should never be disgraced or humiliated, but should be treated with proper respect. He should, however, never be liberated and given independence.
20. Steps should always be taken to acquire what you have not got; to preserve what you possess; and to increase what you have got. You should always spend the increased income on spreading education, religion, promoting the welfare of the state, and on the maintenance of the orphans and such other good works.
21. Money should always be spent on the education of one's progeny, but not on marriages and deaths, etc.
22. He should always keep away from frivolities, keeping prostitutes or mistresses, dances and hearing false praises from jesters and flatterers and charans, and see that others are also kept away from these things.
23. After attaining full youth, i.e., attaining the age of twenty five years, he should marry a girl whom he likes and selects. He should have sexual intercourse only with her, and only on suitable occasions. If by mistake he has married more than one wife, he should treat them all impartially.
24. He should see that no ill-feeling arise amongst them; and he should treat them all with equal regard and affection in the matter of cloths, ornaments etc.

25. The co-wives should realise that if one of them is blest with a son, all of them should regard themselves as mothers.
26. It behoves the king and the queen to do all that increases mutual love, and love between them and the people, and do nothing to the contrary.
27. He should always keep himself fully acquainted with the good and the bad attitudes of both the officials and the public, through well-tried emissaries. He should take such actions as would increase their good intentions and decrease their evil ones.
28. If an officer commits a crime, he should be punished more severely than the common people; for it is more desirable to stop the evil doing of a lion than that of a goat.
29. The system of taxation should be so framed as to promote the happiness of the peasants and others. The king should treat them as a father treats his own son, remembering that they are the main cause of the welfare of the State.
30. When an enemy cannot be overcome by appeasement, conciliation or creating discord, then he should be punished.
31. He should never quarrel with or antagonize any righteous person : but should do so with a rogue without hesitation.
32. All things should be done in accordance with the opinion of the majority of the righteous persons. The public should be consulted in all matters in which they are concerned. Good and bad points of all such measures should be brought out by holding discussions with them, after which the beneficial regulations should be adopted and the contrary ones rejected.
33. He should regulate his or his family's ordinary and extra-ordinary expenditure according to fixed rules.

34. If he gives a monthly allowance or landed property as religious charity or in recognition of merit, he should allow the grantees to enjoy the grants during their lifetime only, or till the donees make proper use of the property, bu not afterwards.
35. If the ancestor had been given a grant for a particular purpose, and if the holder does not abide by its conditions, the grant should be resumed; for, whenever a *Sanad* is granted it is granted for a good cause.
36. If, however, a grant has been made for religious or charitable purpose and those in possession act unjustly, still the grant should not be resumed. It behoves him (ruler) to take it away from the evil doer and give it to some righteous person. If even he misuses it, the grant should be given to someone else. Where there is no worthy man in the grantee's family, it should be given to some other able person even though he may belong to another family.
37. If, however, the descendants of a grantee are more capable than the grantees themselves, their grants should be increased by giving them a share out of the grants of the unworthy ones.
38. If the dispense of justice (Ruler) becomes unjust, those connected with the government, and the good people from the public, should expostulate with him; but if he does not listen to them, then he should be removed and some other person of his family who is fit to be a just ruler, should be appointed in his place. But such appointment should be made impartially; for, the ruler is invested with powers for the good of the State, the promotion of education and the propagation of religion and not for abuse of them.
39. The Ruler should set aside and spend one tenth of the income of the state for religious and charitable purposes,

With this money, teachers and preachers should be engaged to spread the Vedic religion and right education. In time of adversity, it should be used for the protection of the State.

40. Out of the nine tenths of the income, two ninths should be taken to the Reserve Fund; two ninths should be spent on royal family; three ninths on the army. one ninth on public works, and one ninth in scientific and technical matters.

41. The Ruler should not entrust the affairs of the State to any one person. They should be administered by agreement between the officials and the public.

42. No one should show the slightest disrespect by thought, word or deed to whoever is appointed to be the Ruler. Even when a subordinate be more capable than his superior in any respect, still all should treat with respect their superiors in every respect, and the ruler should be respected as second only to God.

43. All officials should regard the orders of the State as more important than their own lives. They should never show partiality in the performance of State duties, though those duties affect intimate friends and nearest relatives. Disobedience of the orders of the State or negligence in carrying them out, should be punished as hostility to the State.

44. In the first place, orders should be issued after most careful consideration of public welfare : then all efforts should be made to see them fully carried out.

45. The Ruler or the official should not take into consideration his own body and soul, but took upon public policy as the ruler and the chief authority.

46. For the proper conduct of the State, three councils should be appointed, viz, The State Council, the Educational Council, and the Religious Council.

47. Both the official and the public should be appointed on these Councils. The officials should look to the interest of the State, while the public representative should look after the interests of the general public. Laws should be enacted from time to time in accordance with the opinions of the above mentioned Councils.
48. None should break the regulations passed by these Councils. If anyone breaks them he should be be degraded and punished.
49. All officials should understand the meaning, the objects and the practical aim of the seventh, the eighth and the ninth chapters of the Manusmriti which treat of politics and of duties to be performed in emergencies, and know the teachings of the sage Vidur, and act in accordance with them, and should always do what they can to spread knowledge of these.
50. Whatever laws or regulations are to be passed, they should be passed with the agreement of the above said Councils and in accordance with the teachings of the Vedas.

There is no gainsaying the fact that whatever disposition, behaviour, zeal and strength are shown by the ruler, the same will appear in the conduct of the common people. It is, therefore, the duty of the chiefs always to act in righteous and just manner, and give up unrighteous acts and conduct; for, the righteous and the unrighteous conduct of the fief is taken as an example by the common people and copied by them. The chief becomes responsible for their conduct and must bear the consequences of it. The chiefs should therefore conduct themselves after fully considering what they do.

These regulations were drawn up and given to His Highness Maharana Sajjansingh to regulate his private life and to guide him in administering the affairs of the State of

Mewar. Some of these were drawn up so as to suit and be of use in the local circumstances of the State; but most of them embody principles of wide application. Some of them show high statesmanship, and contain precepts which the most up-to-date and enlightened rulers may adopt with profit to themselves and as conducive of the highest interests of their States. Take for instance, rule nineteenth. Such rules are of permanent value and may with advantage be adopted by the most advanced rulers.

It is clear from the foregoing narration that Swami Dayanand deeply influenced the Maharana during his presence in Udaipur. But such influence could not prevail long time. The following narration makes it clear as follows :

On 11 July, 1883, Krishna Singh, an adviser to Sajjan Singh, wrote to Dayanand (when the latter was at Jodhpur) that the Maharana needed his help to counter the Christian propaganda. He reported that a large number of missionaries had descended upon the state to convert Hindus. The maharana wanted a learned preacher to be deputed to refute their propaganda. However, the preconditions laid down were that the preacher should refrain from attacking idol worship and pilgrimages, and should not give any hint that he had been 'tutored' not to touch upon these sensitive issues. He should only expose the weaknesses inherent in Christianity. Moreover, he should give no indication that he had any connection with the state or the Arya Samaj. Finally, he should make no attempt to set up an Arya Samaj. Dayanand could not have appreciated the maharana's preconditions. He culd not condone idolatry, not would he have approved of the maharana's timidity and his distancing himself from the Arya Samaj. In his reply, of 20 July 1883, he pointed out that to find an Arya preacher of such a description was impossible. Idol worship and pilgrmags were the very features of Hinduism which the missionaries generally targeted. These were not only indefensible but also unVedic. He had better ask one of his court pundits to take up the job; there were quite a few of them idling away their time. Dayanand also sent by registered post a hurriedly prepared short critique of Christianity and Islam and advised that it could be printed and distributed.[103]

Thus, the influence of Swami Dayanand began to decline for three reasons. One, the Maharana was not an independent and sovereign ruler and was functioning under the subordination and supremacy (paramountcy) of the British. Therefore, he could not work on the advice and guidelines of Swamiji. Second, Swami Dayanand's ideas of *Swadeshi, Swabhasha* and *Swadharama* were not in consonance of with the British empire. He openly offended the Christianity which was flourishing in India under the patronage of British empire. In the eyes of the British Swami Dayanand was a kind of rebellious *sadhu.* Therefore, Maharana or any princely ruler could not afford to support Swamiji's ideas. Third, the people were hard believer of *Pauranik* religion based on mythology. Each of the ruling house had its' adorable or favourite deity, goddess and clan deities etc.. Therefore, rulers could not discard the the traditional religious structure irrespective of their inherent evil practices and superstition. Moreover, the Maharana Sajjan Singh's untimely death on 23 December, 1884 proved a setback for the growth of Aray Samaj movement. Afte him there was no one to take care of the works of Dayanand Saraswati. His successor Maharana Fateh Singh did not had any inclination towards Arya Samaj, even he declined his appointment as President of Paropkarini Sabha. He did not allow the continuation of the head quarter of the Paropkarini Sabha at Udaipur and the executive was compelled to transfer its' head quarter at Ajmer.

During the Chittor visit (October-December 1881) of Swami Dayanand Raja Nahar Singh of Shahpura (a feudatory of Mewar) came into contact. He requested Swami Dayanand to visit his place Shahpura, but due to his busy schedule it could not be possible. He promised the Raja to visit Shahpura during his next visit. To keep his words Swami Dayanand on 1st March, 1883 left Udaipur for Shahpura and after staying about a week at Chittor reached Shahpura on 9th March, 1883.[104] He was received by the officials of the Raja with the utmost possible respect. On the very day of the Swami's arrival at Shahpura the Raja accompanied by all his dignitaries and nobles, waited upon him at dusk, and the conversation that ensued (on dharmic subjects), lasted for some two hours. For the first five days his attendance at *updesh* was repeated but after that it being settled that the daily visit should be of a more profitable character, Raja commenced devoting two out of the three hours he was with the Swami to the study of the Shastras, and he had, following this plan, gone through the Manu Smriti, the Yoga Sutras, and some portion of the Vaisheshak during the two moths and-a-half of the Swami's stay in his dominions. Very often accompanying the Swami in his walks, Raja also learnt from him, practically, the method of *pranayam* (controlling or restraining of breath for and during contemplation).[105]

Swami Dayanand was engaged in practically no public activity like lectures or debates etc. and the keenness of the Raja to learn kept him engaged to the maximum possible time. Thus, the Swami had no time for public discourse. Moreover, their was no challenge from theologists belonging to any religion and sect. But few light incidents happened at Shahpura has been reported by Swami Dayanand's biographers.

Shahpura is the head-quarters of the *Ramsnehi* sect, where its chief Mahatma resides. People asked Swamiji to have a sastrarth with Mahatma Himmatram. Swamiji agreed, but when they went to Himmatram and spoke to him, he said,

"I drink water after straining it, what have I got to do with a sastrarth."

The annual assemblage of the *Ramsnehi* sect took place in 1883 A.D. when Swamiji was in Shahpura. One day, some Ramsnehi Mahajans of Beawar, who had come to the assemblage, came to Swamiji to hear his lecture. The lecture had not begun then. They said *Ram Ram* and sat down. Swamiji said, Namaste, in reply. Swamiji said to them, "You have been reciting *Ram Ram* for so long, what do you expect to gain." They said, "first name, then the object itself : We heard your name first and after search one reaches there. In the same way, a man by reciting *Ram Ram* reaches Ram eventually." Swamiji said that though he never recited their names, yet he had met them and "that a man connot reach God only by reciting His name. One has to take proper steps to reach Him. One connot get *laddus* by simply saying *Laddus* (Sweets). When this was said, some children five or six years old, who sat in the laps of the visitors, got up and, addressing their elders, said, "Babaji, what Swamiji says is true. Can one get laddus by simply saying laddus." The people present there were simply amazed at this, and Swamiji said, "These children are free from prejudice. They have said what they thought without any one prompting them to say so. Their unsophisticated verdict is the award of an impartial umpire on the sastrarth between us."[106]

The Rajpurohit (Royal Priest) of Shahpura Chhavimal Vyas all the time avoided any kind of discussion with Swami Dayanand. One day he came to visit Swamiji. Then Swami Dayanand pulled him in debate and asked him to tell if he had some doubts. Chhavimal Vyas said he is free from all doubts and has not come to you for the removal of such doubts, but only to meet you. Dayanand said that there are only two kinds of people who are free from doubts and recited a verse which denoted the following meaning : Only two kinds of people enjoy happiness, those who are utterly ignorant or those who are fully wise. Those who are neither undergo sufferings. Swami Dayanand asked Vyas to which of the two classes does he belong. He kept quiet for sometime and then said, just as you judge; you are wise.[107]

A Student named Beharilal put three questions to Swamiji.

(1) The 177th Sutra of the second part of the third chapter of Panini contained praise of stone.

(2) Quoting another sutra from Panini, he said that it proved idol-worship, as it mentioned Siva, Krsihna etc.

(3) Is God present everywhere?

Swamiji replied to the questions one by one. In reply to the first question, Swamiji said several things are praised. A mason says : "This stone is good, wood is good. But it does not prove worship of a stone or image." In reply to the second question, Swamiji said that in old days, Siva and Vishnu were names of men and when people went to foreign lands, their images were kept. But that did not prove that they were worshipped. As regards the third question, Swamiji said, "God is present everywhere." On this Beharilal asked if he was justified in worshipping clothes etc. as God was present in them. Swamiji replied, "As God is present in the bell (>ka>j) and in your speech, and throat, why do you beat one part and worship the other part, and if you can make God of a piece of stone by merely thinking it to be God, why do you not eat the sand by considered it to be sugar." Beharilal was convinced and gave up idol-worship and became Swamiji's follower.[108]

In Shahpura Sami Dayanand administered *Sannyas* to a Brahmin boy whom he named Ishwaranand and was directed to go to prayag to prosecute his studies there. He also wrote a letter to the Manager of *Vaidic Yantralaya* to pay him Rs. 5 per month till the completion of his studies.[109]

One day a sannyasi who was Swamiji's pupil became angry with the cook on a question of *chauka*. Swamiji reprimanded him and told him that as a sannyasi, he ought to be above such prejudices as chauka, and that it ought to be his business to abolish differences between the four castes and promote universal brotherhood.[110]

On the departure of Swami Dayanand as a token of goodwill the Raja of Shahpura paid Rs. 250 for the Veda Bhashya and promised to provide Rs. 30 per month to pay for a preacher of the Vedic faith. In the citation and endorsement Raja of Shahapura addressed to the Swami as follows : The repeated and most humble Namaste of the Ruler of Shahpur State to Parmahansa Parivirajkacharya Shrimat Swami Dayanand Saraswati, I agree to funish an *Updeshak* (preacher) to belong to the Vedic Dharma Updeshak Mandli. He shall continue to receive a salary of Rs. 30 a month from my Treasury from to-day. The duty of Udeshak shall be to uphold and preach the Vedic Religion and to expose and denounce false creeds.[111] He also promised for the regular performance of the *agnihotra,* and establish a Vedic school for the sons of Kshatriyas. He remained in regular correspondence with the Swami throughout the following months.[112] Irrespective of unprecedented response from the Raja the Arya Samaj could not be founded in Shahpura.

In his farewell address Raja of Shahpura expressed his sanse of gratitude from his inner core of the heart as follows :

In the service of the bestower of benefit to all, benevolent Paramhansa Parivarjakachaya sri Swami Dayanand Saraswati Maharaj, Sri Rajadhiraj of Shahpura tenders his Namaste. You have kindly stayed two moths and a half here, still my Atma is anxious to hear more and more of your true religious teachings. I had hoped that you would stay here the whole of the summer, but being aware of the strong desire of H.H. the

Maharaja of Jodhpur to have your darsan and to hear from your mouth, teachings of Vedic Dharma in order to accept the truth and give up untruth, and your promise to go there, and considering that you have come to the world to work for the good of millions of people, I have come to the conclusion that you should go there and I, therefore, do not ask you to stay here any longer. I trust you would greatly honour me by favouring me with your visit again. Dated Jeshth Badi 4, S. 1940 (26th May, 1883).[113]

While Swamiji was in Udaipur, he had received invitations from Maharaja Sir Pratapsingh and Rao Raja Tejsingh, inviting him to visit Jodhpur. In reply, Swamiji had written to them promising to go to Jodhpur after his visit to Shahpura. Swamiji again received at Shahpura and invitation from His Highness Maharaja Jaswantsingh of Jodhpur. Swamiji accepted it. Rao Raja Tejsingh and Col. Sir Pratapsingh were particularly anxious to have Swamiji's *darsan* and to listen to his teachings, and had written several times to Swamiji asking him to gratify their desire. Swamiji now fixed 26th May, 1883 as the day of his departure for Jodhpur.[114]

The Raja Dhiraj of Shahpura was aware of the state of affairs at Jodhpur and the influence, a prostitute named Nanni and her entourage had with H.H. Maharaja Jaswantsingh. He, therefore, thought it his duty when he came to know of Swamiji's intention to go to Jodhpur, to give a mild warning to Swamiji, and suggested to him that it would be well if he did not condemn keeping prostitutes in strong terms at Jodhpur. Swamiji, who was always determined to tell the truth and do his duty even when threatened to be cut down by a sword or blown from the mouth of a cannon, treated the warning with indifference and said that he had never tried to cut down big trees with nail cutters, and added that very sharp and powerful weapons were required for that operation.[115]

The success of his stays at Udaipur and Shahpura gave the Swami great confidence that he was indeed beginning to make a serious impact on the native states. In a letter written from Shahpura to Jodhpur, where he had been repeatedly invited by its Maharaja, he exclaimed, I accept with great joy the invitation to come to Jodhpur. And I thank Maharaja Jaswant Singh, Maharaja Pratap Singh, and you, Rao Raja Tej Singh, for the desire you have shown that I Should come to Jodhpur. From this I have come to the firm conclusion that the time has arrived for the advancement of Aryavarta, now that the ruler of Jodhpur and others have become enamored with the true Vedic *dharama* and with ancient statecraft … I pray the Almighty that he may make you all of a determined mind, and that through you he may bring about the uplift of the whole of Ayavarta, so that he may make you share in the glory of that great achievement.[116]

However, Dayanand's enthusiasm was not surprising : after his achievement in one of the greatest states of Rajputana, Udaipur, he was now invited to Jodhpur, which also ranked among the most important of the area. It was the largest state territorially, the largest in revenue, and ranked only second to Jaipur in population. The princely house had an ancestry and a history that rivalled the glory of the house of Udaipur. The ruler, Maharaja Jaswant Singh, was forty-six and had ascended the throne eleven years previously. He was to occupy it till his death in 1895, and he had a good record as a ruler. His younger brother, Maharaja Pratap Singh, was his right-hand man, and acted as Prime Minister of the state from 1876 to 1902, when he was appointed ruler of Idar in Gujarat. Pratap Singh was looked upon as one of the most enlightened princes of India. His half-brother, Rao Raja Tej Singh, the illegitimate son of his father, was his protégé and close associate, and held a jagir from Jaswant Singh.[117] In Jodhpur there was another personality with enormous influence not only on the Maharaja but also on the nobles of the region : the Muslim minister Miyan Faizuila Khan.[118]

Swami Dayanand left Shahpura on the 26th May, 1883 and reached Ajmer on 28th May, 1883 and there stopped for a day. On 29th May he left Ajmer for Jodhpur. In Ajmer too, people were fully acquainted with the conditions obtaining at Jodhpur, and knew that the Maharaja was under the influence of a public woman there. They also knew very well that Swamiji was sure to denounce this evil in strong terms, and that it would create trouble. Moreover, people looked upon the territory of Marwar as barren, physically as well as spiritually. Marwar is called *Maru Bhoomi,* land of desolation and death. Some of Swamiji's devotees, sensing misfortune respectfully entreated him not to go to that *rakhshas* country. But Swamiji was a man of firm resolution and was incapable of going back on his word. He did not listen to their prayers and only said that he was determined to go and preach the Truth there, and cared not even if people made wicks of his fingers and burnt them. This calls to mind Martin Luther's exclamation when he was summoned to defend himself before the Diet of Worms for criticizing Papacy, "I will go there even if there are as many devils there as the tiles on the roof."[119] Little did the Swami anticipate what awaited him in Jodhpur : a bitter disappointment as far as the ruler was concerned, and a tragic illness that would carry him to his death.

Swami Dayanand reached Jodhpur on 31st May, 1883, where he was received by Rao Raja Jawan Singh on behalf of the Jodhpur Darbar. He was put up at the garden house of Faizullah Khan, who was Prime Minister of Jodhpur State. As soon as Swami reached the destination colonel Pratap Singh (popularly known as Sir Pratap) younger brother of the Maharaja Jaswantsingh and Rao Raja Tejsingh half brother of Maharaja visited him to welcome. Colonel Pratap Siingh presented him a gold *Mohar* and silver rupees twenty five to him. But on the pretext of throat infection Maharaja did not visit him.

Baba Chhajju Singh had depicted the conditions prevailed in Jodhpur at the time of visit of Swami Dayanand as follows[120] : Marwar like Mewar, though certainly not on an equally grand scale, not to the same extent, has been rich in heroes and patriots. The history of Rajputana speaks of the achievements and exploits of the Rathores of the true, genuine type in the most flattering terms, and with justice. The sovereigns of Marwar and the chiefs under them have often done and accomplished that which warriors of the very first order alone could do and accomplish. The Muhammadan rulers of India were frequently brought into collision with them, and though they might execrate and curse them ever so much, they could not but admit to themselves on every occasion that the descendants of the great sovereign of Kanauj and their kith and kin were, if possible, their superiors in bravery and far ahead of them in chivalrous feeling. When Sher Shah came into contact with the descendants of Sevaji,[121] their valour made him exclaim : "I had nearly lost the Crown of India for a handful of barely," alluding to the poverty of Marwar!

At the time when the Swami visited Jodhpur, the state was in any but an enviable condition. It was virtually governed by Muhammadans, one Faizullah Khan was the Prime Minister, and the immense influence he wielded was upheld and supported by his co-religionists more or less dominant in the State offices. The Maharaja was on the most intimate terms with a Muhammandan woman of ill-fame, and her voice with him was as powerful as that of his most powerful officials. Indeed, it was considerably more powerful. She was absoulute master in the palace, and she could be such when she chose beyond its walls : in other words, she could interfere in affairs of State when it pleased her. The kinsmen of the Maharaja and Rajputs in general were unnoticed and uncared for. Mismanagement was everywhere, and justice was at a discount. Corruption and extortion were sucking up the life-blood of many an innocent man, and rederess was difficult, if not almost impossible, to be had. The dacoits and highwaymen had their own way all over the land, and it seemed as if the Authorities were all but unable to cope with the pest. Altogether, things in the great principality wore an ugly look, and one might think that the Swami could afford to forego the pleasure of visiting it. Many did think so, and dissuaded the Swami from going to Jodhpur, observing that it was *unsafe* for him to be in the midst of so much unscrupulous selfishness, meanness and villainy, but the swami knew what he was and what he could do, knew what he must do, in duty bound in the interests of his Divinely-ordained mission, at every personal risk. Nor was the Maharaja, whatever his faults, and some of these were certainly great, entirely destitute of great virtues. He was to begin with, a most liberal prince, though his charity for the most part went to feed lazy Brahmans and idle and mischievous representatives of the Sadhu clan.

The Maharaja, accustomed to a different order of things, at first failed to appreciate the greatness of the Swami's personality. He knew that Sadhus and Sannyasis could be summoned at will and dismissed at pleasure. Money and rank had weight with these, and they never lost a chance of courting the same if they could help it. he was under the impression that Dayanand was like one of the Sadhus and Sannyasis in question, that he would be the first to make advances and would win his good-will and pleasure by coming to see him at his palace or at his court. But in this he was mistaken, as he ultimately discovered. Fifteen days passed away without the Maharaja and the Swami seeing each other. His Highness thought that the Sannyasi would come to him, and the Sannayasi on his part, to be true to the traditions of his race, would not have it said that wealth and power were mightier than knowledge and wisdom. At last on the sixteenth day, the Maharaja, either prompted by some noble impulse from within or swayed by the good counsels of men like Maharaja Pratap Singh and others, came to see the Swami, and his coming, be it confessed to his credit, was after the coming of the Arya sovereigns of yore to the huts of sages and saints. As soon as he was face to face with the Swami, he said his *Namaste,* and offering a *nazrana* of five pieces of gold and one hundred rupees, in silver, was about to sit on the carpeted ground, when the Swami asked him to take a chair like his own. His Highness humbly replied that he was not entitled to sit on a chair in the presence of such personages as he, and begged to be permitted to sit on the ground. The Swami would not hear of this, and taking His Highness's hand seated him on a chair. The *updesh* on "Rajdharama" (Duties of Kings) commenced, and lasted for three hours. The Maharaja was extremely pleased with all he heard and, when taking his leave, expressed a desire that the Swami would lecture every day. Agreeably to the wishes of the Maharaja, the swami began a series of lectures, each lecture generally lasting for two hours from 4 P.M. to 6 P.M., and two hours were daily given to the answering of questions and to the removing of doubts asked and expresses. One day His Highness himself asking the question : "How can salvation be obtained?" the Swami replied : "The dispensing of justice rests with you, dispense justice, and that will secure you salvation"[122]

In his public discourse Swamy Dayanand was speaking on various themes buy great stress was on reforming the conduct of kshtriyas. The ruler, *Jagirdars* and various highly place people in the administration were prey of polygamy, drinking, hunting, keeping concubines, mistresses, keeping prostitutes and various evil vices. Thus the nobility and feudatory was not relishing the lectures of Dayanand. Rao Raja Tejsingh requested him not say anything about the Mahraja's conduct. Thus, Swami Dayanand promised that he would condemn the evils in general terms without mentioning any name. He continued condemning the vices of the kshatriya character.[123]

The lectures of Swami Dayanand were not being taken by the nobility in the right earnest, rather they felt offended by his lectures. The Swami's lectures and *updesh* created a stir which Jodhpur had seldom witnessed before. The worst passions of the worst and stick-at-nothing were aroused, and 'vengeance' became the watch-word of this huge and daring fraternity. The Swami questioned the privileges of the undeserving in every department of the State, denounced trickery and fraud of every description, advocated and upheld the cause of virtue with the eloquence of a stern and most earnest enthusiast, in public and in private, and boldly declared that those who 'ate the State's salt' without rendering it good service in return were traitors in the sight of both God and man. Such a man could not be tolerated, and must be made to smart, in some way or another. As to how far the Muslim community was excited by the Swami's true, though unpalatable, utterances, may be judged from the threatening words of Faizulla Khan to the Swami one day : "If it were a Muhammadan government now, you would not live to preach such things!" To which the Swami calmly replied : "If it were so, I would set two Rajputs at your heels!" Whatever plots the enemies of righteousness might hatch and whatever they might say in his hearing or in their secret councils, the Swami was not one to fear them : he feared God, and naught else.[124]

The Maharaja visited the Swami thrice during his sojourn in his State, and thrice did the Swami visit him in return. One of the latter's visits proved to be most unfortunately timed (or, in reality, most fortunately timed) for His Highness. When the Swami arrived at the Mahraja's quarters, his favourite and all powerful prostitute Nannhi Jan was sitting with him. Coming to know that the Swami was at the gate of the palace, His Highness hastily made a sign to his attendants to take the woman away. The attendants placed her in a sedan-chair, and were about to move off when the chair suddenly swayed down to one side with unequal weight and no additional man being near, His Highness became one for the time being, and put his own hand to the conveyance to steady it! But lo! before to retreat from it, the Swami entered and saw what was going on. His astonishment and his pain at the sight no one can describe. The representative of the great Jaswant Singh, of Ajit Singh, humiliating himself so utterly for the sake of a degraded female! Full of indignation he exclaimed : "Alas! that a bitch should share the embraces of a lion. If such associations should not result in the birth of dogs, what else should they result in?" His Highness received this merited rebuke in silence and with a bowed head.[125]

When the words of the Swami came to be reported to Nannhi Jan, as they were bound to be, her rage knew no bounds. "Is this a Faqir or a devil?" said she. "He fears not the Maharaja, and he fear not me!" Perceiving that her interests were at stake she too began to cast about for some plan which should enable her to be more than even with the terrible Sadhu. Men who felt as she did, whose purposes in regard to the Swami's personality were as fell as her own, were forthcoming is scores, and they shared her secrets and assured her of their assistance at the right time.[126]

The opponents of Swami Dayanand began to devise variou strategies to overcome the Dayanand phobia. Initially they tried to get the Swamiji defeated through discussions.

Maharaja Jaswant Siingh himself called *Sahdu* Ganeshpuri to hold *shastrarth* with Swami Dayanand, but he declined.[127] One day Rao Raja Sohansingh came to Swamiji with Nischaldas's book *Parvati Ratnakar* and began to talk about *Jiva* and *Brahma* being one, but could not win over him and after two-three days discussion became speechless before him.[128]

In one of his lectures, Swamiji strongly condemend the Vallabhachari sect, which offended many people. One Pandit Sriram Parvati, a leader of that sect, happening to come to Jodhpur at that time, challenged Swamiji to a sastrarth, but no sastrarth could be held as he insisted on appointing Mehta Bijaisingh, the Revenue Minister, with whom he was styaing, as umpire. Swamiji declined to accept him; for not only was Mehta Bijaisingh a follower of P. Ramlal, but was ignorant of Sanskrit language, in which the sastrarth was to take place. Opposition to Swamiji spread in Jodhpur. Mehta Bijaisingh made common cause with Nanni. The Rajputs, who held high positions, were offended because Swamiji publicly condemned their corrupt and loose conduct. The Muslim became angry as Swamiji denounced Islam in strong terms. The followers of the Vallabhachari sect and tha Pauraniks became his enemies, for he denounced idolworship and thus laid an axe at what was tha means of living for the Brahmins. The courtesan Nanni became alarmed that His Highness may cast her off by listening to the teachings and advice of Swamiji and became Swamiji's enemy.[129]

The presence of Swami Dayanand could not create a team of vocal supporters of him. Thakur Kesrisingh of Kuchaman and his son Kr. Shersingh were men of high character and were full of respect and devotion for him. Maharaja Sir Pratap Singh and Rao Raja Tejsingh were the only great active supporter of him.[130] Mahraja Sir Pratapsingh told Babu Devendranath Mukhopadhyaya that before Swamiji went to Jodhpur, his faith in Hinduism had been shaken, and at times he became very depressed; but that after talking to Swamiji at Jodhpur and listening to his lectures, all his doubts disappeared and his faith in the Vedic Dharama became firm. One day Sir Pratapsingh asked Swamiji if he could obtain moksha. Swamiji replied, "Yes, the way is to do unadulterated justice."[131]

Afte all the preachings of Swami Dayanand could not bring any impact on the conduct of the Mahraja. His character remained unaffected. Neither he gave up the company of Nanhi *Bhagatan* nor he gave up drinking and meat eating.[132]

Since the beginning of his visit Swami Dayanand was not happy with the atmosphere of Jodhpur and after one month he expressed his feelings through a letter to Colonel Pratap Singh as follows : The first part of the letter expressed his concern over the fact that the leaders of such a great state, with such immense responsibilities, were wasting their time and spoiling their health. They should arrange their lives more strictly so that they might be strong and live long to work for the advancement of the people and to share in the glory of the regeneration of Aryavarta. The second part of the letter set out the conditions under which the Swami would be prepared to participate in debates with the local pundits mooted by the court : the princes should be present at these occasions and precise rules of procedure should be drawn up beforehand.[133]

It seems that his happy and pleasant experience at Udaipur and the great success which his work with His Highness the Maharaja of Jodhpur to go to that place. At Udaipur, Maharana Sajjansingh used to visit Swamiji every day and profit by his advise and instruction. So also was the case at Shahpura in Mewar, where the Raja Dhiraj visited Swamiji every day and became his pupil. Thus, when Swamiji received H.H. the Maharaja of Jodhpur's invitation to go to Jodhpur, Swamiji, ever anxious to help in the reformation of the lives of the Rulers of the Indian States by giving them religious instruction, for, on them depended to a great extent the happiness and prosperity of millions of men, accepted the invitation and decided to go to Jodhpur, hoping that as the Maharana of Udaipur had met him every day and Swamiji was able to do some good at Udaipur, the Maharaja of Jodhpur too would meet him frequently, and Swamiji would be able by advice and instruction to influence the Maharaja's life and enable him to do his duty to his subjects. When, however, he reached Jodhpur, he disillusioned. He found that things were quite different there. He reached Jodhpur on 31st May, 1883 and H.H. the Maharaja did not come to see him till the 26th June, 1883, twenty seven days after Swamiji's arrival at Jodhpur. He also saw clearly that the Maharaja had no desire to meet and profit by Swamiji's instruction. Thus, when the Maharaja of Jodhpur, unlike the Maharana of Udaipur, did not give Swamiji opportunities of personally giving him advice and influencing his defective conduct; and Swamiji, fully aware as he was of the corrupt and foul atmosphere in which the Mahraja lived, and the debased and depraved lives that the people who surrounded him led, determined as he was to redeem the Maharaja from his evil habits, decided as the last resort, to write to him and draw his attention to his failings and the grave defects in his character. Swamiji warned him of the serious and harmful consequences of his conduct to himself and to his subjects and told him in a language, courteous and civil, but firm and frank, and a manner deferential and polite, but clear and unmistakable, what his duty as ruler of an important and historic stae was towards his subjects, whom providence had placed under him, and whom it was his sacred and bounden duty to protect, and whose welfare and happiness he was morally and legally bound to secure.[134]

Swamiji wrote a number of such epistles, how many we do not know; but the first and the third of them are available. These epistles prove Swamiji's solicitude for the redemption of the Maharaja, and the welfare of his subjects. They also show that Swamiji made great efforts to reform the lives of the rulers of Jodhpur. He gave private advice and drew the attention of Maharaja Sir Pratapsingh and His Highness and others to the evils in their lives. He publicly denounced in scathing terms, the evils from which the rulers suffered. He made supreme efforts to purify and strengthen the lives of those who were at the helm of the State for their own and the country's benefit, and took all risks, throwing to the wind all caution and care. It looks as if with a full knowledge of the consequences, he deliberately started a campaign against vice, determined to expose and put an end to the corruption and impurity in the lives of the people, on whom depended the happiness and welfare of lakhs of people, caring nothing for his own life and paying no heed to the warning of his followers and well whishers. Swamiji was aware that the entourage of the Maharaja of Jodhpur was infected with the vice of keeping mistresses, from which even Maharaja Pratapsingh and Rao Raja Tejsingh were not free. He, therefore, wrote the following letter to Col. Sir Mahraja Pratapsingh.

"May the highly respected, brave and valiant Maharaja Pratapsingh remain happy. Please show this letter to Baba Sahib too. It causes me sorrow to see His Highness leading a life of indolence and other things. You and Baba Sahib suffer from sickness. Now you people are bearing the burden of protecting and doing good to this State, which contains over sixteen lakhs of people; the improvement or deterioration of the State depends on you three gentlemen. Yet you pay little attention to preserve your health and prolong your lives. This matter is deserving of great consideration. I wish that you would listen to me and reform your conduct, so that you may become known for your good work not only to Marwar but whole of Aryavarta (India). Capable people like you are seldom born in the world, and when born, seldom enjoy long lives. Owing to the lack of such people the country does not prosper. The longer the noble souls live, the greater the benefit to the country. You ought to pay attention to this matter. Now do as you please. Dated Ashwin Badi third, V.S. 1940" (19 September, 1883).[135]

No doubt in the views of Swami Dayanand the Maharaja was good by nature but has been spoilt by the company he keeps. The presence of Swami Dayanand also brought some positive development related to his mission. In August 1883 a branch of the Arya Samaj was established in Jodhpur under the patronage of Pratap Singh. In the same month Hindi was proclaimed the language of the State which was the first in India to take that step.[136] Harbilas Sarda has mentioned that : The only *updesh* (teaching) of Swamiji that the Maharaja and the people accepted was the use of Swadeshi cloth. Every one in the service of the State, from the Maharaja down to the peons - officers, clerks and the elite of Jodhpur adopted the *Khadi* produced in Marwar. Thus, long before Swadeshi became the cry in Bengal, Marwar appeared clad in *Khadi.*[137] It has been rightly summed up by Jordens as follows : When the sick Swami left Jodhpur on the 16 October, Jaswant Singh came personally to bid him farewell. He offered Rs. 2500 to the Swami, and with Pratap Singh and Tej Singh he accompanied the Swamiji's *palki* on foot for some distance. Those facts show that all did not go wrong in Jodhpur. The Swami expected too much, and he found it impossible in his personal relation with the Maharaja to overlook and condone his moral flaws, because in his mind the high personal morality of the ruler was inextricably connected with the prosperity and advancement of the State.

On 28th July,1883 Swami Dayanand wrote a letter to the Maharaja. The first letter to H.H. the Maharaja of Jodhpur is mild, and begins with a quotation from the Mahabharata, in which the sage Vidur tells the blind king Dhritrashtra, that selfish men abound in this world but true men are rare. The letter is as below, Addressed to Srimad Rajeshwar Maharajadhiraj Sovereign of Jodhpur : (Vidur says) "Oh Dhritrashtra in this world : people abound who gain their object by saying flattering things of others. But those who say what is bitter to hear but is very beneficial in the end, and those who gladly listen to them, both such people are rare. As the *Mahabhashya* says : "Just as the victory and defeat of an army is accepted as the victory and defeat of the king, so should your Highness think. Enjoyment which the senses yield, appear like nectar in the beginning but act like poison and rsult in great unhappiness in the end. You ar wise and a word is enough to the wise. It is a matter of good fortune that you posses many praiseworthy qualities, good health and enjoy supreme authority over a kingdom, but it is a matter of sorrow that though you are so intelligent yet you remain occupied in a few things noted below. They are these. You do not give up drinking, association with prostitutes, kiteflyng and other evils, do not devote at least six hours to the work of the State : you do not love your wives, who are the daughters of royal families and who represent Mahalakshmi, prosperity. There are other things about you which cause sorrow and pain. Please rest assured that you will be held responsible for all things creditable or discreditable that your dependents do. If you yourself abstain from drinking liquor, can anyone of your dependents make you do so? Those who are selfish and given to flattery always desire that the Raja should become indolent, so that their purposes be served. But remember that no one will blame them : for, as the *Mahabhashya* says : "Good and bad acts should be taken to be those of the prinicipals and not of their followers". The *Gita* sayas : "Whatever good or bad the high placed people do, the common people copy their example. Whatever standard the great set, the generality of men follow it too". As the saying is, "As the king, so the subjects". As the king is, so the subjects become. It follows, therefore, that high placed people should take careful thought and conduct themselves will, so that they may not be blamed for the degradation of the common people. It is not proper to write at great length to intelligent men. There is no doubt that if long-lived and just Rajas continue to rule, the subjects would be benefited. Drinking liquor and other habits (stated above) undoubtedly do harm to life, intelligence, vigour, health, fame, dharma, prosperity, fulfillment of wishes, and salvation, and prevent parental solicitude for the welfare of your subjects. I trust that you would give up drinking and other evil habits and save those who are near to you. Please give a reply to this just as you like, and do not thinks for a moment that if you give a stiff reply, Swamiji would be displeased.

"I firmly believe that you are truthful and sincere, and you will write to me soon whatever you think of what I have written. This is the first letter I address to you. But if necessary, and if you and I do not meet, it would be only through exchange of letters that we can talk. As I do not delay for even a moment attending to what is urgent or in answering a letter, so will your Highness do.

"If you continue to indulge in the above mentioned evils, then other people shall also copy your example. So long as a man is healthy, keeps good company, and possesses good virtues and is independent, no trouble destructive of happiness appears; for, an intelligent man takes steps to prevent future troubles; otherwise, where is the difference between intelligent and unintelligent people. The difference is that unintelligent people give no thought till the trouble comes; and when the trouble comes they get confused. The intelligent people do not act like this. As the Gita says : "The practice of Brahmacharya and other works appear like poison in the beginning, but later on they act as nectar. What benefits the soul and the intelligence is the happiness which comes from knowledge, good thoughts, good company, and the practice of Yoga and other works."

Manusmriti also says : "Just as when a whole family is poisoned and all members of it die, so when married women who are miserable owing to the treatment meted to them by husbands, fathers, mothers, relations, husband's brothers and others, curse the members of the family, their husbands and others go to rack and ruin".

Manusmriti further says : "Where in a family, the wife is pleased with the husband and the husband with the wife, in that family happiness continues to increase." Just how when a woman has intimate relations, secret or open, with a person other than the husband how miserable the husband become; so does a woman become very miserable, when the husband goes to another woman or a prostitute. The misery of these women destroys the family; while their happiness makes the whole family happy. Therefore, by not giving your valuable time to drinking, associating with prostitutes and other things and by employing it in doing justice, committing righteous deeds and protecting yours subjects, (you should) become deserving of thanks and receive credit from all. It is no good writing more to intelligent people.[138]

The second letter is not available but the third letter written on 8 September 1883 is very important because Swami Dayanand expressed his anguish and dissatisfaction before the Maharaja through this. He also informed the Maharaja that his mission of Jodhpur is a failure and he is thinking of leaving Jodhpur. The said letter had two parts. In the first part Swami gave general advice on administrative reforms and precautions, while second part contained personal advice. The letter was as follows : "His Highness Raj Rajeshwar Maharaja Dhiraj, Sovereign of Jodhpur, be happy.

I now wish to stay here only twenty or twenty five days more, unless some special occasion arises. It is my belief that by coming here, I have caused useless expenditure of your money; for no benefit has accrued to you through me, though all proper hospitality has been shown to me. As your Highness appreciates good qualities, I have, as I found occasions made submissions to you in writing. As you take these submissions in good part, I take an opportunity to write to you for the third time.

1. The administrative work you are doing, you should continue to do till the end; and, if possible, more attention should be paid to it; for it is the prime duty of rulers to treat the subjects with justice.
2. Care should be taken of the food and other things of the Maharaj Kumar. He should be given every day half a pound of cow's milk mixed with one *masha* of dry ginger, placed on fire for a while and then cooled; some *Brahmi* (a medicine plant) should be put into it so that the Maharaj Kumar's intelligence, vigour, energy be increased and his life prolonged.
3. Maharaj Pratapsingh is your Highness's and State's well wisher and should be allowed to continue doing administrative work.
4. This State suffers from scarcity of rainfall. If therefore, on my advice, you perform *havan* every day and use ghee and other things of the value of Rs. 10,000/- a year, and during the season perform it more frequently, possibly there will be more of rain and less of disease.
5. You posses many praiseworthy qualities. If you employ them in administration, the country will benefit and will get credit in the world."

Then Swamiji gives private advice. The letter continues :

SECRET (PRIVATE) ADVICE

1. Your Highness possesses praiseworthy virtues : they are, however, tainted by the following :
2. To love a prostitute named Nanni, much association with her, and little love for your wivs are most improper for Maharajas like you.
3. As it is most difficult to get rid of the poison when bitten by a mad dog, so keeping prostitutes, drinking, wasting time in kite flying, playing *chaupar* and doing other frivolous things and associating with flatterers are harmful and destructive of life and credit, and the State. It causes me great amazement that, possessing as you do great intelligence, courage and other good qualities, you do not keep away from such things.
4. Things such as going to the prostitute Nanni's house, and enquiring after her sick mother and others, as well as going on foot holding the reins of a horse in the marriage of a son of a Muslim servant of yours, are disgraceful acts, and in no way redound to your credit. If, instead, you had gone to see Mehta Vijaisingh who was ill, or if you go on foot in the marriages of Sardrs of Marwar or the members of the Royal family who are the well wishers of your Highness and the State, praise, profit and progress will be the result.
5. When I hear from somebody, or read in papers, censure of you, great pain and sorrow are caused to me. If you do not commit, such blameworthy acts, there will be no cunsure of you and we will not feel ashamed before the Europeans. If the late Maharaja, who was your Highness's father, had not married several wives, kept mistreses and prostitute, you would not have done the same. In the same way, the

Maharaj Kumar and others see your conduct, they also will have the same inclinations; for, it is easy for people to copy others' vices but difficult to learn their virtues.

6. Please do not appoint a Muslim or a Christian as Tutor to the Mahraj Kumar : otherwise, the Maharaj Kumar will learn their vices and will remain ignorant of your traditional policy; nor will he believe in the Vedic religion, for the instructions received in childhood take a firm hold, and it would be difficult to get rid of the effect.
7. All *Sanskars* (sacrificial rites) of the Maharaja Kumar should be performed according to the Vedic injunctions. He should be kept a Barhmachari till he is twentyfive. He should learn Devanagari first, and then should be taught Sanskrit and Arsha literature. This would take less time and labour and give great benefit. After that, English and the literature in it should be taught.
8. As you have given up the company of Ganeshpuri and others who only teach evil habits, why don't you keep away from prostitutes and sweet tongued cheats? As you have, by putting on a cap, payjama, alien dress, coats and pants like the Muslims and Christians, kept yourself away from noble thoughts, you should not in the same way, waste your valuable time and lose your virtues by keeping company with prostitutes etc. You must remember that your person is not for pleasures of the senses and luxury, but for doing good to millions of people, by hard work and doing justice to them. Please see what do-able and undo-able things are prescribed for Rajas in the seventh, eighth and ninth chapters of the Manusmriti. I trust you will be pleased to listen to these things which are bitter, but which will promote your welfare and will bring salvation to you. It is unnecessary to go into details when writing to most honourable men."[139]

In fact Maharaja Jaswant Singh was not a bad ruler and he was obviously inclined towards the ideas of Swami Dayanand. His public preachings in Jodhpur were highly encouraged by the Maharaja himself. The Maharaja was also convinced with the reforming ideas of Swami but his over expectation from the Maharaja could not be fulfilled. Though, the Maharaja encouraged the Swami to work among his people, but he had no desire to become personal pupil of him or to drastically change his own life style on the avice of swami Dayanand. Moreover, it was the greatness and humility of Maharaja that he received the last letter from Swami Dayanand humbly and calmly without resentment. It has been rightly analysed by Harbilas Sarda as follow : Never before in his life, had Maharaja Jaswantsingh to face such unpleasant plain-speaking and sever rebuke. It shows the innate nobility of his character, his high-mindedness, and his magnanimous forbearance that he did not resent the bitter reproaches and the severe condemnation of his conduct which Swamiji's third epistle contained. Unpalatable and galling as these letters must have been to the Maharaja, he took them in good spirit, keeping before his mind the apostolic character of the great teacher. He appreciated the benevolent spirit which actuated Swamiji to write those epistles, and accepted with becoming humility and reverence, the bitter truth that was for the first time presented to him in such scathing terms. Swamiji shewed rare courage and apostolic zeal in rudely awakening the Maharaja to the bitter realities of his life; and the Maharaja showed a truly kingly forbearance and a noble tolerance at the castigation he received, as befitted the elevated position he occupied as the head of one of the most important and historic States in India.[140]

Harbilas Sarda has mentioned that : Swamiji's teachings carried intellectual conviction to His Highness and he accepted their truth, as is proved by two incidents which occurred long after Swamiji's death. In the census of 1891 when Sardar Har Dayalsingh, a minister of the State, asked as to what he should enter as His Highness the Maharaja's religion, the courtesan Nanni, who was present, said it should be entered as Vaishnavism. His Highness himself said no, his religion was Vedic. Another incident took place eight or nine years after Swamiji's death. One evening, during a talk between Nanni and Bhati Arjun Singh, the former alluded to Swamiji in disrespectful language, when His Highness felt offended and told them that they did not know Swamiji : he knew Swamiji's greatness, and said that if Swamiji had been alive at that time, he, as the true son of H.H. Maharaja Takht Singh, would have given up the kingdom and gone with Swamiji after taking *sannyas.* Though Swamiji's teaching wrought a change in the Maharaja's beliefs and he accepted the Vedic Dharama, yet they produced no effect on his conduct and daily life. His character remained unaffected. He did not give up the company of the courtesan Nanni.[141]

Swami Dayanand decided to leave Jodhpur soon as a letter of 20th September, 1883 indicates. In leter on 24th September, he announced his decision to leave on the first October and on 27th September he asked Rao Raja Tejsingh to make the necessary arrangements for his departure. It was in these last days that he was struck down by the illness from which he was not to recover. On the night of the 29the September he took milk as usual which caused stomach pain and vomiting. He than suspected that someone has poisoned him. On 1st October the doctors began to treat him but could not revoke and his health deteriorated very fast. On 15th October Doctor Alimardan advised the Swami's removal to Abu. Obsergving the change of climate may do him good. But his real reason, according to Devendranath Mukhopadhyay was his belief that Swamiji would not survive and that if Swamiji died at Jodhput, the whole blame would fall upon him.[142] Mukhopadhyay has also doubted the role of Dr. Alimardan in the conspiracny against Swamiji. On the day of Swamiji's departure, the Residency surgeon was called and he too advised Swamiji's going to Abu. Therefore, 16th October was fixed as the day of departure.

On 16th October at the time of departure Maharaja Jaswant Singh with his brothers Pratap Singh, Tejsingh and dignatories of the State, made his appearance, to pay his respect to the Swami, and to see him off. The Maharaja presented Rs. 2500 and two shawls to him. Some royal tents, six camels, three chariots, one phaeton were to accompany the Swami, who himself was to travel in a Palanquin, attended by a number of courtiers, one of these being Doctor Suraj Bhan. The parting moment came, and it was clear to all present that His Highness, as also his brother, was in real distress. Who could say how the desease would terminate and if His Highness's worst fears were realized and the illness had a fatal ending, neither he nor his descendants could, for generations, hold up their heads when the sad event was mentioned in their presence. His Highness felt after the noble race from which he came. What has not the true Rajput done and dared to prevent a slur being cast upon his fair name. His Highness with his own hands tied his own special belt found the swami's waist, and to mark his appreciation of the invaluable lessons he had received form the Swami and of the profound respects in which he held him by reason of his lofty virtues and his unique attainments, he walked some two hundred paces by the side of the palanquin before he eventually took leave of its occupant.[143] With moist eyes and flowing tears and in a trembling voice, the Maharaja said : Swamiji, your departing in your present condition of health is a disgrace to me. How I wish you have left the State after regaining your health. Please do come again.

Swami Dayanand reached at Mount Abu on 21st October and from there he was brought to Ajmer on 26th October, where Dr. Lakshamandas immediately resumed his treatment. But things had gone bad to worse as the Swami had now contracted double pneumonia. On the 30th October Hakim Pir Imam Ali (popularly known as Pirji) came and saw the Swami and after having thoroughly examined him, he gave his opinion that he had been poisoned. He said that if the Swami instead of going to Abu had come direct to Ajmer the fatal substance would very probably have been got out of the system.[144]

The civil surgeon Dr. Newman was called who also confirmed the double pneumonia and graveness of Swamiji's illness. In the evening of 30th October, 1883 Swami Dayanand knew that his end was near and he asked all the Aryas to come to his room to bid a final farewell. He recited some Vedic mantras, and his last words were, 'Oh merciful and almighty Lord, such is your will, yea, such is your will, let this thine will be fulfilled, you have perfomed a good lila'. And simultaneously with closing the prayer, he turned in his bed and, controlling the out-going breath after the manner of yogis, cast it out utterly with one vigorous effort and brought his earthly existence to an end.[145] It was Deepawali, 30 October 1883. Out of Gujarat Swami Dayanand began his journey form Abu in Rajasthan in 1852 and also breathed his last in Rajasthan. Thus, India's greatest Sadhu, seer and reformer of modern times expired.

On 31 October Swami Dayanand's funeral was held. Two *Sannyasis* came to claim the Swamiji's body in order to bury it according to the usual rites for Sannyasis. But their claim was refused by Aryas and told them that Swami Dayanand had made it clear in his will that he wanted his body to be cremated according to the rites prescribed for all Hindus in his *Sanskarvidhi.* This rite was performed in the presence of Aryas from all over India, who were stunned by the immense loss they had suffered. The next day i.e. 1st November, 1883 Pt. Mohanlal Vishnulal Pandya took possession of the Swami Dayanand's belongings in the name of the Paropakarini Sabha.

It may be concluded that Swami Dayanand's visits and presence brought many positive effects on the life and thoughts of people. But he could not aqchieve his desired goal of making the rulers of Rajasthan at the helm of affairs of Arya Samaj to lead his reform movement. There were certain limitations of the rulers under the British paramountcy as they could not move indepently. His ideas were more revolutionary as he questioned hereditary rule and preferred a republican form of government. The qualifications of kings defined by Swami Dayanand were rigorously framed. He declared that the king has no absolute powers, he merely wielded them on behalf of the people, not as a representative of god, as was claimed. In the chapter - 6 of Satyarth Parkash entiltled 'Raja Dharama or Science of Government' has given a detailed discourse on 'Rajniti'. Swami Dayanand was of the view that if a king does not work for the welfare of his people, he should be dethroned. He always emphasized on the duties of rulars towards their subjects. He also stressed upon that a king should not waste public money on self indulgence. The king should not waste his time in amusement and sensual activities.

The ruling aristocracy of Rajasthan welcomed Swami Dayanand as a Vedic scholar and saint, but not his ideas due to a series of reason, which can not be explained fully here due to shortage of space in the present study. The princely rulers disassociated themselves form their responsibilities towards their subjects and became responsible to their British masters, whom they tried to appease since their very existence depended on them.[146] The British maintained the princely states to fulfill their own colonial purposes as all dicisive political power was in British hands. The post-mutiny policy of the British towards the princely states was clarified by governor-General Lord Canning on 30 April, 1860 as follows : 'It was long ago said by Sir John Malcolm that if we made all India into Zillahs (or British Districts) it was not in the nature of things that our Empire shold last fifty years; but that if we could keep up a number of Native States without political power, but as royal instruments, we should exist in India as long as our naval supremacy was maintained. Of the substantial truth of this opinion I have no doubt; and the recent events have made it more deserving of our attention than ever.[147]

The princely states were puppet in the hands of British and Swami Dayanand was expecting more from them by considering them sovereign states. The princely rulers were being tempted by the western culture and learnt many vices from them. The colonial administrators induced the princely rulers into western culture. The nationalistic and *Swadeshi* thoughts of Dayanand might have presented the challenges before the British and their supporters. He denounced the profligacy of rulers, *jagirdars* and feudal aristocracy. None of them became true disciple of Swami Dayanand and few of them facilitated him in their areas out of curtsy and their *samskaras.* Since the inception they were taught to honour and worship *Sadhu*, Brahman and cow. Thus, Swami Dayanand was a Sadhu and also a Brahman. It has been rightly analysed an Arya Samaj author as follow : He found devotees among the princes, but, as person, not to his ideas. They suspected the Arya Samaj. In fact, when it was founded at Jodhpur Pratap Singh did not let it function independently. He kept an eye on it constantly. He himself became its president and, after him, Tej Singh took over. The Arya Samaj at Jodhpur was nothing but a weekly get-together for reciting hymns and praying to god. Maharaja Sajjan Singh of Udaipur kept himself aloof from the Arya Samaj. He did not want it to be set up at his capital.

His most sympathetic remark was that "it would come up in course of time on its own". When he wrote to Dayanand to send a preacher who could counteract Christian propaganda, he explicitly asked him to ensure that his candidate had no connection with the Arya Samaj and should not try to set it up. In Jaipur state, Dayanand's followers named their organization the Vedic Dharma Sabha because of the hostile attitude of the Maharaja. That the Arya Samaj was an inconvenient proposition was not a mere suspicion; soon it emerged as a nationalist and patriotic movement in British India. In conclusion, it can be said that Dayanand was welcomed to Rajasthan, but not his ideas.[148]

Surprisingly none of the ruler, *jagirdar* or member of feudal aristocracy did come to Swami Dayanand during his illness to ask his wellness and health conditions. It may also simply be understood that who was responsible for the negligence in treatment of Swamiji. The situation has been rightly narrated by Prof. Jordens of follows : The account of the Swami's tragic last weeks leaves two strong impressions. The first is that of the remarkable willpower, resilience, and heroic patience of the Swami. The second impression is one of regrettable medical mismanagement. The Swami certainly had too many doctors, and probably also some ill-advised medicines, at least in the massive doses. His departure from Jodhpur was badly timed, and the fearful journey aggravated his condition; he might have had a better chance if he had left earlier or stayed on a little longer. For a man in his condition a journey of some four hundred miles was nearly fatal in itself. As the Swami weakened, too many people became involved in the decision-making. By the time he was brought to Ajmer, where he would have received the proper treatment, his condition had deteriorated to such an extent that the additional complication of double pneumonia culd not be overcome even by a man of the Swami's constitution and willpower. It is impossible, however, to point the finger at any particular person for incompetence or malice, because the reports depend too much on hearsay from a later date.[149]

After the death of Swami Dayanand the members of royal houses, *Jagirdars* and members of the feudal aristocracy withdrew from his mission. It is of noteworthy that the members of newly emerged middle class entered into the Arya Samaj movement in Rajasthan. The earlier efforts of princes and *Jagirdars* could not went in vain and their importance as first step can not be ignored. Thus, they too play their limited role in positive direction.

Notes

1. For more details see chapter II.
2. J.T.F. Jordens, *op.cit.*, p. 227.
3. *Ibid* and Harbilas Sarda, *op.cit.,* p. 28. Virjanand charged no fees. The expenses of the Pathshala were met by donations given by three Ruling Princess, Maharaja Balwantsingh of Bharapur, Maharaja Ramsingh of Jaipur and Maharaja Vinaisingh of Alwar.
4. Pandit Lekhram's *Life of Dayanand Saraswati* says that it was Maharaja Ramsingh who had invited Swami Virjanand to Agra and accommodatd him in his camp, and that P. Kedarnath Sastri of Bundi, P. Parandrasingh of Rewa, P. Ramjivan Ojha of Tirhut, the last a great scholar of Nyaya, were present when Virjanand spoke to Maharaja Ram Singh about the *Sarvabhom Sabha.*
5. J.T.F. Jorden, *op.cit.,* pp. 37-38.
6. Harbilas Sarda, *op.cit.,* pp. 35-36.
7. *Ibid,* p. 36.
8. J.T.F. Jorden, *op.cit.,* p 132.
9. Harbilas Sarda, *op.cit.,* pp. 162-63.

10. Bhawanilal Bhartiya, *op.cit.,* p. 493.
11. J.T.F. Jorden, *op.cit.,* p 228.
12. Devendranath Mukhopadhyay, *op.cit.,* p. 96; Pandit Lekhram, *op.cit.,* p. 32; Harbilas Sarda, *op.cit.,* p. 44 and Baba Chhajju Singh, op.cit., Part 1, pp. 36-37.
13. Devendranath Mukhopadhyay, *op.cit.,* p. 99. It has been also reported by Mukhopadhyay that when Swamiji called Pandit Maniram foolish the Maharaja got annoyed and asked the Swamiji to leave the *Rajprasad.*
14. *Ibid.*
15. The Autobiography, *op.cit.,* p. 58. The name of this Sadhu was Gudadia Baba. Though the Maharaja was not a Kabirpanthi but he had great honour to this Sadhu.
16. Devendranath Mukhopadhyay, *op.cit.,* p. 100.
17. *Ibid.*
18. *Ibid,* p. 101.
19. *Ibid.*
20. Baba Chhajju Singh, *op.cit.,* part I, p. 37.
21. Devendranath Mukhopadhyay, *op.cit.,* p. 105 and Harbilas Sarbda, *op.cit.,* p. 47.
22. The Autobiogrphy, *op.cit,* pp. 58-59. The fact being beiliever of Shaivism has been refuted by Harbils Sarda as follows : It has been wrongly stated both in Babu D. Mukhopadhyay's and P. Lekhrm's Jiwan Charit of Swami Dayanand that Swamiji supported Siva worship at Jaipur. It is inconceivable that Swamiji after rejecting the worship of Shiva at Tankara, his home and particularly after his contact with Virjanand Saraswati, should advocate Shiva worship moreover when Swamiji condemned the worship of Siva at Pushkar only a fortnight after leaving Jaipur, it can hardly believed that he supported it at Jaipur (H. Sarda, *op.cit.,* p. 47, footnote).
23. Devendranath Mukhopadhyay, *op.cit.,* pp. 100-105.

24. J.T.F. Jorden, *op.cit.*, p. 41.
25. Devendranath Mukhopadhyay, *op.cit.*, p. 106 and Harbilas Sarbda, *op.cit.*, p. 47.
26. *Ibid.*
27. *Ibid.*
28. Baba Chajju Singh, *op.cit.*, Part I, pp. 37-38, Harbilas Sarda has mentioned the name Venkat Shastri and Mukhopadhyay has mentioned Vyankat Shastri.
29. Devendranath Mukhopadhyay, *op.cit.*, pp. 107-09.
30. *Ibid*, p. 109 and Harbilas Sarbda, *op.cit.*, p. 48.
31. Devendranath Mukhopadhyay, *op.cit.*, p. 109.
32. Harbilas Sarbda, *op.cit.*, p. 48, Mukhopadhyay named it as garden of *Sarishtedar* Vanshidhar.
33. Bhawanilal Bhartiya, *op.cit.*, Part I, p. 71.
34. Most of the biography had written Rev. Rabson but Baba Chhajju Singh has mentioned Rev. Robinson.
35. Baba Chhajju Singh, *op.cit.*, part I, p. 39, Colonel Brooke happens to be the Agent to Governor General in Rajputan.
36. Devendranath Mukhopadhyay, *op.cit.*, p. 113.
37. *Ibid.*
38. *Ibid.* P. 115
39. *Ibid*, Rai Daulatram was saristedar (State officer) in whose garden Swamiji was staying.
40. *Ibid*, P. 117 and Harbilas Sarbda, *op.cit.*, p. 50.
41. *Ibid.*
42. The Autobiography, *op.cit.*, p. 59.
43. Baba Chhajju Singh, *op.cit.*, part I, pp. 39-40, In his autobiography Swamiji himself mentioned that it was the *darbar* of Lieutenant Governor of the North-Western Provinces, while Devendranath Mukhopadhyay and Harbilas Sarda has

mentioned it a great darbar of Lord Lawrence who was the Viceory of India at that time.

44. J.T.F. Jorden, *op.cit.,* p. 207, Jordens has reightly analysed the status of reform ideology in the preincely States, but could not explain the reason behind this state of things. In fact such princely rulers were puppet in the hands of Birtish and a fear of instability of their power persisted. Therefore, they did not supported and promoted the reforms in their dominions concerned.
45. Devendranath Mukhopadhyay, *op.cit.,* pp. 373-74.
46. *Ibid,* P. 375.
47 Baba Chhajju Singh, *op.cit.,* part II, p. 9.
48. J.M. Sharm, *op.cit.,* pp. 197-98 and Harbilas Sarda, *op.cit.,* p. 212.
49. J.T.F. Jorden, *op.cit.,* pp. 186-87.
50. Baba Chhajju Singh, *op.cit.,* part II, pp. 10-13.
51. A report of this debate appeared on pp. 98-100 of "The Theosophist, Vol. 1, No. 2 (A Journal of the Theosophical Society).
52. Devendranath Mukhopadhyay, *op.cit.,* p. 480.
53. *Ibid,* P. 481.
54. *Ibid,* P. 483.
55. *Ibid.*
56. *Ibid,* P. 485 and Harbilas Sarbda, *op.cit.,* p. 214.
57. *Ibid.*
58. The Autobiography, *op.cit.,* p. 67.
59. Devendranath Mukhopadhyay, *op.cit.,* pp. 485-86.
60. The Autobiography, *op.cit.,* p. 67 and Harbilas Sarda, *op.cit.,* p. 215.
61. Baba Chhajju Singh, *op.cit.,* Part II, p. 42. Devendranath Mukhopadhyay has also mentioned that only one lecture could

be held. He mentioned his stay at Jaipur from 20 March to 4 May, 1881. He has also written in the meantime an Organisation Vedic Dharm Sabha was founded which was later changed into Arya Samaj. Same fact has also been mentioned by Harbilas Sarda (op.cit., p. 260) and Bhawanilal Bharity (op.cit., p. 426). But Swami Dayanand had said nothing about it. Moreover, he is silent on insignificant visits of Bharatpur and Jaipur.

62. *Ibid.* R.B.P. Bhagram was Judicial Assistant commissioner, Ajmer.

63. The Autobiography, *op.cit.,* p. 73, Bhawȧnilal Bhartiya (op. cit., p. 441) has mentioned that Pt. Munnalal Upreti Sharma original resident of Agra came as Draftman in Rajputana - Malwa Railway. He was appointed the Secretary of Arya Samaj, Ajmer and also the first editor of the organ of Arya Samaj the Deshiteshi in 1881.

64. Devendranath Mukhopadhyay, *op.cit.,* p. 590-91 and Harbilas Sarbda, *op.cit.,* p. 261.

65. *Ibid,* Mukhopadhyay, p. 592 and Sarbda, p. 262.

66. D. Mukhopadhyay, p. 591.

67. Harbilas Sarbda, *op.cit.,* p. 262.

68. Baba Chhjju Singh, *op.cit.,* Part II, p. 42.

69. *Ibid,* Mukhopadhyay, p. 592 and Sarbda, p. 262.

70. Devendranath Mukhopadhyay, *op.cit.,* pp. 592-97, Jordens, pp. 228-29, Sarda, pp. 263-66 and Baba Chhajju Singh, Part II, p. 43. Rev. Dr. Shoolbred of Nayanagar (Beawar) was English Christian Missionary with Swami Dayanand alongwith an Indian Christian Padree Biharilal. The discussion took place on 28 June, 1881. Both of these Christian Theologist could not stand before Swami Dayanand and on the pretext of shortage of time left the spot for Beawar. The questions forwarded by Dayanand were so hard the Jain Sadhu Siddhakaran was compelled to seek refuge in silence. Before going in silence he also expressed his inability to reply by saying we have no answer, we are Sadhus.

71. *Ibid,* Second *Yajna* was perfomerd on 14th August, 1881 and at that time Sixteen people took *Yagopavit* and more than half of whom were Jain. Rao's *Koth*ari (Incharge of Stores) Chandmal himself was Jain and he took the lead in inducing the Jain community towards Vedic religion.
72. The Said Hindu caste was Rawat or Mer and those were converted to Islam were known s Merats.
73. Mukhopadhyay, *op.cit.,* p. 599.
74. Munshiram Jigayasu (ed.), Rishi Dayanand ka Patravyvahar, Vol. II, Gurukul Kangri, 1935, pp. 73-85
75. J.T.F. Jorden, *op.cit.,* pp. 229-30, Swami Dayanand stayed about for three weeks in Raipur. The enthusiasm shown by Thakur Raipur while inviting Swamiji could not remain continue and the Thakur remained apathetic towards him.
76. Harbilas Sarbda, *op.cit.,* pp. 270-71.
77. J.M. Sharm, *op.cit.,* pp. 201-02.
78. Pandya was then the Secretary of the Udaipur State council and Shymaldas Personal Secrelary to Maharaj Sajjan Singh.
79. Rajputana Gazetteer, Vol. II, Ajmer, 1908, p. 28 and Harbilas Sarbda, *op.cit.,* pp. 271-72, also Jorden, p. 230.
80. Devendranath Mukhopadhyay, *op.cit.,* pp. 604-06 and also Jorden, pp. 230-31.
81. James Tod, Analas and Antiquities of Rajasthan, Vol. III, London, 1920, p. 795.
82. Devendranath Mukhopadhyay, *op.cit.,* p. 605 and Jorden, p. 231.
83. *Ibid.* p. 606, Since the inception the Mewar (Chittor-Udaipur) ruling family had adherence in Shaivism as Ekling was the owner of the State and Maharanas ruled it as his representative or Diwan. Therefore, Maharana Sajjansingh did not want to annoy Sadhu Jeewangui a Shaivite
84. Mukhopadhyay, p. 606 and Sarda, p. 273.

85. Baba Chhajju Singh, *op.cit.,* part II, pp. 75-76. Swami stayed in the Naulakha Bagh also known as Sajjan Niwas or Gulab Bagh
86. J.T.F. Jorden, *op.cit.,* p. 231.
87. *Ibid,* p. 232, Mukhopadhyay, pp. 618-23, Baba Chhajju Singh, part II, pp. 76-80.
88. Harbilas Sarbda, *op.cit.,* p. 282 and Mukhopadhyay, pp. 620-21.
89. Devendranath Mukhopadhyay, *op.cit.,* pp. 622-23.
90. *Ibid.*
91. *Ibid* and Jorden, pp. 232-33. The practice of performing the *Havana* on daily basis in the palace could continue only till the life time of Maharana Sajjansingh and his successor Maharana Fateh Singh discontinued it by considering it ill omen. (Mukhopadhyay, pp. 619-20).
92. Devendranath Mukhopadhyay, *op.cit.,* p. 624.
93. Harbilas Sarda, *op.cit.,* p. 282, Mukhopadhyay, p. 621.
94. *Ibid,* Mukhopadhyay, p. 621. Here Swami Dayanand had not talked of religion but *Dharma* which means the moral duties of human being.
95. Sarda, p. 284, Mukhopadhyay, p. 263.
96. *Ibid,* p. 285 and *Ibid,* p. 624.
97. *Ibid.*
98. *Ibid.*
99. Harbilas Sarda, *op.cit.,* pp. 290-95. The Autobiography, *op.cit.,* pp. 75-79 and Mukhopadhyay, *op.cit.*, p. 631-34.
100. The Autobiography, *op.cit.,* p. 75.
101. Harbilas Sarda, *op.cit.,* p. 304 and Mukhopadhyay, p. 635.
102. *Ibid,* pp. 295-304, Y. Mimanshak, *Rishi Dayanand Saraswati ke Patra aur Vigyapan, 2nd edition*, Amritsar, 1955, pp. 449-52, also Mushiram Jigyasu (ed.), *Rishi Dayanand ka Patra Vyavahar,* Vol. II, pp. 135-43.

103. Y. Mimanshak (Ed.), *Rishi Dayanand Saraswati ke Patra aur Vigyapan,* Bahalgarh, 1982, p. 409 and J.M. Sharma, *op.cit.,* pp. 225-26.

104. Baba Chhajju Singh, *op,cit.,* Part II, p. 79.

105. *Ibid.*

106. Devendranath Mukhopadhyay, *op.cit.,* p. 637 and Harbilas Sarbda, *op.cit.,* pp. 305-6.

107. *Ibid,* pp. 639-40 and pp. 306-7, respectively, J.M. Sharma has written the name Chhat Mal Vyas (Royal Priest), *op.cit.,* p. 226.

108. *Ibid,* pp. 638 and p. 307 respectively.

109. Devendranath Mukhopadhyay, *op.cit.,* p. 637, Baba Chhajju Singh wrote that Ishwaranand was sent to *Kashi, op.cit.,* p. 80.

110. *Ibid,* p. 639 and Sarda, p. 308.

111. Baba Chhajju Singh, *op.cit.,* Part II. pp. 79-80.

112. J.T.F. Jorden, op.cit., p. 235 also Y. Mimanshak, *op.cit.*, pp. 436-37 and Munshiram Jigyasu, *op.cit.*, Vol. II, pp. 24, 34, 36

113. Harbilas Sarda, *op.cit.,* pp. 308-9, Devendranath Mukhopadhyay, *op.cit.,* pp. 640-41, Baba Chhajju Singh, *op.cit.,* Part II. p. 80.

114. Devendranath Mukhopadhyay, *op.cit.,* p. 640 and Harbilas Sarda, *op.cit.,* p. 308.

115. *Ibid.*

116. Y. Mimanshak, *op.cit.*, p. 410 and J.T.F. Jordens, *op.cit.*, p. 236.

117. Rajputana Gazetteer, Vol. III A, Allahabad, 1909, pp. 74-76 and J.T.F. Jordens, *op.cit.,* p. 236.

118. J.T.F. Jordens, *op.cit.,* p. 236 and Devendranath Mukhopadhyay, *op.cit.,* p. 642.

119. Harbilas Sarda, *op.cit.,* p. 309, Devendranath Mukhopadhyay, *op.cit.,* p. 641. Mukhopadhyay has designated the Jodhpur as *Moolasur ka Desh*, (Country of Mool Demon).

120. Baba Chhajju Singh, *op.cit.,* Part II. p. 81,

121. Seoji or Sevaji was the nephew of Jey Chand of Kanauj, who, on the overthrow of his unfortunate uncle's kingdom, emigrated with hanaful of his brethren into Marwar or Marrowar (the region of death) From the Rajasthan of James Tod.

122. Baba Chhajju Singh, *op.cit.,* Part II. p. 82.

123. Devendranath Mukhopadhyay, *op.cit.,* pp. 642-43, Harbilas Sarbda, *op.cit.,* p. 311, Baba Chhajju Singh, *op.cit.,* Part II. pp. 82-83, J.M. Sharma, *op.cit.*, p. 229. J.M. Sharma has written that the main theme of his lectures was what constituted an ideal Kshatriya life. He condemned drinking, gambling and womnising prevailing among the princes. Baba Chhajju Singh had mentioned that : No one need doubt that an individual who could take a sovereign to task before his very face, and that in no mild terms, would not spare his vassals. The licentiousness of these was commented upon daily, and they were constantly exhorted to turn over a new leaf. "If", said the Swami more than once, the Hindu States have not yet been blotted out of existence, it is because the Hindu Ranis are still patterns of virtue. But for this the debouchery of the nobles and chiefs would long have worked their ruin.

124. *Ibid.*

125. *Ibid.*

126. *Ibid.*

127. Devendranath Mukhopadhyay, *op.cit.,* p. 647, Harbilas Sarbda, *op.cit.,* p. 313.

128. *Ibid,* p. 648 and p. 313 respectively.

129. *Ibid,* pp. 644-45 and p. 315 respectively

130. *Ibid,* p. 650 and p. 314 respectively.

131. *Ibid,* J.M. Sharma, *op.cit.*, p. 228 informs that colonel Pratap Singh younger brother of the Maharaja Jodhpur had once toyed with the idea of converting to Christianity but his interaction with the Swami that idea was abandoned.

132. Devendranath Mukhopadhyay, *op.cit.,* p. 650.

133. Y. Mimanshak, *op.cit.,* p. 430.

134. Harbilas Sarda, *op.cit.,* p. 316, Swamiji's letter to Raja Dhiraj Naharsingh of Shahpura dated 30th June, 1883, P. Bhagwaddat's *Patra aur Vigyapan,* p. 462.

135. *Ibid,* p. 317, Baba Chhajju Singh, *op.cit.,* Part II, p. 84.

136. J.T.F. Jordens, *op.cit.*, p. 240.

137. Harbilas Sarda, *op.cit.,* p. 323.

138. *Ibid,* pp. 317-20, The Autobiography, *op.cit.,* pp. 80 and 83, J.M. Sharma, *op.cit.,* pp. 232-33 and Bhagavaddatta, *op.cit.*, Part II, p. 744-47.

139. *Ibid,* J.T.F. Jordens, *op.cit.*, pp. 238-39, The Autobiography, *op.cit.,* pp. 80 and 83, J.M. Sharma, *op.cit.,* pp. 234-35 and Bhagavaddatta, *op.cit.*, Part II, pp. 779-82.

140. Harbilas Sarda, *op.cit.,* pp. 322-23.

141. *Ibid,* p. 314.

142. Devendranath Mukhopadhyay, *op.cit.,* p. 658.

143. Baba Chhajju Singh, *op.cit.,* Part II, p. 86.

144. *Ibid,* p. 88.

145. Devendranath Mukhopadhyay, *op.cit.,* p. 667.

146. B.K. Sharma, *Mass Movements & Freedom Struggle in Rajasthan*, Book Treasurer, Jodhpur, 2013, p. 9.

147. *Ibid.* Preface.

148. J.M. Sharm, *op.cit.,* pp. 238-39.

149. J.T.F. Jordens, *op.cit.*, p. 243.

4

Arya Samaj Organisations and Religious - Social Reforms

The establishment of the Arya Samaj proved a miracle for Rajasthan. Except the British province of Ajmer and Merwara whole of Rajasthan was under the possession of monarchical princely states. These states were nominally autonomous in internal affairs, while all the powers were in the hands of the British. Therefore, the masses were burdened with arch reactionary semi-feudal and semi-colonial form of governance. Obviously, the society was also victim of this unholy alliance of British imperialism and native feudalism. Thus, the society too was rigidly structured in caste hierarchy. The public institutions and organizations were non-existent. The Hinduism was divided into number of sects and *panthas* and superstitious practices were dominant in religion. As far as the religious conditions are concerned the ignorance and evil practices were prominently visible. Swami Dayanand visualized very strong challenge of Christianity to Hinduism in Rajasthan. Therefore, he devised appropriate strategy to meet the challenge.

Swami Dayanand established the authenticity and supremacy of the Vedas. He called on Hindus to go back to Vedas because only these contained the original and pure form of Hindu theology. He rejected the plurality of the Hindu Gods. He also denounced idol worship, superstitious practices and irrelevant ritualistic practices. Therefore, it is pertinent to discuss the impact of the Arya Samaj on religious reforms in Rajasthan. Arya Samaj initiated crusade against caste system, untouchability, social discrimination, slavery, *Sati,* girl infanticide, child marriage, unmatched marriage, polygamy, dowry, sex discrimination, pardha etc.. It encouraged widow remarriage, educational and vocational training of women, self-sufficiency of women, simple marriage rituals etc.. The educational scheme devised by Swami Dayanand was based on scriptures suitable to the indigenous conditions and need. After Swamiji the leaders of the Arya Samaj took the mission of establishing Vedic pathshalas and Gurukulas. Later on a progressive group within the Arya Samaj devised the Anglo-Vedic scheme of education.

Dayanand Saraswati was the first reformer who gave complete scheme of *Suddhi* and opened a powerful channel to reclaim the Hinduism for the people who were converted to Christianity and Islam. Thus, the *Suddhi* movement came into being. Along with *Suddhi* the Arya Samaj also initiated the *Dalitoddhar* movement to prevent the conversion of Dalit Hindus to Christianity and Islam. In fact the whole programme of Arya Samaj was basically focused against British rule and Christianity, therefore it adopted all such means which were being taken by the Christian missionaries. Therefore, Arya Samaj established educational institutions, hostels, orphanages, widow homes (*Vidhwa Ashramas),* destitute homes, famine relief committees. In 1882 Swami Dayanand also formed the Cow Protection Association.

The Nineteenth Century is also known as the century of social and religious reform movements in Modern Indian History. These movements paved the way for rise of nationalism and freedom movement. During this period there were three streams of socio-religious movements viz. conservative, liberal and radical. The Arya Samaj movement belonged to radical stream.

In the light of the foregoing description the religious and social reform activities and achievements of the Arya Samaj has been discussed in this chapter.

Establishment and Expansion of Arya Samaj Organisations in Rajasthan

Though the Arya Samaj organisation came into being in 1875 but it could not appear in Rajasthan before 1881. It has been confirmed by the biographers of Swami Dayanand that he stayed in Jaipur from 20 March to 4 May, 1881 and during this period an organisation named *Vedic Dharma Sabha* was founded by his followers, which was later changed into Arya Samaj.[1] In fact the Maharaja of Jaipur was annoyed with Swami Dayanand, therefore his indifference towards Arya Samaj organisation was obvious. Swami Dayanand reached Ajmer on 5 May, 1881 from Jaipur. Baba Chhajju Singh had mentioned that at Ajmer the local Arya Samaj (established, February, 1881) was considerably strengthened by the Swami's lectures and presence.[2] Swami Dayanand had himself mentioned that : I am at Ajmer since May 1881, in the Kothi of Seth Fateh Mal. I have been giving lectures daily for two hours in the night. A small Arya Samaj has been established here. May god effect its growth.[3] Thus, it is not clear that the Branch of Arya Samaj at Ajmer was founded before the arrival of Swami or during his this visit is not clear because Swami had also not given any date of its foundation.

It is difficult to ascertain that which one was the first Arya Samaj organisation in Rajasthan, but it is clear that at both the places viz. Jaipur and Ajmer the Arya Samaj was founded in the year 1881. Here it is interesting to analyse that the Arya Samaj at both the places were founded in different conditions. Jaipur city was the headquarter of a princely state under the autocratic monarchical ruler under the protection of mighty British imperialists. The level of education of masses was very low and the people were under the influence of ignorance and superstitious practices. The Maharaja of Jaipur was opposed to the Arya Samaj and Swami Dayanand. Therefore, the followers of Swami Dayanand founded the Vedic Dharma Sabha in Jaipur.

The credit of launching the programmes of Arya Samaj (in Jaipur) goes to Pandit Kaluram of Ramgarh Shekhawati popularly known as Sethon ka Ramgarh in present Sikar district. It has been said that Pandit Kaluram was born in a Gaur Brahmin family there. He meet Swami Dayanand in January, 1877 at Meerut and before that he made some correspondence with Swamiji. As has already been said that Thakur Ranjeet of Achrol became the disciple of Swami Dayanand in 1865 during the visit of Swamiji in Jaipur. The fact was known to Pandit Kaluram, therefore after visiting Swamiji at Meerut he came back to Jaipur and meet Thakur Ranjeet Singh. With the help and support of Thakur Ranjeet singh, Thakur Nandkishore Singh (Minister of Jaipur State) and Heeralal Kayasth the *Kamdar* of *Thikana* Achrol Pandit Kaluram founded the Vedic Dharma Sabha on 16th June, 1877.[4]

It was not an easy task to establish an organisation against the will of authorities of a princely state. Thus, under the cover of Vedic Dharma Sabha the activities of Arya Samaj were being carried on in a very slow pace. There activities were limited to *Sandhya* and *Hawan.* But with the growing activities and influence of this *sabha* the *Pauraniks* and Sanatanis began to oppose it and under their influence Maharaja Madhosingh threaten the Aryasamajists to expel them from his State. On this

Thakur Raghunathsingh of Achrol strongly told the Maharaja that I am Aryan and devotee of Mahrishi Dayanand and first expel me from the State. Thus the policy of oppression of Aryasamajists was abandoned.[5] Finally, since 28 March, 1882 the Vedic Dharma Sabha began to be known by name the Arya Samaj.[6]

As has been already mentioned that Arya Samaj was founded in Ajmer in February, 1881 but it became viable in May, 1881 undere the blessings and direction of Swami Dayanand himself. Therefore, it is said that Swami Dayanand himself established the branch of Arya Samaj at Ajmer in 1881 and it became main centre of Arya Samaj in Rajasthan. The conditions at Ajmer were more congenial and favourable for religious and social reforms in Rajasthan in comparison to princely states. Being part of British India Ajmer fetched many benefits like modern education, modern jobs, legal infrastructure, printing, publications, news papers, public institutions etc.. Under the influence of British rule Ajmer was emerging as an important centre of modern education since 1818. Introduction of rail transportation also proved the courier of modernisation and with the beginning of Railway workshop in Ajmer it also became the centre of technical-training and education. Modern or western way of governance also insured the peoples legal birth rights. The Ajmer also became the centre of the activities of Christian missionaries under the support and protection of British power. The Christian missionaries had posed various religious, cultural and social challenge before the Hindus. Therefore, Arya Samaj was more demanding organisation to combat the challenges posed by the missionaries. Swami Dayanand had constantly confronted with the Christian theologists and clergy at Ajmer and he devised a complete scheme of combating them on ideological, religious, educational and social service levels. Obviously, the

Ajmer also emerged as main centre of Arya Samaj movement in Rajasthan. Moreover, Swami Dayanand Saraswati breathed his last at Ajmer on 30th October, 1883. Thus for the Aryasamajists Ajmer became a sacred place.[7]

It is clear from the foregoing that due to a series of factors the Ajmer became the main centre of Arya Samaj movement in Rajasthan. Therefore, the other associated institutions and organisations of Aryasamaj also came up in Ajmer. All the coordinating bodies of Arya Samaj were headquartered at Ajmer. Even the Vedic Yantralaya (vedic printing press) which was headquarter at Prayag was shifted to Ajmer in 1891.[8] In the same manner the Paropkarini Sabha which was founded in 1883 with its' headquarter at Udaipur was also shifted to Ajmer in 1894.[9]

For a long time Udaipur remained centre of the activities of Swami Dayanand, but till his death the formal Arya Samaj organisation could not be founded there. And about for years later the death of Swamiji the Arya Samaj was formally founded by Mohanlal Vishnulal Pandya in 1887 (Kartik Amavasya V.S. 1944) at Udaipur. Its meetings and sessions were held at the residence of Pandya till 1993 when the Arya Samaj temple was built and formally inaugurated.[10] The Arya Samaj in Jodhpur was also founded after the death of Swamiji.[11] It has been reported by the historians of Arya Samaj that Vedic Dharma became the State religion of Jodhpur State. After the establishment of Arya Samaj many reforms were made by the Maharaja of Jodhpur under the influence of Swami Dayanand. In the Census of 1891 when Sardar Hardayal Singh, a minister of the State, asked the Maharaja about his religion, he himself told that his religion is Vedic.[12] Sir Pratapsingh younger brother of Maharaja had expressed that his faith in Hinduism had been shaken, and at times he became very depressed; but that after talking to Swamiji at Jodhpur and listening to his lectures, all his doubts disappeared and his faith in the Vedic Dharma became firm.[13]

At an early stage the progress of Arya Samaj at Jodhpur was appreciable because in August, 1883 itself Hindi was proclaimed the language of the State which was the first in India to take that step.[14] Harbilas Sarda a noted Arya Samaji and author of Swamiji's biography has mentioned that : The only *updesh* (teaching) of Swamiji that the Maharaja and the people accepted was the use of Swadeshi cloth. Everyone in the service of the State, from the Maharaja down to the peons, officers, clerks and the elite of Jodhpur adopted the *khadi* produced in Marwar. Thus, long before swadeshi became the cry in Bengal, Marwar appeared clad in *kahdi.*[15]

The establishment of Arya Samaj organisations in Ajmer, Jaipur, Jodhpur and Udaipur by the 1887 paved the way for its future expansion. Though, there were 21 princely states in Rajasthan but more than 50% of population and also the geographical area was under the four administrative units viz. Ajmer-Merwara, Jaipur, Jodhpur and Udaipur. The branches of Arya Samaj began to be founded in various towns of these areas. The enlightened people established the Branches in other princely states on their initiative. By the year 1911 the province of Rajputana had the fourth largest number of Branches of Arya Samaj. In 1911, there were in the Punjab, 373 Samaj; in the United Provinces, 266; in Bombay 55; in Rajputana 47; in Bengal 36 and in the Central Provinces and Berar 35.[16] The number of Arya Samaj organisations in Rajputana including Ajmer-Merwara reached upto 200. In 1947 there there were about 20 branches in Udaipur State, 15 in Jodhpur State, 35 in Jaipur State, 38 in Ajmer-Merwara including princely State of Kishangarh, 10 in Bharatpur State, 20 in Alwar State, 15 in Bikaner State, 8 in Kota State, one each in Sirohi, Karauli, Dholpur, Dungarpur, Pratapgarh and Jhalawar. It is notable fact that the princely states of Bundi, Jaisalmer and Tonk had no branch.[17]

Arya Pratinidhi Sabha : Due to a sufficient network of the Samaj in the province, Rajputana was provided with the provincial representative assembly called the *Arya Pratinidhi Sabha.*[18] In 1888 the Rajasthan Pratinidhi Sabha composed of the representatives of the various regional Arya Samaj bodies was founded with headquarters at Ajmer.[19] It was named as *Arya Pratinidhi Sabha,* Rajasthan and Malwa because the jurisdiction of this *sabha* was extended upto the Malwa area of present State of Madhya Pradesh. The Malwa area was also dominated by a number of princely states. The objective of the Arya Pratinidhi Sabha was to coordinate and extend the activities of different Arya Samaj oragnisations. The Pratinidhi Sabha took the work of propagation of the principles of the Arya Samaj through propagators known as Arya Samaj *Pracharakas*.

The Paropakarini Sabha was founded by Swami Dayanand as a prime body of Arya Samaj and was also entrusted with the responsibility of dissemination of Vedas, Vedangas and other like *sastras* through commentary, study, teaching, hearing and publication. It has been elaborated that the teaching and preaching of Vedic Dharma, by organizing a body of teachers and lecturers to work in India and other countries, so that truth may be accepted and falsehood may be rejected.[20]

Arya Directory has suggested that after two months of the Swami's death the first session of the Sabha (Paropkarini Sabha) was held at Ajmer on 28th December, 1883 where Mahadeo Govind Ranade realized that Sabha alone would not be able to accomplish much. He, therefore, proposed to establish Arya Pratinidhi Sabha in the provinces and accordingly the Pratinidhi Sabha was established in Punjab on 29th December, 1886[21] and in U.P. and in Rajasthan in 1888.[22] Under the guidance and direction of Pradeshik Partinidhi Sabha the workers and preachers of Arya Samaj accelerated the work of propagation and preaching.

Paropkarini Sabha : Much has already been written about the Paropkarini Sabha in chapter III as it was the brain child of Swami Dayanand Saraswati. He in his life time at the time of its formation nominated this as his successor. Initially it was established at Meerut on 16th August, 1880. It consisted of fourteen members with Rai Bahadur Sunderlal as Secretary. It was also registered there.[23] But when, Swami Dayanand came to Udaipur he made another will by cancelling the Meerut will and got it registered in the office of the State Council of Udaipur State on 27th February, 1883.[24] A governing council of twenty three eminent dignitaries was constituted. In this galaxy of dignitaries nine from Rajasthan and out of nine eight were from Mewar (Udaipur State) itself and only one was from Ajmer. Two were from Punjab each from Ludhiana and Lahore and eight were from U.P. one each from Meerut, Aligarh, Moradabad, and Kanpur and four from Farrukhabad. Accordingly one from Danapur in Bihar and three from Maharashtra, two from Poona and one from Bomaby.[25] And obviously, the headquarter of the Paropkarini Sabha was made Udaipur. But it seems that Maharana Sajjan Singh unwillingly accepted the position of President of Paropkarini Sabha because he did not attend the first meeting of the Sabha held on 28th December, 1883 at Ajmer. The Sabha could not make any appreciable progress at Udaipur. Moreover, sad demise of Maharana on 23rd December, 1884 proved a setback to the growth of Sabha. His successor Maharana Fateh Siingh declined to accept the position of President of the sabha. Unfortunately the Sabha remained without President till 1891, when Sir Pratap Singh of Jodhpur accepted the position.[26] In 1894 the headquarter of the Paropkarini Sabha was shifted to Ajmer.

Though the Paropkarini Sabha was prime body of Arya Samaj but it remained an independent and autonomous body and functioned independently. It was an all India body, therefore its jurisdiction was whole India. At the same time it was entrusted with the duty of propagation of the principles of Arya Samaj globally. Thus, the Paropkarini Sabha was an international body of Arya Samaj. Since the inception it has its separate organizational structure and constitution, but it worked in collaboration of other bodies or organisations of Arya Samaj. Being headquartered at Ajmer it had more activities there. Thus, the Rajasthan reaped maximum benefits from the Paropakarini Sabha.

In 1888 the Rajasthan Arya Pratinidhi Sabha came into being but it did not interfere in the affairs and activities of Paropkarini Sabha. The *Sarvdeshik Arya Pratinidhi Sabha* was founded in 1908.[27] The Sarvdeshik Sabha in its constitution gave the status of associated subordinate to the Paropkarini Sabha. But, in the session of 1925 the Sarvdeshik Sabha redelibrated the issue and being the successor of Swami Dayanand the Paropkarini Sabha was given the status of as an autonomous institution. Even the members of two opponent groups of Punjab Aryasamaj viz. the Gurukul party and college party were equally represented in the Paropkarini Sabha. Thus, the Paropkarini Sabha remained free from factionalism.[28]

In the session of 1895 a decision regarding the registration of Paropkarini Sabha under Act No. 21 of 1860 was taken. In 1896 the task of preparing a memorandum of Association was handed over to Raja Jaykrishandas, Pt. Mahadev Govind Ranade, Barrister Roshanlal, barrister Ramgopal and Rai Mulraj. The memorandum was approved in 1906 and finally the Paropkarini Sabha got registered on 31st August, 1908 in the court of Ajmer Registrar.[29] Dayanand Ashram, Vedic Pustkalaya and Vedic Yantralaya were kept under the

Paropkarini Sabha. A monthly journal *Paropkari Patrika* was also began by the Sabha.[30]

Arya Kumar Sabha : It was an organisation of youths and students who believed in the principles of Swami Dayanand and Arya Samaj. In July, 1905 the Arya Kumar Sabha was founded in Ajmer to propagate the principles and teaching of Swami Dayanand and Vedic religion.[31] In 1909 the Arya Kumar Sabha of Ajmer was affiliated and associated with the Bharatvarhiya Arya Kumar Parishad at Rawalpindi. Chand Karan Sharda was its main leader and organizer in Ajmer. The Arya Kumar Sabhas were also founded in 1914 at Jaipur, in 1932 at Bikaner, in 1936 at Jodhpur, in 1938 at Ladnun, in 1939 at Chhoti Sadri, in 1940 at Nandrai (in Mewar State), Tamkor (Jhunjhunu Jaipur State) and Abu Road.

In 1942 the Arya Kumar Sabha was established at Sirohi.[32] Such other organisations like Arya Veer Dal, Arya Sewa Dal, Arya Mitra Sabha, Arya Bal Sabha also came into being at different places of Rajasthan from time to time during 1905-1947. This has been the period of active national and freedom movement. Thus, the such activities has been described and analysed at length in chapter V.

The Arya Kumar Sabha initiated the programmes of allround personality development for the youths and students. They were induced in various physical and mental activities. The games, sports, debate, essay writing etc. activities and competitions were also organized. The members of this Sabha were also engaged in maintaining peace and discipline during fairs and festivals. They were also given practical training of theology and rituals. During 1915-1920 the active members of this organization were known by the name *Om Sevak Mandali.* The member of this *Mandali* were under strict discipline. Their selfless devotion towards the service of humanity was appreciable. The membershsip of Arya Kumar Sabha was open to the youts and students between the age of 12-25 strictly.[33] The sabha also rendered valuable services at the time of famines, flood, epidemic etc. to the victims and needy people. It's members also participated in the Suddhi, antidowery and liquor prohibition campaign. They also provide help in rehabilitation of refugees who came from Pakistan.[34]

It is interesting to note that Seventeenth Arya Kumar *Sammelan* was held at Bharatpur on 29th December, 1928. It was inaugurated by Prof. Indra Vidyavachaspati. He struck a note of aggressive nationalism and preached revolution to attain Swaraj. Paying rich tribute to Lala Lajpat Rai for his supreme sacrifice, Prof. Vidyavachaspati made it clear that in view of the present political turmoil, the Arya Samaj could not remain confined to the religious bounds alone.[35]

Stree Samaj : The Stree Samaj was the women's wing of the Arya Samaj. J. Ried Graham has argued that there were constant complaints in the journals of the Samaj that the "Arya Samaj consisted of men who can talk in terms of social reform but that women in the homes till hold the orthodox ideas and insisted on the orthodox ceremonies. Therefore, the Arya Samaj's efforts at reform were not able to go forward. It was evidently to help meet this situation that the Stree Samaj was founded in 1912."[36] Sangeeta Sharma has infromed that : However, Stree Samaj had come into existence long before 1912. By 1912, there were as many as 60 Stree Samajs.[37] Probably early Stree Samajs were not formally structured, therefore, looking to the growing needs of the issues of women's emancipation these were founded in 1912 with organisational setup. The ealiest Stree Samaj was founded in Ludhiana and Lahore followed by Ajmer.[38] Gulab Devi was the Pradhana of Stree Samaj Ajmer. In 1933 on the occasion of celebration of 50th death anniversary of Swami Dayanand all India Arya Mahila Sammelan was held, which was hosted by the Ajmer Stree Samaj and Gulab Devi was the Pradhana of Reception Committee.[39]

In addition of the aforesaid organisations there were some other ancillary organisations and institutions of Arya Samaj, which were at the implementation end. Their details has been given iin the future pages of the present chapter and as well as in next chapter. The aforesaid organisations were the core and basic which were responsible for conceptualizing the programmes policies and their implementation. The foregoing description about the Aryasamaj organizations is clear evidence of sound foundations of the Aryasamaj. There were various odds in the way of progress of the Arya Samaj movement in Rajasthan but these organizations were capable to carry on the mission.

Religious Reforms : The religious ideas and thoughts of Swami Dayanand has been discussed at length in the previous pages. Swamiji's slogan was 'back to Vedas' because in his view Vedas are the fundamental scriptures. He rejected the pauranic ideas and idol worship. He vehemently refuted all forms of Tantraism and superstitions. He also condemned the Shaivism, Vaishnavism, Shaktism, Jainism, Buddhism, Islam and Christianity for their misconceptions and evil practices. Thus, in his view only Vedas contained pure form of religion, philosophy and theology.

As far as Rajasthan is concerned it may be said that it was only Swami Dayanand Saraswati who initiated the process of religious and social reforms. Because in British India the mission or organizations like Brahma Samaj, Prarthana Samaj, Satyashodhak Samaj etc. came into being under the influence of English and western education. These could not come in Rajasthan due to various factors. The early thoughts of Dayanand promoted and supported the religious revival activities by refuting the wrong and untrue thoughts. Swamiji adopted the method of *shastrarth* and *pravachan* for the foundation of his ideas. But in Rajasathan Swami did not faced any major challenge because the knowledge of pundits was so meager that they could not stand before him. Though, some efforts were made by *sanatani* and *pauranik* pundits at Jaipur, Pushkar, Ajmer, Udaipur and Jodhpur but they could not succeed in their efforts. Few discussions were also held with Jain, Muslim and Christian theologists, who could not proved their points before Swami Dayanand. He was revivalist and reformer both. He was of the clear views that the religious evils existed in the Hinduism had weakened it and it has paved the way to Christianity and Islam in India. Therefore, he took the task of revival and reform the Hindu religion.

The work of religious reform and revival was entrusted too Paropkarini Sabha which is clear from its rules and objectives. Through propagation of Vedic literature and philosophy it took the task of religious reforms. The Aryasamaj organization was also an essential instrument to reform the religious practices. Each Aryasamaj founded the Aryasamaj temples to give it a definite form of a religious sect, where regular Agnihotra in the morning and evening were performed. The preachers used to deliver regular speeches in these temples on the need and ways of religious reforms. Without any social and religious discrimination these were open for all. It is a well known fact that Swamiji vehemently supported the rights of untouchables and women to study Vedas. Under the traditional Hindu religion large numbers of people were deprived of the right of worship and professing religion due to prevalence of social discrimination. Swamiji and Aryasamaj not only condemned this but also brought the large masses in the orbit of Hinduism. These efforts also discouraged the dalit Hindus from conversion to other religions.

Ajmer was made the centre of religious revivalism and reform in Rajasthan. The Aryasamaj was supposed to struggle hard on various fronts because initially it had the challenge from the traditional Hinduism. The Aryasamaj did not believe in idol worship and pauranik religious literature. It had also denied various rituals related to the human life from birth to death. Even Arya Samaj proved the futility of *shradh* after death, *vratas* (fasts), pilgrimage and many superstitious practices. The major challenge before the Arya Samaj was posed by the Christian missionaries who were converting the Hindus into their sect under the political and administrative protection and support of the British. Ajmer was also the centre of Christian missionaries, therefore the Arya Samaj had the great challenge at Ajmer. Thus, the Rajasthan Arya Pratinidhi Sabha was established in 1888 with its headquarter at Ajmer. This *sabha* recruited and prepared the preachers, teachers and propagators of Arya Samaj. They themselves used to go in the field and preach the principles and practices of Arya Samaj. They were also sent in Hindu fairs where they propagated and disseminated the Vedic religion through lectures and preaches in Sanskrit, Hindi and local dialects. They induce the people in Vedic religion. The said sabha's activities were not confined to Ajmer only rather these were also extended in whole Rajasthan.[40]

The Arya Samaj Ajmer specially established its branches at the places like Beawar (1884), Masuda (1885), Naseerabad (1890) and Kedal, Pushkar, Pisangan, Ladpura and Saradhana (1900-1901) where Christian missionaries were active. The *Desh Hiteshi* had reported that the Christian missionaries used to create obstacles with the help of police in the propagation of Vedic religion in the fairs of Teej, Kartik Purnima, Tejaji and Ramdevji.[41] The preaching activities in the fairs had been the speciality of Rajasthan Arya Samaj. In 1909 Rajasthan Arya Pratinidhi Sabha also framed the rules of Shastrarth for the guidance of Arya Scholars.[42] Rajasthan Pratinidhi Sabha also established Shri Virjanand Sadhu Ashram at Mathura on 7

September 1910, where Sanskrit language and Vedic *Shastras* were taught free of cost.[43] It became a centre for education and training for preachers and teachers of Arya Samaj.

With the establishment of Rajasthan Arya Pratinidhi Sabha the progress of Arya Samaj was notable as at the time of its establishment the number of Arya Samaj affiliated to it was eight. The number of Arya Samaj reached upto 21 in 1907, 38 in 1914, 47 in 1921, 160 in 1927 and 165 in 1931.[44] This progress also shows the progress in the number of its followers and progress in its acceptability by the people. Thus a sizable population of the Aryasamajists came up. The fact is also proved from the following census data from 1891 to 1931 as upto the census of 1931 the followers of the Arya Samaj got entered their religion as Arya. The details were as follows[45] :

Rajputana States				*Ajmer-Merwara*		
Year	*Total Aryans*	*Male*	*Female*	*Total Aryan*	*Male*	*Female*
1891	371	251	120	1157	662	495
1901	632	376	256	366	225	141
1911	1891	1732	760	884	524	360
1921	3143	1752	1391	1509	882	627
1931	11471	6196	5275	2602	1392	1211

The above data shows a steady growth of Arya Samaj movement and population. In my view this is a rough estimate because during the reporting period there was no clear distinction between Hindus and Aryas. There were the people who were following the both. Only the staunch and strict Aryasamajists number is included. But in 1941 the Aryans too entered their religion as Hindu on the direction of Sarvadeshik Sabha.

For the propagation of Vedic religion the Dayanand Ashram at Ajmer in 1885 was established. It was also a residential Vedic pathshala where the education of Sanskrit language and Vedic literature was imparted. Later on a Ashram school was also founded.[46] The religioous reform efforts of Arya Samaj began to yield positive result. The workers and preachers also gave stress upon Vedic rituals based on the Sanskar Vidhi written by Swami Dayanand. The rituals were simple, logical and without any pageant and complication. Even the *sanatanis* also began to observe Aryan rituals. The Aryasamajists allowed and offered Yagopavit to the people of all the castes and classes. Accordingly they performed *Yajnas* and *Agnihotra* which were also attended from all walks of the society without any discrimination. The women were also given the right of Yajna and Agnihotra. They began to study Vedas which was forbidden to them since a long. Now the women also began to perform religious rituals independently.[47]

The Pratinidhi Sabha appointed Pt. Brahmadatt Sharma in 1904 to take up the propagation work at Jodhpur. He began to perform the rituals in Vedic way on the occasion of birth, marriage, death, naming the child, beginning of education and other *sanskaras*. He also established the Vedic *Pathshala* for the study of Sanskrit language and Vedic literature.[48] Since then the Vedic religion was revived in the Jodhpur State. The preachers propagated the Vedic religion in the towns of Ladnun, Nimaj, Sojat, Nagaur, Pipad, Falodi and Barmer. It has been reported in the Arya Samaj records that the *Seths,* traders, intellectuals and state employees founded the Arya Samaj in Barmer.[49] The progress of Vedic religion in Marwar under the Arya Samaj took speed and the Aryasamajists created a progressive and powerful social group to transform the society into scientific instrument for the good of humanity.

After Ajmer the Jodhpur State became second important centre of Arya Samaj because it got the state patronage since the arrival of Swami Dayanand in Marwar in 1883. Though, during the visit of Udaipur in 1883 Swami Dayanand received unprecedented response in Mewar and Maharana Sajjan Singh built Yajnashala in the palaces, but his successor Fateh Singh became non responsive towards Swamiji and his ideas. In the absence of state patronage the individual enlightened people supported the movement of Arya Samaj. The newly emerged modern middle class people were among its supporters. The trading class was the another group which joined Arya Samaj.

Shyamji Krishan Varma a noted revolutionary nationalist and staunch disciple of Swami Dayanand served for the Maharaja of Udaipur as a State Council member from 1893 to 1895. Before joining this position he was practicing as an advocate in Ajmer. During his term of Council member the educated people including state emplyees also joined Arya Samaj. The Arya Samajist preachers also reached upto small towns and villages such as Sardargarh, Kapasan, Badnore, Bedla and others. The preachers taught the people to perform *Agnihotra,* Sandhya etc.. They also administered *Yagopavit* and *Sanskaras.*[50]

In the states of Udaipur and Jodhpur the Arya Samaj got state support upto the end of 19th Century only. In the beginning of 20th Century the newly emerged middle class people attracted towards Arya Samaj. By the first dicade of twentieth Century the Arya Samajes were also founded in the state of Dungarpur, Banswara, Sirohi and South-Western Rajasthan.[51] The process of founding of Arya Samaj and religious reforms were supplementary of each other.

The extension of Arya Samaj works in eastern Rajasthan took different path since the inception as its programmes and ideology attracted the attention of educated people. In the states of Jaipur, Alwar and Bharatpur the Arya Samaj movement grown without the state support, but the Arya Samaj did not faced any opposition from the states. Only after 1920 most of the states all over Rajasthan began to oppose the activities of Arya Samaj. In the state of Dholpur the Arya Samaj came into confrontation with the Maharaja in 1914, because the state banned the sessions and deliberation in the Arya Samaj temple. The propagation and preaching works became standstill. The Arya Pratinidhi Sabha took the matter and tried to resolve it and finally with the help of Swami Sharaddha Nanda the matter was settled in 1918.[52]

In Kota the Arya Samaj movement took smooth footing as the State did not interfered in its affairs.[53] The Arya Samaj faced opposition of the State in the Bikaner State where Arya Samaj came into being in 1912. The official history of the Arya Samaj has depicted that the relations of Arya Samaj with princely states were not smooth. Maharana Sajjan Singh was appointed the President of the Paropkarini Sabha becaus it was expected that being the land of Maharana Pratap the religious reform work may take fast speed. But after the death of Maharaja the progress in Udaipur became standstill.[54]

The religious reforms works of Arya Samaj originated the Vibrations in the religious spheres in Rajasthan. In the initial stage the other religious groups such as Pauranik or Sanatanis, Jains, Muslims, Christians etc. felt challenges from the Arya Samaj and they began to question and confront with them. But their opposition could not sustain because of their inherent evil religious practices. Like Punjab the Sanatani could not pose organized opposition to the Arya Samaj in Rajasthan. Though orthodox Sanatanist movement also came up with the rise of reform movements. For instance in the year 1873 when Dayanand was at Calcutta, there a *Sanatan Dharm Rakshini Sabha* was formed.[55] In 1887 a Sanatanist organisation, the Bharat Dharm Maha Mandal was founded in Punjab under the leadership of Pandit Din Dayal.[56] The said maha Mandal sponsored debates, lectures and publications in defense of orthodoxy. These efforts of Maha Mandal created counter reformation movement against the Arya Samaj. In 1890 Sanatan Dharm Sabhas came into being throughout the Punjab province.[57] The Sanatan Dharm Sabhas were also founded by the Punjab group of Pandit Dindayal at Delhi and Haridwar.[58] In 1896 Swami Gyananandji started a campaign at Mathura called 'Nigamagama Mandali'.[59] In 1900 a national conference of Sanatani organsations was held at Delhi under the chairmanship of Maharaja Darbhaga. The people of Rajasthan were aware of such movements but they could not organize in the way of Northern India in British provinces. The setup of princely states was not congenial for the growth of organizations. Though, the Arya Samaj faced the opposition of Sanatanis in Rajasthan but not to the extent of Punjab and United Province.

The conflict between Sanatanis and Aryasamajists could not became sharp because both the streams came together in defense of Hinduism. The Sanatanis themselves initiated religious reforms by weeding out many religious evils and superstitious practices under the influence of Arya Samaj. The Sanatanis also began to oppose the untouchability. They also took the programme of cow protection. The Suddhi movement initiated by the Aryasamjists also attracted the sanatanis. The religious and social reforms introduced by the Arya Samaj were also adopoted by the Sanatanis. The main difference between the both existed on idol worship. Swami Dayanand and Arya Samaj had not accepted the Puranas as religious scriptures. Therefore, the sects originated from the Puranas were not accepted to the Arya Samaj. Thus, the Sanatanis had broad understanding with the Arya Samajists. It is interesting to note that in 1923 the Aryasamajists founded the Provincial Hindu Sabha and the works of Suddhi, Yagopavit, temple entry of untouchables, inter-caste feasts, collective religious sessions, *satsangas, Kirtans, Kathas* etc. were being organized.[60] Chandkaran Sharda a staunch supporter and leader of Arya Samaj at Ajmer was also the leader of Hindu Mahasabha.[61]

Social Reforms : The religious reforms of Arya Samaj prepared a solid ground for social reforms. Initially, the Arya Samaj movement began as a religious renaissance movement. Through the study of Vedas and ancient scriptures Swami Dayanand refuted the wrong and untruth religious conceptions and practices. In his view the evil existed in the religion are responsible for decline of Hinduism and Indian society. Thus, the religious reform was the key of social reforms. Obviously, the religious reform ideas and practices prepared a ground for social reforms. For instance Swami Dayanand advised the people not to observe the sex, caste and race discrimination in religious affairs and practices. Basically it was a sort of social discrimination rather than religious. Therefore, Swami Dayanand also initiated the efforts for social reforms.

Removal of Untouchability : Swami Dayanand was supporter of equality of human kind at all levels. And also in his view untouchability was the main factor of decline of Hindu society which led to the social and national disunity. The Christian missionaries by taking the advantage of the social factors were converting the untouchables to their religion. Thus, before the establishment of the Arya Samaj Swami Dayanand began to teach the people to uplift the poor and untouchables. One interesting episode has been depicted by Harbilas Sarda that in around 1868 when Swami Dayanand was on his way on the banks of Ganges in Western U.P. a Sadhu entered into a discussion on *Atma* (soul). In a long discussion Swami Dayanand asked the Sadhu : have you ever given thought to those millions of men who go hungry from day to day? There are thousands who have never had a full meal, who have only rags to cover their bodies. Millions of men, poor villagers like cows and buffaloes, pass their lives in huts surrounded by dirt and rubbish. Hundreds die by the roadside, uncared for. Mahatma, if you want to love Atma, think of them and look after them as you do of your own limbs. They alone who do this are mahatmas and entitled to be called lovers of Atma.[62]

The concept of *Shuddhi* was basically aimed to uplift the dalits. Though, Swami Dayanand never used the word exclusively for inclusion of non-Hindus into Vedic Religion. In the chapter ten of Satyarth Prakash Swami Dayanand had explained the conduct (Desirable and Undesirable) and Diet (Permissible and Forbidden).[63] In this he had discussed the concept of clean and unclean. He advised the clean conduct by behaving according to what is sanctioned by the Vedas and scriptures. He had also stressed upon good habits of food and living. He clearly supported the idea that the food can be taken cooked by a Shudra if he keeps himself clean physically. The innocent people are not aware of it, therefore must be taught the cleanness. Even he abandoned the concept of *Chauka,* because food may be cooked at any clean place. By supporting the foreign visit Swami Dayanand had written that there is no sin in touching with the foreigners and heretic. His concept of *Shuddhi* and Dalitoddhara seems to be inter related.

There are many instances when Swami Dayanand did not observed untouchability in accepting food without any caste discrimination. At a time when he was hungry, a *manjhi* (boatman) gave him half of his *roti* (chapati) which Swamiji ate.[64] Once he accepted food from a member of *Sadha* community whom Brahmins considered untouchable. The Brahmins deprecated Swamiji taking food given by the Sadhs. Swamiji said food becomes uneatable only in two ways : first when it is procured with the money obtained by inflicting sufferings on people, and secondly, when it is dirty.[65] Swami Dayanand had also refuted the concept of *Sakharee* (katcha) and *Nikharee* (pacca) foods.[66] But he strongly condemned the non-vegetarian food which causes uncleanliness. Thus, the cleanliness and purity in conduct, food and living habits is *Shuddhi.* As there is scope to clean the unclean in the same way impure can be made pure. Therefore, the Arya Samajists began their *dalitoddhar* programme with sincere zeal to ameliorate the conditions of downtrodden people.

The Arya Samaj movment founded by Swami Dayanand Saraswati more effectively attacked the caste system. It became more popular among the middle castes but its influence was more deep upon the fourth fold of Indian society. The Aryasamajists in Rajasthan also took the task of removal of untouchability. A noted Sociologist Prof. Shyamlal has narrated that[67] : The Arya Samaj had become popular by the turn of the twentieth century in Rajasthan and many untouchable lower castes and communities came under its influence. A notable leader Kisan of Top-khana was associated with the activities of Arya Samaj during his early days in Jaipur. His father Gunji and mother Jagadevi were very simple and poor Chamars with progressive ideas. His father had four sons and three daughters. While Kisan was living with his father at Top-khana, he came in contact with Swami Raghuwar Das, who was an active member of Arya Samaj. Kishan was influenced by his teachings. This gave Kisan an opportunity to participate in Arya Samaj's programmes thereby gaining self respect and prestige in the eyes of others. His participation in Arya Samaj provided him instant of social awakening. Now Raghuwar Das changed Kisan's name and he was called as Kisan Das.

Prof. Shyamlal has made his point on the positive role of Arya Samaj in the upliftment of dalits on the basis of oral sources tapped by him vigorously. His beirf description and analysis is worthy to reprodue here as follows.[68]

In Jaipur at Chhipo-ka-Mohalla near Jat-ka-Kauwa, Swami Muktananad a popular Vedyaraj and most influential Arya Samajist, was living there. When Kishan Das met Swami Muktanand, he came under his influence. Soon after this, he became his disciple. Swami Muktanand rechristinised his name as Munishwarnand. From 1920 onward Arya Samaj started supporting Chamars and others untouchable castes in many ways in Jaipur. They had started working for the upliftment of Chamars and others. In 1921, Munishwaranand opened the first "Vedic Pathshala" at Top Khana Jaipur to impart elementary education to the children of Chamars, Raigars, Dhanka and others. The expenditure to be incurrd on these students was borne by Kapoorchand Patni, who was then a businessman of Johari bazar, Jaipur. Patni collected the donations form public. The teachers of school included Nand Kishore and another teacher popularly known as "Madrashi Baba". They were paid Rs. 15/- per month in the year 1921, another school for Bhangis children was opened at Nadi area, Harijan bastee, Jaipur. Arya Samajists not only cooperated with Munishwaranand in opening the schools for Chamara and Bhangis, but also did efforts to bring socio-religious changes amongst the down-trodden masses.

Swami Munishwaranand, Chamar, himself toured the different parts of Rajputana and other places and propagated the adoption of good habits, Vedic rituals and encouraged the community to send their children to schools. Because of his fighting with the then Government, a Primay school for boys was opened at Babu-ka-Tiba, near Ramdev temple. Similarly a primary school for girls was also started in a rented house of a Chamar at the Babu-ka-Tiba, Jaipur. Thus Chamars, Raigars, Dhankas and others in Jaipur had the government schools. However, it is necessary to point out here that later on these schools were shifted to Hida-ki-Mori due to shortage of children/ accommodation.

The Arya samaj became popular force among the untouchables in general and Chamara in particular. A notable feature was the spread of teachings, beliefs and rituals of Arya Samaj amongst the Chamars in Jaipur and adoption of sacred thread. It led to a movement called the 'Jeneu movement' because group of male adults adopted the sacred thread in public. Later, some caste Hindus particularly Brahmins forced them to remove the sacred thread since untouchable lower castes were not allowed to wear the sacred thread. On the contrary, Swami had asked his followers not to yield to the pressure but to continue with it. It was an agitation against the discriminatory practices and to end the monopoly of caste Hindus with regard to the use of sacred thread. It is note-worthy that the attitude of the Jaipur government towards the efforts of Chamars to overcome their religious disabilities were softened and this led to the increasing enthusiasm amongst the Chamars. For instance, the drive for 'Juneu' took a positive turn when Thakur of Jobner Sh. Narendra Singh, who was the then Education Minister, once visited the Vedic Pathshala and asked the students about the principles to wear the sacred thread. Thus Hon'ble Narendra Singh gave the Chamars the rights to wear the sacred thread. Besides, he declared Rs. 2/- per month as a donation to the school. Adoption of Arya Samaj beliefs and ritual meant several changes in the life style of the Chamars. It is necessary to point out that emergence of an awareness amongst the Cahamars was a gradual process occurring at different regional levels, with the different degree of intensity.[69]

The *dalitoddhar* and *Shuddhi* efforts of Arya Samaj continued together. During 1930-37 the Arya Samaj, Ajmer perfomed *Janeu sanskar* for Chitahs, Rawats and Mehrats in the adjoing areas of Ajmer. The Arya Samaj in collaboration of Rajasthan Prantiya Hindu Sabha opened small *Pathshalas* in rural areas of Ajmer to inculcate the principle of Hinduism. The students of D.A.V. school and orphanage educated the untouchables of Harijan Bastis about the sanitation and health care. The Arya Samajists of Ajmer also supported the Gandhian movement for *harijanoddhar*. When on 5 July, 1934 Gandhiji visited the Secretary, Arya Samaj and students of D.A.V. school accompanied Gandhiji to Harijan Bastis. Gandhiji appreciated the works of Arya Samaj in these Bastis.[70]

Under the influence of *dalitoddhar* the princely State of Jhalwar took the lead in removing the untouchability officially in 1933. The Maharaja of Jhalawar was the first who opened the State temple to the Harijans.[71] The Arya Samaj in Johdpur played an important role in eradication of untouchability. Prof. Shyamlal has written that : The decade of 1920 saw the emergence of the Bhangis leadership vis-à-vis social reform movement as a conscious and organized force in the socio-religious life of the Bhangis of Rajasthan. Here, the reform movement of Arya Samaj emerged more distinctly in the Bhangi basites of Jodhpur city. Being influenced by Arya Samaj movement in the region, the Bhangi reform movement concentrated on socio-religious evils. The aims of the movement were as follows:

1. To wean the Bhangis away from eating beef, dead animals, left overs and consumption of alcoholic drinks.
2. To inculcate the idea of cleanliness in them and give them a sense of improved standards of living.
3. To create feeling of Hinduism, and
4. To eradicate Muslim influence from their socio-religious spheres.[72]

More precisely, there emerged the Arya Samaj movement in 1923 in Jodhpur which challenged the influence of Muslim culture on the Bhangi community. With the result, the Bhangis relinquished the Muslim influence in almost every walk of life and laid the basis for influencing Bhangi's socio-religious life and movement including the process of sanskritisation.[73]

The social and cultural consciousness created by the Arya Samaj among Bhangis prepared grounds for their political development. In 1942 an organisation of sweepers known as Safai Mazdoor Union came into being. Subsequently, in 1945 Marwar Mehtar Sudhar Sabha ws founded.[74] Later on the cause of untouchable took over by the workers and leaders of Praja Mandals allover Rajasthan. And alongwith the growing public agitations the princely state became liberal and considerate towards the untouchables. The Sanatanis also changed their behaviour and attitude towards dalits. In 1923 Hari Narayan Sharma who belonged to an orthodox Brahmin family of Alwar opened the doors of his own temple to untouchable people.[75]

In order to educate the Bhangis, Arya Samaj made history by opening a school to exclusively benefit the Bhangi children in the year 1923.[76] Again in 1940 after an interval of few years, Arya Samaj started a primary school at Udaimandir Bhangi Basti.[77]

Prof. Shaymalal has concluded the efforts of Arya Samaj in the direction of removal of untouchability as follows : Their main aim was initially to improve the socio-religious conditions of untouchables in the urban areas. It was against socio-religious discrimination by upper caste Hindus. By 1920-21, a few 'sacred thread' ceremonies were performed in Jaipur. By this time, the Arya Samajists had expanded their area of influence mostly among the untouchables namely, Chamars, Raigars and Bhangis. Soon After, the untouchable communities discovered that this made no difference to their low position in caste hierarchy because caste Hindus continued to treat them untouchables. Lacking organisation and leadership, it remained an isolated outburst but it did contribute to social awareness.[78]

The Arya Samaj could not enlist among its follower from the lower castes particularly untouchables. It was the supporter of fourfold division or *Varna* system of the society. Therefore, the communities belonging to *shudras* opposed the Arya Samaj.[79] It was the clear view of the conscious section of shudras that the caste system is the extension of varna system. Thus, the supporters of *Varna* system had full faith in the caste system. Therefore, the caste abolition efforts of such people and organisations were nothing than hypocrisy. I have come across an archival document that an organisation named *'The All India Jati Sudhar Maha Sabha'* passed the following resolution in the meeting of Executive Committee on 18th October, 1931. Resolution No. 2 "This Committee declares that it has no confidence in the All India Shradhanand Dalit Uddhar Sabha, the Achhut Uddhar Committee, Allahbad, U.P.; and the Dayanand Dalit Uddhar Mandal, Hoshyarpur, Punjab. It strongly condemns the policy of the above mentioned organisations which profess to uplift the depressed classes of India, but are in fact run by high-caste Hindus for their own benefit; their efforts are directed to retard any improvement or progress that the depressed classes may try to achieve."[80]

The above organisation belonged to the depressed or Dalit castes and the resolution mentioned above is their perception of Arya Samaj and high caste Hindus. This perception clearly seems divisive one politically and socially. The Arya Samaj was an anti-British organisation, while the said depressed class organisation was pro-British. This was clearly reflected in the resolution No. 5 as follows : "This committee looks forward to the British Parliament to make its decision and release the depressed classes from the ageold slavery and degenerating thraldom into which the caste distinctions and high handedness of the so-called high-caste Hindus have thrown them. If the British Parliament complies with a constitution according to the wishes of the Hindus without conceding the legitimate demands of the depressed classes, the burden and responsibility of their serfdom will rest on its shoulders.[81]

Irrespective of all the Arya Samaj opened the way for removal of untouchability. It was the first oganised effort in the modern Indian History to eradicate the stigma of untouchability on Indian society. The efforts of Arya Samaj also inculcate self confidence among the *dalits.* Since 1931 onwards Gandhiji and his disciples took the cause of depressed classes in bigway through Harijan Sewa Sangh. In Rajasthan a number of such organisations and Ashramas came into being as the result of efforts of Gandhian social and political workers. The Prajamandals since 1938 also played leading role in removal of untouchability. But the role of Arya Samaj can not be undermined in this direction because it not only sown the seeds of this but also nurtured it.

Shuddhi : The word *Shuddhi* means purification. Initially, it envisage to purify the untouchables to bring them in the main stream of Hinduism. The Arya Samaj initiated the Shuddhi movement to prevent low caste Hindus from embracing Christianity or Islam and to purify them for their inclusion of Hinduism.[82] The foregoing is an official view of imperialist government. But in the course of time the Shuddhi movement developed into the movement for reclamation of Hinduism by the people who had embraced Christianity and Islam. Thus, in religious terminology it began to apply for (i) Reconversion of those who have recently or at a remote period adopted one of the foreign religions, (ii) Conversion to Hinduism of persons belonging to foreign religions, and (iii) Reclamation, i.e. raising the status of the depressed classes.[83] Swami Dayanand was the first reformer who gave complete scheme of *Shuddhi* and opened a powerful channel to reclaim the Hinduism for the people who were converted to Christianity and Islam. Thus, the Shuddhi movement came into being. Along with *Shuddhi* the Arya Samaj also initiated the Dalitoddhar movement to stop the conversion of Dalit Hindus to Christianity and Islam. Thus, apart from reclaiming Hindus who had converted to other religions, it was used for raising the status of the untouchables.[84]

In his remarks Lala Lajpat Rai had briefly explained that the *Shuddhi* movement was also aimed to bring back the Hindu who were converted to other faiths, but it got great success in raising the social status of depressed classes. In his own words he had defined it as follows : Literally, *Shuddhi* means purification, but when used by Arya Samajists it also includes reclamation and conversion. The Arya Samaj, being a Vedic church, and as such a Hindu organisation, engages itself in reclaiming the wandering sheep who have strayed from the Hindu fold, and converts any one prepared to accept its religious teachings. In this undertaking it comes into direct conflict with the proselytizing work of the Musulman mullah and the Christian missionary. The Musulman fanatic and the Christian zealot abhor it, and even the sober minded moulvie and the broad-minded Christian have no liking for it. Yet the Samaj has achieved a considerable measure of success in reclaiming Hindus converted to other faiths, and in stemming the tide of conversion. But its greatest success consists in raising the social status of the depressed classes among the Hindus and preventing them from forsaking Hinduism for other religious denominations. In regard to the reconversions, the Census Commissioner of the United Provinces of Agra and Oudh remarks : "Special efforts are directed to the reconversion of converts from Hinduism to Christianity or Islam, while persons who are Christian or Mahomedan by birth are also occasionally converted."[85]

Most of the Biographers of Swami Dayanand had mentioned the fact that Swamiji himself initiated the work of

Shuddhi in Ajmer. It had been written by Harbilas Sarda that : During Muhammadan rule, some Hindus, Rawats or Mers by caste, had become Muslims in Masuda and in Merwara and were called Merats. But the Mers (Rawats) who were Hindus still gave their daughters in marriage to these converts. Swamiji told them that it was improper to Hindus to do so. They, then gave up the practice.[86]

The purification of dalits was also administered through the process of *Shuddhi.* Their *Yagopavit* ceremonies were performed and they were renamed as per the Vedic rituals and *Sanskaras.* They were brought in the social category of *dwija.* And also the right to study and reciting the Vedas. But the conversion of non-Hindus to the Vedic religion had slightly a different procedure. Mr. Burn, I.C.S. the Census Commissioner of Punjab has reported the procedure as follows that : the ceremony of conversion is simple. They would be Aryas lives on milk alone for a period of fifteen days[87], this being known as the Chandrain birth. Admission into the Samaj is made an occasion for a public meeting, at which the converts declares his adherence to the Ten Principles of the Samaj, a great *homa* sacrifice is performed, passages from the Vedas are recited, and the covert distributes sweetmeats to those present.[88] In some instances a certificate of *Shuddhi* is issued, which facilitates social intercourse with Hindus.

The *Shuddhi* movement in Rajasthan was different in comparison to Punjab and United Provinces. Being mainly under the rule of princely states the atmosphere for such new or modern public activities was not favourable. For a long time Ajmer remained the centre of *Shuddhi* movement in Rajasthan. The Muslim and Christian officers in the government services were very influential in the princely states. Therefore, the princely states did not support the religious conversion of Muslim and Christians to Hinduism. The Arya Samaj units located in the princely states used to send the people for conversion to Ajmer. The people desirous to accept Vedic religion were brought to Ajmer and there they were inducted into Hindu society. The work of *Shuddhi* by the Arya Samaj was being done on the slow pace mainly at Ajmer. These activities were limited to the individuals or individual families. The larger groups were not persuaded for conversion. Hence the conversions on mass level were not administered.[89] Thus, from 1883 to 1923 the *Shuddhi* remained limited to individual level and collective *Shuddhi* could not be done.

On 13th February, 1923 the Bhartiya Hindu Shuddhi Sabha was established under the President of Swami Shraddhanand and Lala Hansraj became its Vice-President.[90] I have not come across any reference of its branch in Rajasthan. But the programme for collective shuddhi adopted by the said *sabha* also influenced the *Shuddhi* movment in Rajasthan. The Arya Pratinidhi Sabha, Rajasthan in collaboration of Rajasthan Prantiya Hindu Sabha launched the movement for collective shuddhi. Hence, the nature of *Shuddhi* movement invented and initiated by the Arya Samaj got changed as since 1923 with the establishment of the Bhartiya Hindu Shuddhi Sabha the Arya Samaj went in background and the Hindu Mahasabha became main force behind this. Earlier the Shuddhis were inducted into the Arya Samaj and converts were supposed to follow the principles and rule of the Arya Samaj. But after 1923 all such conditions for conversion and convert were abandoned and even the condition of not believing in idol worship was also given up.

In Rajasthan the *Shuddhi* movement achieved success in checking the advance of Christianity. Though, some converts from Hinduism to Christianity were reconverted to Hinduism but such cases were scattered and sporadic. The first *Shuddhi* was administered on 25th August, 1883 by Pandit Kamal Nayan

Sharma the Secretary, Arya Samaj, Ajmer in which one woman two children were converted to Hinduism from Christianity.[91] And on 26th August, 1883 itself one another woman was converted to Vedic religion.[92] In 1891 three Muslms were made *Shuddhis* in Bandikui by the Arya Pratinidhi Sabha, Ajmer.[93] The said *sabha* also established the *Shuddhi* Fund in 1910 to accelerate the Shuddhi work.[94] On 19 February, 1928 the Arya Samaj Ajmer performed a Shuddhi ceremony at Ajmer in which family of Biharilal Gupta converted Christian was inducted into Vedic religion.[95] One Christian named Strocke was made *Shuddhi* by Ajmer Arya Samaj on 4th March, 1932 and he was given the name Satyanand.[96]

The newly founded Bhartiya Hindu Shuddhi Sabha took the task of converting the Malkana Rajputas to Hinduism. The Malkana Rajputs were scattered in many villages between Agra, Mathura, Farrukhabad in Western U.P.. They were nominally Muslims, but their actual cultural and ritual customs were a strange mixture of Muslim and Hindu practices. On 25th February Swami Shraddhanand himself was present at the first ceremony of reclamation of Malkanas to Hinduism at the village of Raibna[97], near Agra, and he spent the next two months in the field, going from village to village. In those two months about a hundred villages were covered. Within the first month five thousand Malkanas were reclaimed, and by the end of the year the total had risen to about thirty thousand.[98] The Malkana Rajputs were also inhabited in the Bharatpur and Alwar princely States and during 1926-30 they became Shuddhi due to the constant efforts of the Arya Samaj and Hindu Mahasabha. Though, the *shuddhi* Sabha came into being in Bharatpur also in February, 1923. The said sabha was founded by the local Arya Samajists and Sanatani Brahmin Pandits. Bharatpur Maharaja Kishan Singh (1918-1929) himself was the supporter of *Shuddhi* movement. Hence, he not only contributed to the upliftment of depressed classes but also to the Hindu cause.[99]

The Hindu *Shuddhi* sabha Bharatpur also founded the '*Shuddhi Kosh*' on 30th December, 1926 in the memory of Swami Shraddhanand, who was assassinated by one Muslim fanatic on 23rd December, 1926.[100] The leaders of *Shuddhi* concentrated on the *Shuddhi* of such communities who were following the mixed Hindu and Muslim traditions and culture. Among these the Malkana Rajputs were prominent. The Maharaja advised the people to treat the shuddhis equal by establishing social interaction. During my field work I came across a villages, Tasai, which was densely inhabited by Malkanas on the border of Bharatpur and Alwar states, where about 100 families of Malkanas embrace Hinduism. When the Sanatanis became against their entry into the temples, the Shuddhi Sabha created a temple known as *Shuddhiyon ka Mandir* with grant of Birla trust, hence it is also known as Birla Mandir.[101]

The Shuddhi movement initiated by the Arya Samaj paved the way for *Shuddhi* of untouchables and Hindu converted Christians and Muslims. Through concept of *Shuddhi* Swami Dayanand checked the advance of Christianity in Northern India. This was an ancient Hindu concept, referring to the quality of purity necessary for the proper performance of *dharma,* which includes ritual and social duties. By extension the term also indicated the rite by which pollution is removed, and access to *dharma* is restored : it gives back the right to perform the rituals and to participate in the social life of the caste.[102] In the nineteenth century the term first appeared among the reformers in the context of crossing the *kala pani,* the black waters. Those who had journeyed outside India would necessarily have had many contacts with polluting materials and persons. They were, therefore, in their return required by orthodoxy to submit to a rite of purification. Many reformers repudiated this rule, and so did Dayanand.[103] The second use of the term was for the reinstatement of a 'lapsed' Hindu, perhaps somebody who had been converted to another religion. Orthodoxy was very reluctant to accept such reinstatement.[104] The pundits forgot that it was an ancient custom : the *Atharvaveda* and the *Brahmanas* prescribe the rite of *vratyastoma* for readmittance of those fallen beyond the pale of Aryan society, and the later law-books like the *Devalasmriti,* probably written after the early Arab raids, prescribe lengthy provisions for the re-admission into Hinduism of people forcibly converted.[105]

Though, the provision of reconversion in Hinduism existed since ancient time, but it had gone out of memory and practice. Hence, Swami Dayanand not only refounded the concept of *Shuddhi* firmly but also made it functional and applied. Through this concept the religious and social rigidity existed in Hinduism began to erode.

Women's Emancipation : There existed innumerable hindrances in the way of emancipation or uplifment of women. They, were surrounded by a number of miseries. When the Arya Samaj came into being the conditions of women were deplorable. They were deprived of exposer to education. They were the victim of their dependence on man hood, early marriage, puradah, unmatched marriages, polygamy, widowhood, caste vices etc.. The Brahmo Samaj was the first organisation which took the cause of women's emancipation. No doubt the movement of Brahmo Samaj was influenced with western education and thoughts. After Raja Ram Mohan Roy Swami Dayanand gave serious thought to the problems of womanhood. He was of the opinion that deterioration in woman's position in the Hindu society is the result of decline in the ancient Hindu ideals of womanhood.

The perception of Swami Dayanand and the Arya Samaj on the issue of woman's deplorable conditions had been briefed by Lajpat Rai as follows : English education and Western ideas have played an important part in engendering this change, but an equally great, if not even greater, part has been played by an appeal to the ancient Hindu ideals of womanhood and to the teaching of the ancient Hindu religion in the matter of the relations of the sexes. A study of ancient Hindu literature made it abundantly clear that the present unenviable lot of Indian women was due to a deterioration of their old ideal. In Ancient India, both in the theory and practice, women were placed on a pedestal in society - equal to that of men, if not higher. As regards education and marriage they held an equal position. The girls were equally entitled to receive education, and no limitations at all were set on their ambition in this direction. Study was equally enjoined for the girls as well as the boys. The only difference was that, in the case of girls, their period of education expired sooner than in that of boys. The minimum age of marriage for girls was sixteen, as compared with twenty-five for boys. This was based on Hindu ideas of the physiological differences between the sexes. It is presumed that as regards the choice of a mate, both parties enjoyed equal freedom and equal opportunities. The ideal marriage was monogemic, and one contracted with the mutual consent of the parties. Yet, so many varieties of legal marriages are known to Hindu law as to leave no doubt as to the sensitiveness of the Hindus to the extreme difficulty, indeed unnaturalness, of attempting to impose a single law upon both sexes. Some forms of marriage suggest that courtship was not altogether unknown in Hindu society, and furthermore, it was not regarded with any grave disapprobation. Though as a rule subject to control by parents, husbands and even sons, Hindu mothers, wives, sisters and daughters occupied a higher position than their counterparts ever had in Christian Europe before the nineteenth century. In the family the position of the mother was higher than that of the father. According to Manu she is entitled to a thousand times greater respect and reverence than the father. She was in supreme control of the house and at the helm of household affairs, including finances.[106]

When the Arya Samaj was brought into existence the condition of woman was deplorable. They had lost their higher position in the family as well as in the society. Women began to maintain purdah and depended on their male relations. Early marriage became almost universally prevalent among them and monogamy was replaced by polygamy. Swami Dayanand and his Arya Samaj were no less generous and no less bold in their crusade against social evils adversely affecting the life and conditions of woman. Hence, the Arya Samaj advocated for complete emancipation of women.[107] Therefore, the campaign and struggle was launched on all the fronts to ameliorate the conditions and position of women.

To address the issues of women's emancipation the *Stree Arya Samaj* was founded in Ludhiana and Lahore followed by Ajmer, Dehradun, Meerut, Badayun, Lucknow, Kanpur and various other places.[108] The primary objective of the Stree Samaj was to uplift the woman. The Ajmer Stree Samaj came into being in 1904. It was founded by Smt. Gulab Devi Maheshwari.[109] After getting the rights of performing *Yajnas, Sandhya-havan* and *Vedadhyan*, and conducting religious rituals independently by the women workers of the Stree Samaj were promoted. As a result of such activities the awareness and confidence developed upto the optimums which encourage them to oppose social evils.[110] The Beawer Stree Samaj was extension of Ajmer Stree Samaj. After Ajmer another Stree Arya Samaj was founded in Bharatpur.[111] By 1930 the Stree Arya Samajes also came into being in Jaipur, Alwar, Jodhpur, Bikaner etc.. The Stree Arya

Samajes founded girls and women's schools, *Vanita Ashramas, Vidhwa Ashramas, Mahila Sewa Sansthan, Mahila Mandals, Purdah Niwarak Mandlis, Vidhwa Vivah Sahayak Sabhas* etc.. Thus, the Stree Arya Samaj contributed immensely in the direction of women's emancipation.

The social evil of child marriages were adversely affecting the female and male but females were heavily victim of this evil. In his lectures and discourses Swami Dayanand vehemently criticized the child marriages. In his views the practice was highly injurious to the physical, mental, and psychological growth of boys and girls. It also caused to social and national degeneration of Hindus. He suggested the minimum marriageable age 25 for boys and 16 for girls. The Arya Samaj was not in a position to launch a movement against the child marriage particularly in the princely states of Rajasthan. Therefore, the Arya Samaj propagators through weekly assemblies, Arya conferences, and regular lectures created an atmosphere against this ill tradition. They encouraged the Arya Samajists and educated people to voluntarily give up this social evil and call them to motivate the others too.

With the efforts of Arya Samaj the caste associations began to oppose the child marriages since 1920. The educated middle class was taking keen interest in the abolition of the evil. Under the influence of growing awareness against this evil the feudal and elites also began to think on the problem. Therefore, the collective efforts of all such groups impressed upon the princely states to put legal restrictions on such dangerous evil tradition which was adversely affecting the future generation. The State of Bharatpur in 1926 fixed age of Marriage 11 years for girls and 15 years for boys.[112] In July 1926 the State of Kota also fixed it 11 and 15 for girls and boys respectively.[113] In Karauli in 1927 it was fixed 13 for girls and 16 for boys[114], in 1928 the Bikaner State made it 11 and

15[115] and in 1930 the State of Jodhpur fixed 13 and 16 for girls and boys respectively.[116]

The age of consent Act 1891 was enacted in the British India on 19 March 1891, which raised the age of consent for sexual intercourse for all girls, married or unmarried, from ten to twelve years in all Jurisdictions, its violation subject to criminal prosecution as rape. The said provisions were not applicable in the princely states of India. Thus, in Rajasthan it was applicable only in the British province of Ajmer-Merwar. Har Bilas Sarda a prominent Arya Samajists and President of Paropkarini Sabha made serious efforts to make a law to prevent child marriages. He happens to be a member of the Central legislative Assembly. He moved a Bill in the Assembly as the Child Marriage Restraint and the same was introduced for deliberations on 15th September, 1927. The primary object of the Bill was to put a stop to child widowhood. The second object was to remove the principal impediment to the physical and mental growth of the youth of both sexes and the chief cause of their premature decay and death.[117] Sarda moved this Bill as private Bill of an individual member. Therefore it faced stiff opposition from the Government. But with the constant efforts he mabilzed support to the Bill nationally and internationally. Finally, the Bill was passed on 23rd September, 1929 and the Child Marriage Restraint Act came into being. The same came into effect from 1st April, 1930. It fixed 14 and 18 years age as the marriageable age for girls and boys respectively of all communities.

As far as Rajasthan is concerned the said Act was applicable only in the British province of Ajmer and Merwara. The orthodox Hindus opposed the enforcement of Sarda Act in all the princely states. But the Aryasamajists vigorously and aggressively campaigned for its implementation in the princely states. Initially the Sarda Act could not become effective immediately in the province of Ajmer-Merwara as the inhabitants of this territory desirous to perform child marriages began to solemnise the same at the places located in the territories of the princely states. Later in 1938 through an amendment in the Child Marriage Restraint Act the child marriage solemnise by the inhabitants of British provinces in the princely states became publishable offense.[118] During 1933-1945 most of the princely states incorporated such provisions in their marriage laws.

The problem of widowhood was another problem confronted by the womenfolk. It was the problem of upper castes among which the widow remarriages were not allowed. The Arya Samaj took the issue and campaigned in favour of widow remarriage. Apart from compassionate grounds, the Arya Samajists were largely moved by the fact of mass conversion of widow to Christianity and Islam.[119] The establishment of Vidhwa Vivah Sahayak Sabha in 1915 imparted a fillip to the widow remarriage movement spearheaded by the Arya Samaj movement.[120]

Since 1920 onwards the widow remarriages began to be solemnised in Rajasthan for which credit goes to the Arya Samaj organisations. Bandikui Arya Samaj conducted remarriage of Meerabai a *bal vidhwa* belonging to Brahmin caste with Ramgopal Sharma on 4th July 1928.[121] In this widow remarriage function about five to six hundred people were assembled.

Here it is interesting to note that the princely state of Bharatpur took the lead in the direction of widow remarriage. The State government passed "Social Reforms Act" in 1926 thereby permitting widow remarriage in the State.[122] Apprehending deprivation of the parental property to the off-springs of the remarried women, the Maharaja emphatically declared "the off-springs of such a wedlock would be considered sacred and eligible claimant to the father's property".[123] Taking advantage of the "Widow Remarriage Vidhan", a number of widow remarriages took place in the State. Of these, the marriage of Haridas Gayadin, an officer of the Baretha circle with a sixteen year old Brahmin widow on 8th July, 1927, occupied an important place in the social history of the State.[124] The marriage party procession, including principal Sardars of the State and escorted by the military bodyguard. Maharaja was also present. Thus, under the state patronage the widow remarriage became an acceptable event, which encouraged it in future. The social acceptability of the widow remarriage opened the ways of women's emancipation. The Sanatanists also began to support the widow remarriage all over the Rajasthan. Thus the joint efforts of Arya Samajists and Sanatanists made the remarriages a social reality.

To mitigate the problem of widows various steps were taken by the Arya Samaj. The Arya Stree Samaj founded the widow homes and *Vanita Ashramas.* The first widow home came into being in 1891 at Lahore, which was founded by the Lahore Stree Samaj.[125] Though the Arya Samaj, Ajmer also started to give shelter to destitute widows. The Ajmer orphanage was taking the care of them. The first *Vidhwa Ashram* was founded in October 1909 by the Ajmer Arya Samaj in the Dayanand orphanage. The Ajmer *Vidhwa Ashram* began with eight widows whose number reached upto 22 in 1922. Among these inmates of this widow home the women from Muslims were also included.[126] In 1926 at Jatiawas in Ajmer a "*Vanita Ashram*" was founded by the educated Arya Samajists by raising donations from public. It was not purely a widow home but the poor and destitute women were also given shelter. Apart from philanthropic activity it was also aimed to prevent the conversion of such women into other religions. Hence the Vanita Ashram's objective was also to make them self reliant and to rehabilitate them.[127] The said Ashram was started with 35 women whose number reached upto 153 in first year.[128] The *Vanita* and *Vidhwa Ashrams* also gave shelter to destitute women and those who were persecuted by their husbands and families.[129] Rajasthan Vanita Ashram, Jhansi Vidhwa Ashram, Saharanpur Vanita Ashram and Dayanand orphanage specified thus very clearly in their advertisements that harassed women, whether widow or not, were welcome in the homes. In most of the cases such persecuted women were sent back to their guardians.[130] These institutions also performed remarriages of eligible women inmates.

The Arya Samaj also opposed the unequal marriage. Though, in the opinion of Swami Dayanand the best form of marriage is that by choice know as *Swayamvara.*[131] He gave stress on compatibility between husband wife. In many cases the old aged people were got married with young girls of their daughters and granddaughters age. In such cases the girls married to men of their fathers and grandfathers age were worst hit, because their widowhood at an early age was sure. Therefore, Arya Samaj created awareness against such marriages. The educated people not only gave up such marriages and they began to look down towards men who were entering into such unmatched wedlocks.

The Arya Samaj also confronted the problem of the custom of dowery. The countless marriage rituals were also in practice. In the previous chapters the thoughts of Swami Dayanand on the issues of marriages and remarriages has been discussed. Many evils became part of marriage rituals. Coupled with the senseless obligations of dowry and countless of rituals were highly unproductive and economically costly. A noted Arya Samajists scholar had said that : To have a daughter in the family is to constantly burn in the fire of hell. Where to get money from? No money no marriage. Several families have met a tragic end.[132] The Arya Samajists mounted a vigorous campaign against the Hindu orthodoxy for the simplification of marriage rituals and this formed one of their earliest efforts to reform the institution of marriage. Dayanand's *Sanskar Vidhi* had already provided his followers with a series of simple Vedic ceremonies. However, the process was both long and different as the Samajists had to fight a grim battle with the Hindu orthodoxy for the acceptance of reformed and simple Vedic rituals.[133]

Polygamy was another evil which was prevalent in almost every part of India and Rajasthan was not exception to it. The polygamy was widely prevalent among the rulers and *jagirdars*. Having more wives had become the status symbol among them. The rulers and *jagirdars* also wished to give their daughters in the families higher to their status. During his visits of Rajasthan Swami Dayanand pursuated the rulers and *jagirdars* to give up the system of polygamy. It had also effects on these people.[134] Even after the death of Swamiji the Arya Samajist also kept their efforts continued to oppose the polygamy.

Purda system was also an impediment in the way of emancipation of women. Due to Purda the movement of women was confined within the four walls. They were deprived the opportunity of getting education. The Arya Samaj gave equal right of education to the women. Thus, by exercising the right of education the women began to resist the *purda* system. Gulab Devi and Manorma Devi of Ajmer Stree Arya Samaj were the chief motivators and activists of the *Purdah Niwaran Mandli* in Ajmer. The *Purdah Niwaran Mandli* was founded in 1928 at Ajmer.[135] Parvati Devi (wife of Harbilas Sarda), Sukhda Devi (wife of Chand Karan Sharda) and Gulab Devi (Pradhana of Ajmer Stree Arya Samaj) participated as the representative of Ajmer in the session of all India women's conference held in January, 1930.[136] The Samajist leaders denounced the practice of *purda.* In an article entitled 'Awakening of women', H.B. Sarda enumerated the disadvantages of the customs of *purda* and made a strong plea for its removal .... He remarked that : *Purda* must be abolished .... *Purda* and innumerable disabilities imposed on her are insurmountable obstacles in the way of her fulfilling her desire and prevent her from performing what she regards as her duty .... Whatever their origin, these handicaps must now be removed and removed without delay...............make her free and she will break man's chains.[137] The women from the Arya Samajits families took lead in abolition of *Purda.*

Promotion of women's education by Arya Samaj has been a noble attempt for overall and complete emancipation of women. Lala Lajpat Rai a prominent and stalwart leader of Arya Samaj has explained the problem of education as follows : It must be frankly admitted that when the Arya Samaj came into being the lot of Hindu women was deplorable. In certain respects it was even worse than that of men. A proportion of the men (though comprising only a very small percentage of the population) had received some sort of education, in the schools and colleges opened by the Government, the Christian missionaries and other private agencies, but very little had been done to further the education of Indian women. The system of Government introduced by the British necessitated the education of Indian men for administrative reasons.[138] Among the agencies that have worked for improvement in this respect, the Arya Samaj occupies a high position in the Punjab and the United Provinces of Agra and Oude(Oudh). It can be safely said that there has occurred a metamorphosis in the outlook of men towards women.[139]

Swami Dayanand the founder of the Arya Samaj envisaged education of both, men and women, as the key to the resurgence of Hinduism. The women were under deprivation since the centuries as far as their education is concerned. Swami

Dayanand and his Arya Samaj initiated crusade for emancipation of women. Both advocated the complete emancipation of women. They advocated that women should be educated. Like Annie Besant, they believed that the regeneration of India was possible only through the proper education of her women. Until girls were educated, until they were taught and trained, until they knew the glory of the past and taught the children of their knees what India was and what she might be, until Indian mothers were also worthy of the Indian women of the past, until they became patriots as well as the men and loved the land as well as their husbands - until these things were done in India, India must remain weak.[140] Dayanand and his Samaj laid stress on proper type of female education. It has been aptly remarked by O'Malley that feminism and nationalism had gone hand in hand.[141] The Samaj believed that proper and equal education should be given to female and male. It believed that if men were educated and women uneducated or women educated and men uneducated, then the house would be a place of constant warfare between the gods and demons and there would be no happiness.[142] Dayanand clearly advocated that a Brahmin woman and a Kshattriya women should learn all sciences; a Vaishya woman would learn commerce and Shudra Woman the art of service.[143] Just as men should learn at least grammar, theology and the principles of their profession, similarly women should necessarily learn grammar, theology, medicine, arithmetic and art. Without this much it was not possible to ascertain what was right and what was wrong, what sort of treatment should be offered to the husband and others, how household affairs should be carried on, how food should be prepared by hygienic methods, and how disease should be kept out and happiness secured in the family.[144]

The Punjab Arya Samajists took lead in developing huge educational infrastructure. But looking to the size of Arya

Samjists in Rajasthan the efforts were appreciable. As usual the Ajmer was the centre of educational activities of Arya Samaj. The Paropkarini Sabha took initiative in this direction to establish Dayanand Ashram in the memory of Swami Dayanand Saraswati at Ajmer.[145] It was founded on 29th December, 1887 by Rao Bahdur Singh of Masuda.[146] On 10th February, 1888 the Dayanand Ashram School was opened in the Arya Samaj Bhawan, Kesarganj, Ajmer.[147] In April 1889 the subject of English was introduced in a academic curriculum of the school. Thus, since April 1889 it was known as 'Dayanand Ashram Anglo-Vedic School'.

For a long time the Arya Samaj could not began formal schools for girls' education. Some primary level Arya pathshalas also came up with the individual efforts of educated and enlightened Arya Samajists in the city of Ajmer where co-education was given.[148] On 27th February, 1898 the Arya Samaj Ajmer established the first girls' school known as *Arya Putri Pathshala* in *Purani Mandi* Ajmer. The objective of the school was the overall physical and mental development of girls. Along with theological aspects modern education was given. It also aimed intellectual development of girl students and to make them aware of Vedic culture.[149] The curriculum of the school was according to government school. It was began with two teachers and eight-nine students. The number of students reached ninety in 1912.[150]

Another Arya girls school known as *Mathura Prasad Gulab Devi Arya Kanya Pathshala,* Ajmer also came into being in 1898. It was founded by Gulab Devi a noted Arya Samajist and woman activist. She was also the founder of Stree Arya Samaj. The school had a modest beginning from July, 1898, when Gulab Devi and her husband Mathura Prasad, leading Arya Samajist of Ajmer began to teach a group of girls and women from their neighbourhood.[151] It was began with 5 students in

1898, whose number reached 68 within a span of two years. In 1900 it was given the status of a middle school and its academic curriculum was according to government schools. In addition to prescribed courses the students were also given the training in different branches of handi-crafts and cottages industry to make them self- reliant. They were also taught religious literature and theological values. The students were required to perform *Sandhya* and *Havan* regularly. In 1941 it had 322 students. The Pathshala became very popular as it was progressively achieving its aim through various learning activities. Thus, it inculcated religious and ethical values and social-national awareness. Till 1912, the Pathshala was under the personal management of Gulab Devi and thereafter its' management was handed over to the Arya Pratinidhi Sabha, Rajasthan.[152] In March 1921 the Arya Samaj, kesarganj, Ajmer took over the management.[153] In 1940, on the advice of Gulab Devi, it was placed under a trust.[154] This Arya Kanya Pathshala flourished under able supervision of Gulab Devi till her death in 1963.[155]

Shrimati Godavari Arya Kanya Pathshala, Beawar was also an important institution promoted by the Arya Samaj for the education of girls. Initially it was an individual effort of Shrimati Godavari Swarnkar who opened the Arya Kanya Lower Middle school at Beawar on 6th March, 1913 in her own residence along with fifteen-sixteen girls. Later in October, 1913 the school was brought under the Arya Pratinidhi Sabha, Rajasthan but its management remained under the supervision of Godavari Devi.[156] Along with normal courses the religious education was made compulsory and the medium of instructions was Hindi and Sanskrit. Religious discourses, performing *Yajya, Hawan* and *Sandhya* were the regular activities. In 1936 the school was promoted upto Upper Middle level.[157] Godavari Devi was also a women activist and was main leader or the Stree Arya

Samaj, Beawar. She donated her property to Kanya Pathshala in Beawar.[158]

The extension of girls education in other parts of Rajasthan also took place. After Ajmer the State of Bharatpur took lead as Arya Samaj Bharatpur began Arya Kanya Vidyalaya on 1st July, 1906 with seven students. In 1912 the number of students reached 112.[159] Another Arya Kanya Pathshala at Ballabhgarh (Bharatpur) came into being on 1st July, 1932 and in April 1937 Arya Vedic Kanya Vidyalaya was founded in Bhusavar (Bharatpur).[160]

After 1930 the Arya Kanya Schools came up in larger areas of Rajasthan. In 1931 Arya Putri Pathshala middle school at Jodhpur was began.[161] The Arya Kanya Pathshalas were also established in Bikaner proper and towns such as at Ratangarh, Churu and Sujangarh.[162] In the Jaipur State Arya Kanya Pathshalas were founded at Bandikui (1938), Mandawa (1934), Phulera (1936) and Jaipur (1946). In 1941 Shri Vedic Kanya Pathshala at Abu road was established.

The establishment of the *Mahila Seva Sadan* in Jaipur in the year 1942 began a new era in the direction of women's emancipation : From 1942 to 1945 the *Mahila Seva Sadan* provided shelter to 541 girls.[163] Efforts were also made to make the inmates self-reliant and intellectually enlightened. Mahila Shilp Vidyalaya was set up to impart formal education and vocational training. The scope of Mahila Seva Sadan's Shilp Vidyalaya, its activities can be inferred from the fact that in 1950, it had 400 students and 11 teachers.[164]

It may be summarised that from 1877 to 1883 the rise and growth of Arya Samaj organisations remained on slow pace, but after the sad demise of Swami Dayanand Saraswati the devotees and believers of Vedic religion accelaratd their efforts. There were certain obstacles in the way of Arya Samaj in the princely states, because the attitude of the majority of rulers towards it was indifferent. But the educated and enlightened people took the mission of spreading the organisational network of Arya Samaj and by the end of nineteenth century they covered almost all the corners of Rajasthan. Due to various factors Ajmer emerged as most important centre of Arya Samaj activities. Being a British province it had many advantages. In 1888 the Arya Pratinidhi Sabha Rajasthan and Malwa with its headquarter at Ajmer came into being. The Pratinidhi Sabha through preachers and propagators strengthened the Arya Samaj organisations. The headquarters of Vedic Yantralaya and Paropkarini Sabha were also transferred to Ajmer. The Arya Kumar Sabha, Arya Veer Dal, Arya Stree Samaj, Dayanand Ashram, Vidhwa Ashram, Orphanage etc. a number of associated organisations and institutions facilitated the missionary works of Arya Samaj.

Religious reform works of Arya Samaj were prominent as priority was given to them. The Christian Missionaries presented challenges before the Hinduism. Swami Dayanand devised a scientific form of Vedic religion based on *Arsha* literature and scriptures. He not only denounced the pauranic foundations of Hinduism but also criticized the pauranic religious practices. After his disciples took the mission of propagation of Vedic religion. They refuted all the superstitious practices and denounced the idol worship. Simple and scientific religious rituals were introduced by the Arya Samaj. The Sanatanists also began to be influenced from the Arya Samaj and they too introduced logical rituals by reforming the evil practices and rituals.

The social reforms of Arya Samaj were equally important. Through various means the Arya Samaj attacked the social evils. The removal of untouchability was an important programme of social reforms. Through the removal of untouchability programme the social unity could be achieved. Shuddhi movement initially envisage the shuddhi of *dalits* and later on through this a channel of reconversion of such people began, who embraced Christianity or Islam. After 1920 the Hindu Mahasabha and Sanatani organisations also adopted the programmes of *dalitoddhar* and Shuddhi. They also joined hands with Arya Samjists. The Arya Samaj also took an ambitious programme of women's emancipation. The Stree Arya Samaj took the lead in this direction. The evil of child marriage was confronted and Arya Samaj finally achieved its' goal by getting the Sarda Act passed in 1929. Various steps were taken to mitigate the problems of widowhood. The Vidhwa Ashrams and women homes were founded. The campaign of widow remarriage also got success which was also taken over by other Hindu organisations. The educational programmes of Arya Samaj created awareness among girls and women.

Notes

1. Baba Chhajju Singh, *op.cit.* Part II, p. 42, Harbilas Sarda, *op.cit.*, p. 260 and Bhawanilal Bhartiya, *op.cit.*, p. 426.
2. Baba Chhajju Singh, *op.cit.*, pat II, p. 42. The fact has also been confirmed by the other biographers.
3. *The Autobiography of Dayanand Saraswati, op.cit.*, p. 73.
4. Satyaketu Vidyalankar (chief editor), *Aryasamaj ka Itihas,* Volume Two, Arya Swadhyay Kendra, New Delhi, First Edition, 1995, p. 507. Thakur Nandkishore Singh was originally resident of Kasganj (UP) and he was minister in the State council of Jaipur. He was well versed in Hindi, English and Sanskrit. He was the person who prevailed upon the Maharaja to withdraw the orders of expulsion of the Aryasamajists from the territories of Jaipur State.
5. *Ibid.*
6. *Ibid.*
7. For details see chapter III.

8. *Report of Vedic Yantralaya, 1906,* Vedic Yantralaya, Ajmer, 1907, p. 1
9. V.K. Vashishtha, *Arya Samaj Movement in Rajasthan during the Nineteenth Century,* published in S.C. Malik Ed. Dissent Protest and reform in Indian Civilization, Indian Institute of Advanced Study, Simla, 1978, p. 229.
10. Satyaketu Vidyalankar, *op.cit.,* Volume Two, pp. 410-11.
11. *Ibid,* p. 413. While J.T.F. Jordens has written that in August, 1883 a branch of the Arya Samaj was established in Jodhpur under the patronage of Pratap Singh (*op.cit.,* p. 240).
12. Harbilas Sarda, *op.cit.,* p. 314.
13. *Ibid.*
14. J.T.F. Jordens, *op.cit.,* p. 240.
15. Harbilas Sarda, *op.cit.,* p. 323.
16. Ried, Graham J., *Arya Samaj as a Reformation in Hinduism, with Special Reference to Caste,* Yale University, Ph.D. Dissertation, p. 426, quoted from Pratibha Jain, Sangeeta Sharma and Archana Garg, *Liberation of Women - An Aryasmajist Perspective,* Project Report Centre for Women's Studies, University of Rajasthan, Jaipur (Year is not mentioned), p. 19.
17. Calculated from various sources and majorly from Satyaketu Vidyalanakar, *op.cit.,* Volume Two, pp. 405-25.
18. Ganga Prasad Upadhyay, *op.cit.,* pp. 91-92.
19. V.K. Vashishtah, *op.cit.,* p. 229.
20. For details see chapter III and also Shrikaran Sharda, *Svami Dayanand's Will and Trust : The Paropakarini Sabha, Ajmer, Dayanand Commemoration Volume,* Edited by Swami Satya Prakash Sarsavati, Maharishi Centenary Celebrations, Ajmer, 1983, p. 49.
21. *Arya Directory,* published by International Arya League, Delhi, 1941, p. 47.
22. *Ibid,* p. 53.

23. Harbilas Sarda, *op.cit.,* p. 254.
24. *Ibid,* pp. 290-91.
25. *Ibid,* pp. 291-92.
26. Shrikaran Sharda, *op.cit.,* p. 53. Also see Kaviraj Dharmsingh Kothari, *Paropkarini Sabha ka Itihas, Dayanand Commemoration Volume,* Edited by Svami Saty Prakash Saravati, Maharishi Centenary Celebrations, Ajmer, 1883, p. 27.
27. Indra Vidyavachaspati, *Aryasamaj ka Itihas,* Volume Second, Sarvadeshik Arya Pratinidhi Sabha, Delhi, 1957, p. 45.
28. Kaviraj Dharamsingh Kothari, *op.cit.,* p. 26. It is interesting to note that Swami Shradhanand from Gurukul faction and Mahatma Hansraj from college faction were the councillor of Paropkarini Sabha.
29. *Ibid.*
30. *Paropkari,* 1889, Editor - Shivdayal Singh, Vedic Yantralaya, Prayag.
31. *Arya Darshayitri Aur Yantri,* Imperial Native Press, Delhi, 1906, pp. 94-96.
32. *Arya Directory, op.cit.,* pp. 135-36, 148-49 and Arya Darshayitri Aur Yantri, *op.cit.,* pp. 94-96.
33. *Arya Kumar Sabha ki Niyamavali,* Vedic Yantralaya, Ajmer, 1915 and *Pancham Bharatvarshiya Arya Kumar Sammelan ki Karyavahi,* Vedic Yantralaya, Ajmer, 1924, pp. 5-6.
34. *Arya Directory, op.cit.,* p. 148, *Arya Martand,* July-August, 1940 and 15 January, 1947 and *Arya Prantiya Sabha,* Rajasthan, 1948-49, Annual Report.
35. S.C. Misra, *National Movement in a Princely State,* Pointer Publishers, Jaipur, 1993, p. 22.
36. J. Ried Graham, *op.cit.,* p. 145.
37. Sangeeta Sharma, *op.cit.,* p. 146.
38. Vishnulal Shastri, Handbook of Arya, Tract Department of the Pratinidhi Sabha, United Provinces, 1912, p. 88.

39. Indra Vidyavachaspati, *op.cit.*, Volume Two, pp. 176-77.
40. *Arya Pratinidhi Sabha, Rajasthan and Malwa, Annual Report, 1890-1900,* p. 1, Rajputana Press, Ajmer, 1900, Indra Vidyavachaspati, *op.cit.*, Volume Two, p. 82.
41. *Desh Hiteshi,* May 1882, Paropkarini Sabha Annual Report, 1892-93.
42. Indra Vidyavachaspati, *op.cit.*, Volume Two, p. 82
43. *Ibid,* p. 83.
44. *Ibid,* p. 81 and 214.
45. Computed from *Censuses of India, Rajputana States and Ajmer-Merwar for the year 1891, 1901, 1911, 1921 and 1931.*
46. Indra Vidyavachaspati, *op.cit.*, Volume One, p. 282.
47. *Stree Arya Samaj, Five Years Report 1928-33,* pp. 25-26.
48. *Report of Arya Samaj,* Jodhpur, 1905, p. 2.
49. File *Arya Samaj,* Barmer, 15B, 27 August, 1926.
50. *Arya Updeshak Pandit Gangadatt ka Bhraman,* Vedic Yantralaya, 1908, pp. 11-12 and Arya Pratinidhi Sabha, Rajasthan, File No. 11C.
51. *National Archives of* India, New Delhi, Rajputana Agency Record (Mewar) 1906-08, p. 32, *A Report on Mewar Arya Samaj* 1914, A booklet, Udaipur, 1915.
52. Indra Vidyavachaspati, *op.cit.*, Volume Two, pp. 84-86.
53. *Ibid,* p. 84.
54. *Ibid.*
55. Radhey Shyam Pareek, *Contribution of Arya Samaj in the making of Modern India 1875-1947,* Sarvadeshik Arya Pratinidhi Sabha, New Delhi, 1973, p. 105.
56. Kenneth W. Jones, *Arya Dharm - Hindu Consciousness in 19th Century Punjab,* Manohar, New Delhi, 2006, p. 109 and also Sheena Pall, *Din Dayal Sharma : The Formative Phase of the Sanatana Dharma Movement in late Nineteenth Century North*

India, Indian History Congresss, 63rd session, proceedings Volume, pp. 1012-20.

57. *Ibid,* pp. 111-112.
58. Radhey Shyam Pareek, *op.cit.,* p. 105.
59. *Indian Social Reformer,* May 17, 1914, pp. 535-38.
60. *Arya Pratinidhi Sabha, Rajasthan, Report 1922-29,* pp. 12-20, Recitation of *Gayatri Mantra, Om* and performing *Havanas* or *Agnihotra* were common activities of both the groups i.e. Aryasamajists and Sanatanis.
61. Indrda Vidyavachaspati, *op.cit.,* Volume Two, p. 87.
62. Harbilas Sarda, *op.cit.*, p. 62.
63. Chrirnjiva Bharadwaja, *op.cit.,* pp. 311-31.
64. Harbilas Sarda, *op.cit.*, p. 54.
65. *Ibid*, p. 64.
66. Chrirnjiva Bharadwaja, *op.cit.,* p 321. Swamiji had said that the food that is cooked in water is called *Sakharee,* while what is Cooke in milk or fried in butter is called *Nikhaaree* (i.e. nice). This is another fraud invented by these rouge. The food cooked in milk and butter is always pleasing to the taste; they (priestly people) have originated these fraudulent practices in order to fill their stomach with delicious, greasy articles of food, otherwise, whatever has been ripened by heat and time is called ripe (Nikharee) and whatever has not been cooked or ripened is called raw (Sakharee).
67. Shyamlal, *Untouchable Movement in India,* Subline Publications, Jaipur, 2002, p.39.
68. *Ibid,* pp. 40-41.
69. *Ibid,* p. 41.
70. *Harijan,* 2 August, 1934.
71. P.S. Choudhary, *Rajasthan between the two world wars,* Sri Ram Mehra & Co., Agra, 1968, p. 110.

72. Shyamlal, *Untouchable Castes in India*, Rawat Publication, Jaipur, Reprinted 2010, pp. 4-5.
73. *Ibid*, p. 5.
74. *Ibid*, pp. 6-7.
75. Sumesh Joshi, *Rajasthan Mein Swatantrata Sangram ke Senani*, Granthagar, Jaipur, 1973, p. 244.
76. Shyamlal, *Ambekar and Dalit Movement*, Rawat Publications, Jaipur, 2008, p. 19.
77. *Ibid.*
78. *Ibid*, p. 35.
79. Brij Kishore Sharma, *Social, Economic and Political Contribution of Caste Associations in Northern India*, Har - Anand Publications, New Delhi, 2008, p. 16
80. *National Archives of India*, New Delhi, *Home Deptt., File No. 490/31 Public*, 1931.
81. *Ibid.*
82. *Ibid, Home Politial Department (Confidential) Proceedings, Part A*, April, 1912, No. 4.
83. *Punjab Census Report*, 1911, p. 148.
84. *Ibid*, p. 149.
85. Lajpat Rai, *op.cit.*, p. 120.
86. Harbilas Sarda, *op.cit.*, p. 267.
87. Later it was reduced to three days only.
88. *Census Report for 1901*, Punjab, p. 87.
89. In Rajasthan there were three big social groups of Muslims Communities who followed the mixed culture of Hinduism and Islam. Among these the Kayamkhanis, Merats and Meos were included. Though, they were persuaded for conversion, but no encouraging results could be achieved.
90. J.T.F. Jordens, *Swami Shraddhanand : His Life and Causes*, Oxford University Press, Delhi, 1981, pp. 131-32.

91. *Arya Pratinidhi Sabha, Rajasthan*, Annual Report, 1891-92, p. 10.
92. *Ibid.*
93. *Arya Pratinidhi Sabha, Rajasthan, Annual Report,* 1911-12, p. 10.
94. *Ibid*, 1922-23, p. 9.
95. *Ibid*, 1928-29, p. 7.
96. *National Archive of India, New Delhi, Home-Political, Consultation No. 61, Part A, May, 1933.*
97. The Village must be Raibha because the village by name Raibna's reference could not be found.
98. J.T.F. Jordens, *Ibid*, as reference No. 90, pp. 131-32.
99. S.C. Misra, *op.cit.*, pp. 22-24.
100. *A Report on Bharatpur Arya Samaj, 1927-28,* pp. 1-6.
101. The village - Tasai,Tehsil - Kathumar district - Alwer. The Malkanas of this village were linked with the Malkanas of U.P. through matrimonial relations. This helped in easy conversion of Malkana of this village.
102. P.V. Kane, *History of Dharmashastra*, Vol. IV, Poona, 1973, pp. 268-69.
103. C.H. Heimsath, *Indian Natinionalism and Hindu Social Reforms*, Princeton, 1964, *Passim*.
104. C.T. Parvate, *Mahadev Govind Ranadey : A Biography,* Bombay, 1963, pp. 35-36.
105. P.V. Kane, *op.cit.*, Vol. II, Part I, Poona, 1941, pp. 385-87.
106. Lajpat Rai, *op.cit.*, pp. 117-18.
107. *Dayanand Commemoration Volume*, Edited - Svami Satya Prakash Sarasvati, Ajmer, 1983, p. 112.
108. Sangeeta Sharma, *op.cit.*, p. 147.
109. *Ibid*, and *Arya Stree Samaj, Ajmer ka Vivran,* 1906 to 1913, p. 2.

110. Five Yearly report of Stree Arya Samaj, Ajmer, 1906-11, pp. 2-63.

111. *Arya Pratinishi Sabha, Rajasthan, Annual Report, 1906-07*, p. 15 and Also *Arya Stree Samaj, Ajmer, Annual Report, 1913-14*, p. 3.

112. *Bharatpur State Gazette*, 25 October, 1926.

113. *Kota State Gazette,* 1 July, 1926.

114. *Census of India, 1931*, Volume 28, p. 110-11.

115. *Bikaner State Gazette (Extra Ordinary)*, 10 December, 1928.

116. *Jodhpur State Gazette,* 1 March, 1930.

117. *Speeches and Writings : Har Bilas Sarda*, Ajmer, 1944, pp. 33-40.

118. *Gazette of India*, 15th March, 1938, An Amendment in Child Marriage Restraint Act No. 7.

119. Sangeeta Sharma, *op.cit.*, p. 111.

120. *Ibid*, p. 106.

121. Prakash Vyas, *Rajasthan ka Samajik Itihas*, Panchsheel Prakashan, Jaipur, 1988, pp. 286-87.

122. The Hindi weekly Journal *Bharatveer* (a government publication). Its publication was started by the state Administration under the able guidance of Maharaja Kishan Singh of Bharatpur from 16th November 1926. The information about the Social Reforms Act available in the *Balkank* of Bharatveer, No. 3, 1927. p. 2-3.

123. *Ibid*, Also see S.C. Misra, *op.cit.*, p. 15.

124. S.C. Misra, *Ibid.*

125. Sangeeta Sharma, *op.cit.*, p. 111.

126. *Anath Rakshak*, 10 May, 1922. A Report on Vidhwa Ashram, Kesar Ganj, Ajmer.

127. *First Report of Vanita Ashram*, 1926-27, Vedic Yantralaya, Ajmer, 1927, pp. 1-2.

128. *Ibid.*

129. *Vidhwa Bandhu*, December, 1927, pp. 11-12, Arya Martand, 4 July, 1928, *Arya Mitra*, May, 1925.

130. Sangeeta Sharma, *op.cit.*, p. 113.

131. Chirajiva Bhardwaja, *op.cit.*, p. 93.

132. Ganga Prasad Upadhyay, *op.cit.*, p. 100.

133. Sangeeta Sharma, *op.cit.*, p. 141.

134. See Chapter III.

135. *Arya Stree Samaj*, Ajmer, A Report, 1928, Vedic Yantralaya, Ajmer, 1928, p. 2.

136. *The Hindustan Times*, 5 February, 1930.

137. *Speeches and Writings : Harbilas Sarda*, p. 28.

138. The figures of literacy, according to the Census Report of 1911, stood as follows : Males : 100 per 1000; Females : 10 per 1000; an average of 58 per 1000 of the total population.

139. Lajpat Rai, *op.cit.*, pp. 116-17.

140. Sita Ram Singh, *Nationalism And Social Reform in India (1889-1920)*, Ranjit Printers & Publishers, Delhi, 1968, p. 171.

141. L.S.S. O' Malley, *Modern India and the West,* London, 19140, p. 695.

142. Chiranjiva Bhardwaja, *op.cit.*, pp. 110-13.

143. *Ibid.*

144. *Ibid.*

145. *Srimati Paropakarini Sabha ka Pratham Adhiveshan*, Pratham Report, 1883, Vedic Yantralaya, Prayag, 1884, p. 2.

146. *Ibid*, 1887-88, p. 2.

147. G.C. Verma has written that on 8th February, 1888 the Ashram School was opened, G.C. Verma, *Modern Education : Its Growth and development in Rajasthan - 1818-1983*, Publication Scheme, Jaipur, 1984, p. 304.

148. *Arya Pratinidhi Sabha, Rajasthan, Report, 1935-38, Arya Martand*, 1 June, 1948.

149. *Arya Putri Pathshala, Varshik Report, 1898-99*, Vedic Yantralaya, Ajmer, 1899-, p. 1

150. *Administrative Report of Ajmer-Merwara, 1912-13,* p. 82.

151. *Shri Mathura Prasad Gulab Devi Arya Kanya Phathshala, Ajmer, A Report, 1905-06*, pp. 3-8.

152. *Arya Pratinidhi Sabha, Rajasthan Annual Report, 1912-13*, Vedic Yantralaya, Ajmer, 1914, pp. 25-26.

153. *Shri Mathura Prasad Gulab Devi Arya Kanya Pathshala, Ajmer, Trivarshiya Report, September, 1923 to October 1926*, Vedic Yantralaya, Ajmer, 1927. p. 5.

154. Sangeeta Sharma, *op.cit.*, p. 170.

155. Gulab Devi donated her entire life, resources and energies not only to the women education but also to the women's cause. *Rajasthan Stree Shiksha Nidhi* was also founded by her. During 1945-47 she with the association of Bhawari Bai, Siddhkunvar Bai, Sukhda Dev, Ramni Bai and others propgated the importance of education in the rural areas by organizing camps. Hansa Bai and Rameshwari founded a number of small Arya Kanya Pathshalas at Pisangan, Kharwa, Srinagar, Jawaja and other towns. In 1938, she presided over the Arya Mahila Sammelan. Through all these activities she facilitated the resurgence of Hindu womenhood. She was also popularly known as chachiji.

156. *Arya Pratinidhi Sabha, Rajasthan, A Report, 1913*, pp. 16-17.

157. *Ibid*, 1936-37, p. 17.

158. Sangeeta Sharma, *op.cit.*, p. 148.

159. *Rajasthan State Archives, Bikaner, Bharatpur Records*, Deptt. of Education, File No. 13/18, Report by Principal Arya Kanya Vidyalaya to Education Deptt. 6th July, 1928.

160. *Ibid*, File No. 18/B, 12th August, 1945 and 25th August, 1945. Also *File No. 7*, 8th December, 1947.

161. *Arya Samaj*, Jodhpur, A Report, 8th March, 1931, p. 2 (hand written).

162. *Arya Samaj, Bikaner, Varshik Prativedan*, 1914-15, pp. 3-4 and 19285-29, 1932-33 and 1945-46.

163. Pratibha Jain, Sangeeta Sharma and Archana Garg, *Liberation of Women - An Arya Samajist Perspective,* Project Report, Centre for Women's Studies, University of Rajasthan, Jaipur (Date and year are not mentioned), p. 24.

164. Ibid, p. 25.

5

Philanthropy, Education and Mass Consciousness

Swami Dayanand was the great radical reformer. His religious and social reforms were not limited to abolition of evils existed in religion and society. He envisaged over all regeneration of India as leader of humanity. He created spirit of self-respect, self confidence and self-esteemed among the people of India and also generated a new consciousness in all spheres of national life. He himself was a great philanthropist because he envisaged welfare and salvation for larger masses. Swami Dayanand had told : I am not anxious about my salvation . I am particularly anxious for the salvation of those lakhs of people who are poor, weak and are suffering. I do not mind if I may have to take birth again and again. I will attain salvation when these people will attain it. He had also told that : The world is fettered by the chain forged by superstition and ignorance. I have come to snap asunder that chain to set slaves at liberty. It is contrary to my mission to have people deprived of their freedom.[1]

Thus he had strong inclination towards downtrodden, poor, ignorant, destitute, widows, orphans etc.. During his extensive visits of rural and backward areas he came across various unprivileged people and groups who were in dire need of help from privileged and affluent people for survival.

Philanthropy

The concept of philanthropy basically involves the services to the humanity by the capable people. There were certain instances when Swami Dayanand himself did charity and also inspired the others to do so. The Christian missionaries were very active on the front of philanthropy, because through such activities they were converting the poor and destitute people into the Christianity. Swamiji very soon visualised the fact. This had been also a factor for adopting the philanthropic programme by the Arya Samaj. Swamiji's compassion towards humanity and mankind was unparalleled. He had a tender heart. It was full of pity for the people around him, who led wretched and miserable lives. The woes of the people, their extreme poverty and their helplessness due to subjection to foreign rule and priestly domination, caused him pain and made him miserable. He devoted his whole life, his time and his energy to their betterment. He gave no thought to his own comforts or his personal welfare.

In September 1878, while Swami Dayanand was in Meerut condemned the Brahmins and priestly class that they have not the slightest pity on the poor and miserable condition of the people of this country. During the Kumbha fair at Haridwar in 1879 he expressed his pains about sufferings of Indian people that : Brother what can be a more heartrending pain than the fact that this country is being ruined by the sighs of the widows, the piercing cries of the orphans, and the slaughter of cows.[2]

Later, when he heard that an old village woman threw the dead body of her son in the Ganges, as she had no money to cremate it, tears came into Swamiji's eyes, and he exclaimed in his misery, "Ah our country has become so poor that we cannot even afford to have fuel to cremate a dead body". On another occasion Swamiji said "Foreign Rule has so completely drained the wealth of India that the country has now been reduced to utter poverty."[3]

In a discussion with a *sadhu* Swami Dayanand told that : There are thousands who have never had a full meal, who have only rags to cover their bodies. Millions of men, poor villagers, like cows and buffaloes pass their lives in huts surrounded by dirt and rubbish. Hundreds die by roadside uncared for. Mahtma, if you want to love Atma, think of them, and look after them, as you do of your own limbs. They alone who do this are mahatmas and entitled to be called lovers of Atma.[4] Thus, it may be said that though the service to humanity one can see the reality of Atma. Hence, Swami Dayanand gave priority to serve and help the poor, destitute, hungry, orphan, widow, needy, ill etc.. During his life time Swami Dayanand not only initiated philanthropic work but also did his utmost to promote the same. Lala Lajpat Rai has summed up that. Outside Christian circles the Arya Samaj was the first purely Indian association to organize Orphanages and Widows Homes. The first Hindu orphanage was established at Ferozepur, in the Punjab, in the lifetime of the Founder of the Samaj; it still retains its position as the premier Hindu orphanage in India, has splendid commodious buildings, all erected by private charity, and maintains schools and workshops for training boys and girls. There are several other orphanage run on similar lines in northern India, controlled and managed by the Arya Samaj; and, besides these, many Hindu institutions and orphanages spread all over India bear the impress and influence of the Arya Samaj, and are indebted for their birth and efficiency to Arya Samajists.[5]

Since the inception the Arya Samaj was a philanthropic organisation and it's moto was public welfare. Therefore, it had devised various ways and means for the same. The Arya Samaj also organised famine relief works for famine stricken people.[6]

The philanthropic work of Arya Samaj was not, however confined to famine relief, but included various kind of social service. In the time of epidemic it organised medical relief, nursing to sick and helping in the disposal of the dead.

Lajpat Rai has depicted that : At the time of the great earthquake in the Kangra Valley in 1904 it organised relief on a large scale for its victims, and earned the thanks of the people and the Government. In this calamity the Arya Samajists were the first to reach the afflicted area. This example has, within recent years, been largely followed by other organisations, and there is now a network of social-service agencies throughout India. The Arya Samaj was the pioneer in social service work in an organised form and on a large scale, at least in northern India.[7] The social and philanthropic work of Arya Samaj was inspired by the ideas of Swami Dayanand. Dayanand had a feeling heart. One day while he was delivering a lecture, someone brought the news that a fire had destroyed the huts of Bharatpuria Chamars, who lived on the Anasagar Ghati at Ajmer and that they were now homeless. Swamiji gave some money for their relief and asked people present to give money as charity, and good sum was at once collected.[8]

Orphanage : The foundation of the orphanages was one of the major activity of Arya Samaj in the direction of philanthropic works. It was part of the will (*Swikar Patra*) of Swami Dayanand made by him for the foundation of the Paropkarini Sabha. In the third objective it was clearly stated that : Helping and providing in the protection, feeding, and education of the orphans and destitute of India.[9] The problem of orphans was linked with the famines, because due to death by starvation and diseases large number of people perished.[10] Thus, large number of orphans and destitute were left. The Christian missionaries were running the relief work for such people. The Arya Samaj began relief works in Northern India.

Lala Lajpat Rai had mentioned the Arya Samaj was the first non-Christian private agency which started a non-official movement for the relief of distress caused by famine.[11]

The first Arya Samaj orphanage was founded by Swami Dayanand Saraswati himself in 1877 at Ferozpur in Punjab.[12] In January, 1895 the first Dayanand *Anathalaya* in Rajasthan in the memory of Swami Dayanand was founded in Ajmer at Kesarganj.[13] Reading and writing was compulsory to the child inmates of the *Anathalaya* from the seven years age to onwards. After the age of ten years they were given training in weaving of cloth, carpet etc. and sewing, dyeing, embroidery etc. to make them self reliant. The said *anathalaya* was functional from the funds collected in donations from the public mainly from *Thakurs* (Jagirdars), Seths and Traders.[14]

In 1901 the Arya Samaj founded the Victoria Anathalaya in Bharatpur in the memory of Queen Victoria. It was provided the building by the State.[15] In addition to this the orphanages were also founded in Jodhpur, Bikaner, Sujangarh, Phulera, Mandawa etc. by the local Arya Samajes. The Ajmer orphanage also started a monthly journal known as *'Anath Rakshak'* to propagate its aims and activites. The orphanages organized relief works to the famine stricken people during the famine of 1899 known as "*Chhapania Akal*". The intensity of famine in Rajputana was severely felt. Therefore, the Lahore Arya Samaj deputed one of its younger members to proceed to Rajputana and ascertain on the spot in what way and to what extent they could render help, and whether it was possible to enlist local sympathy in their cause in the famine - stricken areas themselves. On this mission Lala Dewan Chand Chaddha travelled to Jodhpur, and stayed at many places (amongst them Kishangarh, Ajmer, Beawar, Pali etc.) to inspect the famine relief camps. He spent altogether a month in Rajputana, and on his return gave a graphic and touching account of his experiences which brought tears to many eyes and stirred almost the whole of Lahore to take immediate and vigorous action for the succour of the unfortunate Hindu waifs and orphans of Rajputana.[16]

In several Native States Arya Samajic workers waited upon high officials, and tried to impress upon them their duty towards the orphans and other destitute children in their territories, explaining how necessary it was, in the interests of the States, to keep the children on their own soil and to save them in that distressing period, not only from perishing by starvation, but also from being carried off to distant places to be converted to alien faiths.[17]

The missionaries were waging a noble battle, and it was not for us to stir up agitation against them in Rajputana. To save even a few hundreds, we found it necessary to convey them to the Punjab, where they were sure to be given sufficient food and clothing for survival till the end of the famine. But the Punjab itself was at this time in crying need of help, as some parts were seriously affected by the famine. Notwithstanding the efforts of the Government, there were still some who required external aid to avert starvation or conversion.[18]

Valuable work was done by the Hissar Arya Samaj and the Bhiwani Hindu Orphanage. Under the leadership of the late Lala Chandu Lal, the President, and Lal Churamani, their Secretary, they relieved hundred of children and fought a noble battle against death and misery. For Rajput children the Relief Committee submitted representations and memorials to the Commissioner of Ajmer-Merwara, who was also the Agent to the Governor-General in Rajputana, and to the Deputy Commissioner of Beawar; but elicited no response. Arya Samajic workers applied in person to the local officers in charge of the famine relief camps, but in vain, although there was reason to believe that large numbers of Hindu children were periodically made over to Christian missionaries and sent by them to distant places in India. In Bombay, workers travelled as far as Surat and Baroda, and strove to arouse the Hindu public to a sense of duty towards the little ones of their own community, who in dire distress, needed their help and sympathy. These visits and the readiness of the Arya Samaj to take charge of as many children as could be entrusted to its care, had due effect. The reasons for our failure to get children from Government famine relief works need not be set forth in detail, the most important being that the missionaries were everywhere too powerful for us.[19]

Lala Lajpat Rai also appeared before the Indian Famine Commission appointed by the Government of India in 1901 and he put the problem related to famines and orphans. When Mr. F.A. Nicholson one of the Commissioners asked him that you are the Honorary Secretary of the orphanage in Ferozepore? Then he answered that I am connected with other orphanages as well.[20] He advanced his argument that the orphans and destitute taken by the different institutions for shelter and relief were converted to the different religions. Agreeing with the views expressed by Lajpat Rai, the Commission recommended that deserted children and orphans should not be made over to persons or institutions of a different religion until all efforts to find persons and institutions of their own religions willing to take charge of them have failed.[21]

Cow Protection

Another very important teaching of Dayanand was the Protection of Cows. This teaching is based not on any religious tenet, cows being no more sacred than horses or any other animals, but on the supreme usefulness of cows to humanity. In the interests of humanity, of mankind as a whole, of men women and children in every country, slaughter of cows for food should be abolished. Wherever he went, he preached this doctrine. Cow Protection is an economic matter of supreme importance to mankind and not a purely religious affair.[22] In a verse of *Yajurveda* it has been clearly mentioned that : In order to get wealth and food grains, may cows, which should never be slaughtered, become more and more numerous. May cows with their calves be free from ordinary diseases as well as such dangerous disease as tuberculosis. May sinful people and thieves never become masters of cows. May the cows of those persons who protect them go on increasing, and may they have long lives. Oh God protect the cattle of the virtuous.[23]

It is to be noted that Dayanand nowhere pleads for the protection of the Cows on the ground that the cow is a sacred animal. His whole argument rests on the usefulness of the cow to man. In man's own vital interest, the cow should be protected. It is not to sentiment he appeals, but to man's material welfare. In order to reach their full physical, mental and spiritual growth, men should give up slaughter of cows.

Dayanand's concerned for cow-protection appeared early in his ascetic life. In 1866, on his first visit to Ajmer he talked about it to colonel Brookes, Agent to the Governor-General in Rajputana. His argument was already clearly established : the killing of cows was bad because of its economic consequence, as a dead cow provided little food whereas a live one provided for many.[24] Colonel Brookes admitted cow killing was harmful, but he was powerless in the matter and asked Swamiji to see the Governor General of India and gave Swamiji a letter of introduction addressed to the Governor General.[25] In 1873 in Farrukhabad he asked Mr. Muir, the Lieutenant-General of the N.W. Provinces, if he would use his influence to promote the ban on cow-slaughter when he became a member of the India Council in London.[26] He referred to the question in two places in his first *Satyarth Prakash*.[27] One of the duties of a king is to prevent the destruction of useful animals, because the people depend on them, an argument he elaborated in the section in which he criticized the British Raj. There he stated in full his economic argument : one cow can in the long run provide food for a hundred thousand, whereas its carcass scarcely feeds a hundred. The cow should not be killed because it is the basic condition of the good health and nutrition of all the people. The Swami restated this theme occasionally in the course of a lecture, for instance in Poona[28] but it certainly was not yet a major concern of his.

It was only in 1877 that cow-protection became a major issue and that Dayanand started to devote special lectures to it. In fact, it was precisely in the beginning of that year that a group of Hindus sent a plea asking the Government to stop the slaughter of cows. When the Government answered that it could do nothing in the matter, Harischandra Bharatendu wrote bitterly about the injustice of a Government that favoured a minority of Muslims and Christians against an overwhelming majority of Hindus.[29] In 1879 the Swami made the following statement in Farrukhabad : "There is no unity among us, that is why cow-slaughter keeps going on. If we petitioned the government all together, could it not come to an end?[30] However, he did not take any specific action at that time.

In early 1881 Swami Dayanand take the decision to launch a systematic agitation against cow-slaughter. In the same period he wrote a pamphlet (booklet) entitled *"Gokarunanidhi"* (ocean of kindness to the cow.). The first half of the booklet sets out at length the case for a ban on the slaughter of cows and other useful animals. The economic argument is elaborated and supported by scriptural arguments, and opponents' points are answered in detail. The fundamental ethical principle is simple : actions that cause injury to others are sinful. The killing of animals, in particular of the cow, leads to harm in two different ways. It causes the ruin of society by undermining the production of the best possible food; it also does untold damage by destroying the ecology : 'by the destruction of the natural order of the universe'. This line of argument shows the Swami's concern for a healthy and pollution-free life, although its economics may be rejected. Animal slaughter, he says, leads to a greater dependence on grains, the cultivation of which increases wastage that pollutes earth, air, and water. Animals, even non-domesticated ones, have an important role in the cycle of nature : they clean up more than an army of sweepers could, and they are at the same time a great source of natural fertilizer. The protection of forests, which promote better rainfall and a purer atmosphere. Dayanand stressed that his argument thus encompassed the protection of the whole animal world, but he stated that the latter could only gradually be implemented. The immediate agitation was for the protection of the cow, which was selected by the ancient Aryans for special care because among the animals it is supremely useful, conferring the greatest benefits on man. In this work the Swami also stated his final attitude towards the consumption of meat : every form of it is sinful. The plea of the opponent, that a ritual context makes it morally right, was now rejected, and it was affirmed that the *Veda* do not prescribe any rite involving killing or meat-eating.[31]

The second part of the pamphlet contains the laws and by-laws of a society called the *Gokrishyadirakshini Sabha* 'for the protection of kine, agriculture etc.', usually shortened to *Gorakshini Sabha.* All men who wish to devote their effort and help by body, mind, or riches, to this work for the benefit of all' were invited to become members, and any society with similar aims was urged to associate itself. The Swami was very concerned that membership be kept open to all, as the explicit instructions to the secretary clearly show : 'It should be borne in mind that a member may belong to any community or group whatsoever, and that any community or organization affiliated should have a representative in the executive committee.' The document gives details of membership, organization and management. Such a society was immediately started at Agra, and several more followed soon, but the exact details are not available.[32]

In his book *'Gaukarunanidhi'* he has explained the benefits of the protection of cows purely on economic grounds. He adopts a mathematical approach to the problem and says that if out of two cows, one yielded two seers of milk and the other twenty, then the mean yield of each would be eleven seers. Thus in a month the quantity of milk would be almost eight maunds and a quarter. Barring the period when the cow ceases to give milk, the quantity of milk will be ninetynine maunds. One thousand nine hundred and eighty persons can be fed on this milk, if it is boiled and sufficient quantity of rice and sugar mixed in it. Thus Dayanand explained in details his view point for the protection of cow.

He further emphasizes the usefulness of the male calves. A farmer can produce, in a year with the aid of a pair of bulls, 200 maunds of corn and with three pairs, 600 maunds. On an average, a bull works for about eight year which means that three pairs of bulls will help to grow 4800 maunds of corn during their life time. Now taking into account the quantity of corn for one meal of a man say, a pond and a half of corn, the corn grown with the help of three pairs of bulls during their life time will be enough to feed 2,56,000 persons at a time. But if a cow is killed only 80 persons can be fed on her flesh. "Hence to kill such a useful animal for the selfish satisfaction of a few and thereby deprive innumerable people of the benefit derived from it is a great crime and great sin".[33]

Apart from the booklet *Gaukarunanidhi* and the Gaurakshani Sabha Swami Dayanand's campaign had a third line of attack : he planned to give impetus and strength to the movement by collecting at least a hundred thousand signatures to a memorial which was to be presented to queen Victoria, the British Parliament, and the Governor General of India. The document published in Bombay on 14 March 1882 outlined the case against cow-slaughter and asked the Government 'to quickly put an end to the slaughter of cows, bullocks and buffaloes'. Hundreds of copies of this appeal were sent with an accompanying letter from the Swami to the Samajes, to leading personalities and institutions, and to the rulers of the princely states. It is difficult to assess the overall success of this campaign as it has to be judged from the few remaining letters that refer to it. In some places, the result was very quick and encouraging. There is a report of 40,000 signatures from Mewar, of 60,000 in Patiala and a letter from Bombay mentions over 15,000. The Swami complained of the slackness of some Aryas, e.g. those of Meerut and also mentioned that his mail was being tampered with. He was trying to communicate a sense of urgency; he felt that the Memorial, to be fully effective, should be presented during Lord Ripon's governorship which was due to run out in 1884. However, his untimely death put an end to his own efforts, but on the whole the agitation generated was strong enough to bother the Indian Government.[34]

The cow protection movement got heavy support in Rajasthan and even the Sanatanis also joined this movement. The Arya Samaj organisation leads this movement. The movement also got the personal support of several ruling princes. Lakhs of signatures were obtained including those of several Ruing Princes such as the Maharana of Udaipur, Maharaja of Jodhpur and the Maharao of Bundi.[35] Though, the movement got setback by premature death of Swamiji, but the direction set by his serious and sincere efforts continued to work in motion. And even after the death of Swamiji the movement continued vigorously. To save the cows from slaughter Swamiji himself established *Gaushalas* in Punjab, Rajasthan and U.P.. The *Gaushala* of Rewari is one of the oldest among the *Gaushalas* established by him. Being inspired by him several workers took up the cause of cow protection and several *Gaushalas* were established at various places.[36]

Education

Much has already been written in the previous chapters on educational activities of Swami Dayanand Saraswati and Arya Samaj. Education received serious attention of Swamiji because it was an important means of salvation of humanity. The task before him was to make the people realize their degradation and ignorance and help them to regain strength, self confidence and a will to break the fetters that bound them and win back their spiritual, social and political freedom. He devoted himself, therefore, to equipping and fitting them physically and morally to fight for their liberty and their inheritance. In a plea for the education of all four classes, of men and women, he predicted that until all were educated, there is no hope for the prosperity of Aryavarta : education had to be the key to its renaissance.

Though Swamiji pleaded for education of all, but his stress was on the education of weaker sections of the society i.e. women and dalits. The educational activities of the Arya Samaj in Rajasthan has been discussed in Chapter - IV of the present study. The other important works and achievements in the field of education which could not be covered are being discussed in the present chapter- V.

Swami Dayanand had devoted chapter - 3 of Satyarth Prakash for education. In the opening para he had said that : Is is the highest duty of parents, preceptors and relatives to adorn children with good sound education, nobility of character, refinement of manners, and amiability of temper.[37]

The wearing of jewellery adds no beauty to the soul. It only arouses vanity and other lower passions, gives rise to fear of robbery and may even be the cause of death. Many a child has been known to lose its life at the hands of cutthroats because of wearing jewellery.[38] Swami Dayanand had said that "Blessed are the men and women whose minds are centred on the acquisition of knowledge; who possess sweet and amiable tempers; who cultivate truthfulness and other similar virtues; who are free from vanity and uncleanness; who enlighten the minds of those who are in ignorance; whose chief delight consists in promoting the happiness of others by the preaching of truth, by generous distribution of knowledge without fee or reward, and who are engaged in altruistic work as prescribed by the Vedas."[39]

Swamiji had conclusively remarked that : knowledge alone is the inexhaustible treasure; the more you spend it, the more it grows. All other treasures run out by spending, and the claimants inherit their shares as well. Thieves cannot steal this treasure, nor, can anyone inherit it. It is the chief duty of the rulers, as well as of the ruled, to protect and augment this treasure.[40]

Though, swami Dayanand gave stress on indigenous education but he was not opposed to the study of English and Western sciences. But his priority was for indigenous education. He himself inaugurated the mission of education in his life time by establishing Sanskrit and Vedic Pathsahals. Much has been written on the educational works of Arya SAmaj in Punjab and U.P., but very less is known about its educational activities in Rajasthan.

As has been mentioned that Ajmer emerged as main centre of the activities of Arya Samaj in Rajasthan. Obviously, the educational efforts of Arya Samaj also began from Ajmer in a systematic way. In the first session of the Paropakarini Sabha on 28th December, 1883 a decision was taken to establish the Dayanand Ashram at Ajmer in the memory of Dayanan Saraswati. It was to be equipped with Anglo Vedik School, library, museum, printing press, book store, orphanage and lecture hall.[41] Here it is important to note that before the said decision of the Paropkarini Sabha the Lahore Arya Samaj on 9th November, 1883, in a meeting unanimously adopted the proposal to found an Anglo-Vedic College in honour of Swami Dayanand's memory.[42] And on 2nd June, 1886 the D.A.V. School at Lahore came into being. Two years later intermediate classes were opened and by 1894 the B.A. classes were added to it.[43] No doubt the decision of the Paropkarini Sabha was also influenced by the decision of Lahore Arya Samaj. Thus the D.A.V. School and College Lahore became a pioneer institution for the educational endeavourer of Arya Samaj in all India.

On 10th February, 1888 the Dayanand Ashram School was opened in the Arya Samaj Bhawan, Kesar Ganj, Ajmer. Initially the Paropakarini Sabha took its overall responsibility including financial burden. In 1889 the subject of English was included in the curriculum of the school, therefore, the school was renamed as 'Dayanand Ashram Anglo-Vedic School'. The objectives of the DAAV school were as follows :

(a) To encourage, improve, and enforce the study of Hindu literature.

(b) To encourage and enforce the study of classical Sanskrit and of the Vedas.

(c) To encourage and enforce the study of English literature, and sciences, both theoretical and applied.

To provide means for giving technical education in connection with the Dayanand Anglo-Vedic Institution as far as is not inconsistent with the proper accomplishment of the first object.[44]

Thus, with the establishment of Dayanand Ashram Anglo-Vedic School the D.A.V. educational movement of Arya Samaj began from Ajmer. This educational movement of Arya Samaj at Ajmer received financial help and encouragement from the *Jagirdars* of Masuda and Shahpura. Pratap Singh of Marwar also supported the educational venture of Arya Samaj with all possible means.[45] Funds were also collected through contribution and donations. The B.B. and C.I. Railways also began to give grant to this school as the children of Railways employees were admitted in this. The education Department (D.P.I.) also extended grant to the school.[46]

The story of its rapid growth from primary school to a multi faculty college during the course of the next half a century appears like a magic tale. The magic however, lies in the high ideals which the sponsors always kept before them and the dedicated spirit with which they worked for its progress. Non-communal in outlook, open to rich and poor alike, due stress on moral and cultural along with secular education these were some of the special features of the D.A.V. School, Ajmer, which attracted towards it students of all castes and creeds resulting in its upgrading to the middle school standard in 1892 with 208 boys on rolls and to the High school status in 1897 with 500 scholars.[47] The number of students reached to 1500 by 1940, hence the school was upgraded upto Intermediate standard.[48] Thus, the D.A.V. Inter College came into being.

In 1915 Arya Sanskrit Pathshala was founded at Vijaynagar by the Arya Samaj. In 1923 Dayanand Vedic Pathshala came into being at Nasirabad which was renamed as Dayanand Anglo-Vedic Madhyamik Pathshala in 1925 when the subject of English was introduced in the studies. Virjanand Primary school was also founded in 1940 at Ajmer which got the status of middle school in 1945. In addition to these about one and half dozen Vedic schools of primary level were functional in

Ajmer till 1947 with the individual efforts of the devotees of Arya Samaj. None of the educational institutes/schools except D.A.V. School/College was given the financial grants by the government.

The Jaipur Arya Samaj inaugurated its educational mission in the opening year of twentieth century by establishing 'Arya Achhut Pathshala' in February, 1901 in the Hathroi basti of Jaipur[49], which was conferred the status or 'Dayanand Arya Middle School'. Seven primary level *Pathshalas* were also established in Purani Basti (1906) and Kolion ki Kothi (1908). The mission for education of untouchable by Jaipur Arya Samaj remained continue and Arya Pathshalas were also opened in Topkahan Desh (1926), Jhotwara Road (1928), Heeda ki Mori (1932), Surbadi (1937), Harijan Basti (1937) and Khatik Gali areas of Jaipur city.[50] In 1939 the Arya Harijan Pathshala was established in Kishanpol.

The Arya Samaj schools were also functional in various villages and towns of Jaipur State. Among these the Vedic and Angol-Vedic schools were founded at Jhunjhunu, Rajgarh, Mandawa, Navalgarh, Bhagwat Garh, Uniara, Bandikui and Phulera. The Arya Samaj school of Jobner had special significance and it rose to prominence second to the D.A.V. school, Ajmer. One of the prominent Thakur of Jaipur State Thakur Karan Singh of Jobner on 3rd April, 1891 founded the Kshtriya Anglo Sanskrit Middle School in the memory of Swami Dayanand Saraswati. In 1911 this school was raised upto the level of High School and it was renamed as 'Dayanand Anglo-Vedic High School, Jobner.'[51]

The Arya Pathshala at Bahdikui had special significance because it was founded in March, 1905 to combat activities of the Christian missionaries. Bandikui was one of the main administrative centres of Bombay, Baroda and Central India Railway, where sizable number of Christian people were working in the railway. These included Anglo-Indians, Anglo and European people. In 1892 a Catholic Padri Mr. John Trail began teaching Bible. In August 1905 two Arya Samaj brothers viz. Madhusudan and Harisudan founded the 'Arya Prathmik Pathshala' in the Arya Samaj Bhawan which received the status of a middle school in 1937.[52]

In eastern Rajasthan the Arya Samaj educational movement flourished in Bharatpur State. The first Arya Sanskrit Pathshala was began by Bharatpur Arya Samaj on 3rd July, 1904 with a grant of Rs. 10/- per month from state's *Dan* department (Deptt. of Octroi). In 1927 another school known as 'Dayanand Arya Pathshala' was established in the Arya Samaj Bhawan, Bharatpur. The Arya Samaj school of Ballbahgarh (a village in Weir Tehsil) had got prominence which was founded in 1923 as a primary school named as Arya Vidyalaya. The said school was given the status of middle school in 1926 and in February, 1947 it became High School. Hence it was renamed as 'Dayanand Anglo-Vedic High School.[53] Arya Pathshala was also established in Deeg in 1923 for the untouchable students. In 1924 a middle school name as Dayanand Brahm Vidyalaya was founded in Bhusawar, which became High School in 1941.[54]

The educational activities of Arya Samaj in Jodhpur began in 1904 with the establishment of 'Dayanand Vedic Pathshala'. In 1912 'Marwar Gurukul' was founded by Swami Darshananand at Mandore.[55] In 1904 'Shrimad Dayanand Arya Vedic Pathshala' was founded at Sojat town which rose to the status of middle school in 1925. In 1931 Dayanand Vedic Schools for boys and girls were founded in Sardarpura colony of Jodhpur. Though, a Vedic Pathshala was also founded in Pali town in 1934 but due to financial constraints the same was closed in 1938.[56] In addition to these the local Arya Samajs at each village and town developed the provision for religious and cultural education and practices.

In Mewar the Raja of Shahpura took the cause of Vedic education and on the advice of Swami Dayanand Saraswati in May 1883 when he promised to appoint a preacher on Rs. 30/- per menses to preach Vedic faith.[57] In 1891 he founded the Vernacular middle school on the pattern of Vedic education.[58] The significant Arya Samaj education centre in Mewar had been the Gurukul of Chittor which was founded in the year 1927. The pattern of Gurukul education was entirely new and revolutionary in the history of Modern Indian education.

It was felt that in the D.A.V. schools/colleges enough emphasis was not being laid on the study of Sanskrit literature and the Vedas. Swami Shraddhanand alias Mahtma Munshiram devised the scheme of Gurukul education. On 26th Novemeber 1898 Munshiram's motion to open a Gurukul was formally accepted by the general body of Arya Pratinidhi Sabha, Punjab.[59] On 16th May, 1900 the Gurukul was officially inaugurated at Gujaranwala with twenty boys, among whom were Munshiram's, sons Harishchandra and Indra.[60] Later on in 1902 the Gurukul Kangri at Haridwar came into being.[61] On 4th March, 1902, twenty Brahmcharis including Munshiram's sons who were studying at Gujaranwala were brought here. Thus, the Gurukul Kangri came into existence with Pandit Ganga Dutt as Acharya.[62]

In 1927 at the time of Silver Jublee celebration of the Gurukul Kangri one Yudhishthar entered into Sanyas Ashram who was given the name Swami Vratanand. He took an oath to devote his whole life for the establishment and functioning of Gurukul at Chittor as desired by Mahrishi Dayanand.[63] On 2nd February, 1927 Swami Vratanand reached at Udaipiur where in his speech he told that it is difficult to found Gurukul at Chittor right now, therefore, I shall try to found the same in Udaipur.[64] Thus, with 8 students in the Arya Samaj Bhawan the Gurukul at Udaipur was founded on 11th July, 1927.[65] The basic objective of the Gurukula was to produce and prepare Arya preachers. On 8th October, 1929 the Gurukul was shifted to Chittor.[66] It was situated on the *Sangam* of Gambhiri and Bedach rivers in Chittor.

An extensive network of Vedic schools of basic primary level education came into being in the princely states of Alwar, Dholpur, Kota, Jhalawar, Bikaner etc.. Through these schools the Arya Samaj created religious, social, cultural and even political consciousness in Rajasthan.

Mass Consciousness

Through religious and social reforms the Arya Samaj created a new mass consciousness which immensely contributed in rise and growth of national and freedom movement. The story of the rise and growth of Arya Samaj movement in Rajasthan is different from Punjab and U.P. and elsewhere due to peculiar social and political conditions. The major part of Rajasthan was under the occupation of princely states where no public society or organization was allowed to be founded. Thus, the Arya Samaj in Rajasthan was the first modern organization which took footings in the areas of Rajasthan ruled by the princely rulers. But due to rigid and narrow political and social outlook of rulers there was limited scope for modern organization to function freely. Hence the progress of the expansion of Arya Samaj remained slow. Initially the princely rulers supported the activities of Swami Dayanand and Arya Samaj but later on they began to put obstacles in the way. Being centrally administered the province of Ajmer-Merwara was under the direct British rule where all kinds of civil rights to the residents were available. Therefore, Ajmer was the most suitable place congenial for the growth of Arya Samaj movement in Rajasthan. All the modern amenities like education, health, market, transport, civic life etc. equipped the city of Ajmer. Thus, under the British influence it was emerging as a modern city in Rajasthan. The sizable number of modern middle class people was among its residents. Introduction of Railway in Rajasthan also helped in the emergence of mass consciousness. The trade union activities in the Railways began in the last decade of 19th Century. This also contributed to the growth of social, national, and political consciousness.

There were two distinctive features in the rise and growth of Arya Samaj Movement in Rajasthan viz. (i) it did not faced any organized or unorganized opposition from the *Santani* and traditional Hindus and (ii) there was not internal rift and split within the Arya Samajists. Moreover, the programmes and activities of Arya Samaj since the inception were planned in the manner that these originated mass consciousness without any extra effort.

Swami Dayanand unearthed or discovered the glorious past and infused a sense of pride and generated self-confidence among the Indians. Before launching his campaign through extensive tours and excursions he could understand the realities of Indian society and nation. Early in life Dayanand became fully aware of the deplorable political and economic condition of India. He realized, as many others have realized since, the degraded, and debased condition of the Aryas (Hindus) in their own country. His heart bled at the sight of the degenerated and desolate condition to which the people of India had been reduced. He saw before him a great country ideally situated, fertile and possessing all the resources which nature can give, a country inhabited by people endowed with intelligence, people numbering millions and millions, yet degraded, debased and helpless.

Like Coleridge's Ancient Mariner who saw "water, water everywhere but not a drop to drink", Dayanand saw men, men everywhere, yet not manly man – human beings, billion of them but not men with courage who will do their duty. He saw all around him people, weak, ignorant, helpless, without strength or determination to help themselves or to protect their heritage. He saw men who had forgotten their glorious past, the magnificent achievements of their ancestors, before stock and stones, tamely follow the directions of ignorant and selfish monopolists of religion, and become hewers of wood and drawers of water for foreigners, quite unconscious even of the misery of their lives, too timid to protect themselves of their rights against aggression or an unjust and oppressive regime. His heart bled to see all this helplessness of the people and the abasement and degeneration of the country :

Clime of the unforgotten brave whose land from plain to mountain cave was freedom's home or glory's grave Shrine of the mighty. Can it be, that this is all remains thee?[67]

The task before Dayanand was to make the people realise their degradation and ignorance and help them to regain strength, self-confidence and a will to break the fetters that bound them and win back their spiritual, social and political freedom. He knew that centuries of worship of false gods and political subjection to men of inferior culture and civilization but strong, courageous and determined to rule had sapped the strength and undermined the morale of his own people. His first task, therefore, was to instill in them spirit and the will to cast off the artificial and self imposed bonds that tied them to their present position, and to remove from their eyes the bandage that prevented them from seeing the light of truth and liberty. He devoted himself, therefore, to equipping and fitting them physically and morally to fight for their liberty and their inheritance.

He saw that he stood alone, while all around him were hostility and opposition. Arrayed against him were the serried ranks of the orthodox Hindus, the fanatic Muslim and the domineering Christians. They comprised firstly the entire Brahminhood of the country, learned as well as ignorant, armed with the weapon of excommunication supported by the Pandits of Banaras, the last Court of appeal in India in religion or tradition holding undisputed sway over the masses who were kept ignorant by the priestly class, and who had therefore Become apathetic and timid owing to centuries of political subjection and submission to priestly domination; secondary, the organised body of Christian missionaries backed by the tacit support of European officials and wielding the powerful weapon of the patronage to all who become converts or were helpful to the missionaries; thirdly the bullying Muslims ready to use violence, and offering the bait of free indulgence in the pleasures of the flesh, and freedom from all social or domestic restraints; and fourthly and lastly those educated in colleges and schools with their recently acquired feeling of pride on emancipation from religious thralldom, and because of the superficial acquaintance with modern European scientific thought looking with contempt on things Indian, and deriding the customs and practices prevalent in the country.[68]

Dayanand calmly surveyed the forces that opposed him, and gauging well their strength and their weaknesses, delivered his assault on them all rendering them incapable of aggressive action and laying bare there weak points.

He, however, knew that the disease from which people suffered was no ordinary ailment, but a disease which must prove fatal unless properly handled. He knew that it could not be cured by ordinary remedies but demanded a course of treatment which was bitter, unpalatable, almost repulsive to the patient, but which alone could purge the system of the poison that had accumulated there and which must be eliminated in order to restore the dying patient to health. He, therefore, determined to give them that course of treatment though he knew well that treatment was fraught with dire consequences for himself. But as he knew that he alone could administer the treatment, which the patient was no mood to accept because of its unpleasant nature, he took the risk to himself, and for the good of the patient, started the treatment. Swami Dayanand felt that he alone had truly diagnosed the disease and new the remedy and that he alone could apply it, just as the younger Pitt said when England was in danger : "I know that I can save England and I also know that no one else can save it." Dayanand began the treatment with results, fatal to himself."[69]

It is a notable fact that he did not try to administer palliatives, as had so often been done by Hindu reformers. He aimed at destroying the disease root and branch, and not merely to chopping here and chopping there. He went to the core of the distemper to effect a radical cure. He discovered the ultimate causes of the trouble and set about to remove it. He came to know that the degeneration and degradation of the Aryas (Hindu) was due to their imbibing false beliefs, accepting false and unsound teachings which stunted their growth and gave them false ideals, made them weak and feeble, kept them ignorant and dependent physically, and spiritually and unable and unwilling to stand on their rights and defend themselves. These false teachings deprived them of self respect, self consciousness and freedom in matter of everyday life, domestic, social and religious, and made them slaves politically, with disastrous economic results. He therefore tried to restore to them their self-respect, make them conscious of their strength and capacity, free them from the domination of the priestly caste, and make them aware that no Purohits, Gurus, Mahants or pilgrimages and beliefs in avatars will bring them *mukti*, as they had failed to bring them worldly prosperity. He taught them that they should first make themselves strong physically. A physically weak people can achieve nothing, neither social and political wellbeing, nor spiritual salvation. He taught them that the teachings of book like the *Sheeghra Bodh* and the Puranas which encourage child marriage, had made them a prey to every invader. He taught them that in order to achieve unity of the nation, the bonds of the caste system which had kept them bound hand and foot and made them condemn some of their own people as untouchables and unassociables, must be broken. He knew fully well that unless the evil practices such as idol-worship, child-marriage, the debasing caste system, untouchability, seclusion of women and making household slaves of them were given up; that unless men and women made themselves strong and vigorous physically and mentally, and until unity was achieved by making all Aryas or Hindus look upon one another as brethren; that until spiritual freedom was gained by discarding dependence on the priestly caste for the performance of religious observation, there was no hope for them.[70]

When the British authorities tried to suppress the Arya Samaj on the pretext of its nature as a political body. During the Swadeshi movement the Arya Samaj leaders were targeted by the authorities. For a long time between 1910–1920 the leaders and activists were dealt under the provision of sedition act. Lala Lajpat Rai on various occasion made the position clear that Arya Samaj is a socio-cultural organization. In an article he had said that : I have proclaimed from housetops and public platforms, through the press and through personal friends, local and foreign, that the Arya Samaj is not a political body. I reiterate that the Samaj is not a political body but a social organisation. At the same time I have no hesitation in admitting that on account of its general spirit and mode of education the Arya Samaj is not free from political bias of sorts. However, I would not like to be dubbed an opportunist by turning a blind eye to the original rules and regulations and aims and objects of the Arya Samaj.[71]

Swami Virjanand the Guru of Swami Dayanand wanted the Hindus to discard the *Pauranik* tomes and resort to the study of the *Vedic* literature which contained the true interpretation of religion. According to him, all the religious books that had gained currency and were being commonly used to impress the Hindu mind were jejune and beyond anybody's comprehension. Having weak eyesight, he had great difficulty in purveying his ideas to the people at large by writing books. All he could do was to convey his ideas by word of mouth. Because of the lack of proper medium, he feared, his ideas would remain in bottled up in his mind, and this thought made him sullen and still more irascible. Perhaps would have died carrying his ideas with him, but luckily during his declining year he found a worthy pupil like Dayanand who was fully in accord with his views and philosophy of life. With the exchange of views between them Swami Virjanand's mind which had started withering blossomed out as a flower. He freely imparted all his knowledge to Dayanand as he was his rightful heir. Swami Dayanand had roved all over the country and he observed how is country was steadily drifting toward ignorance and shibboleths. Till now he had not been able to find a mentor after his own heart. Now he had found true guru in Swami Virjanand. Swamiji was however not sowing the seeds of his learning in a barren land. If he had the acumen to impart his knowledge, Dayanand had the capacity to assimilate it. The benefit was mutual. Both were operating on the same wavelength.

The *summum bonum* of swamiji's teachings was the same as of Dayanand which can be explained as follows :

(1) Swamiji hated slavery of all kinds, mental and physical.

(2) He hated any kind of hypocrisy craftiness and wily machinations and advised to remain miles away from them.

(3) He was convinced, and so was Dayanand, that the education of Hindus was responsible for the traits of slavery in them and their Wiley ways which were grossly reflected in their ways of life.

(4) He and Dayanand both were avid proponents of the *Vedic* religion and culture and held that in complete adherence to them lay the country's salvation. They were also equally great patriots at heart, love of the country being a dominant factor in their lives.

(5) Both of them believed that their mission in life should be broad-based, having the sympathy and support of the widest segment of society, including the elites. They believed that in order to achieve their end they should form associations, societies and organization which could promote their cause in an organised manner. As for their models, they had in mind the societies and Organisations existing in the West. Incidentally, in his lifetime Swami Virjanand tried to form one such association under the patronage of the Maharaja of Jaipur but his effort did not meet with much success. Later on Swami Dayanand got great success in this respect with the founding of the Arya Samaj. The first Arya Samaj was founded at Bombay in 1875. But the similar Samaj was founded on a much firmer basis at Lahore in 1877. The Samajes founded after this were based on the rules and regulation originally formulated by Swami Virjanand and Dayanand and proved to be the precursor of Samajes in different parts of the country. The Samajes grew like mighty banyan trees conferring benefits on innumerable countrymen. Founding of the Lahore Arya Samaj had wide ramifications. After

> that many Hindu orphanages, homes for widows and educational Institutions were founded.[72]

Lala Lajpat Rai had written that : In my article published in the *contemporary review* in 1910, at the very outset I had written that the Arya Samaj wanted to make education broad-based by covering all aspects of a man's life with inevitably included politics also. Man cannot remain unaffected by politics. In Northern India the Arya Samaj and Indian Nationalism are considered synonymous.[73]

Dayanand, therefore, set to work to rid the people of India of those cramping, choking, throttling customs and practices which had their roots in false and emasculating religious teachings. He took in hand the work of freeing Hindus from those handicaps and obstacles which stood in the way of their growing to their full stature, and developing those qualities which are necessary to enable them to find their way successfully to political freedom and prosperity.

He was fully and painfully aware of their degraded, debased, woeful political plight. His heart bled to see the heartrending poverty and the utter helplessness of the people around him. He saw thousands dying for want of food and millions alive but skeletons, with sunken cheeks and hollow eyes, helpless and hopeless; others ignorant, deluded, servile, ignorant even of their sad plight, ignorant of their heritage, ignorant of their potential strength; some others, proud, parasitical, living in luxury and affluence, unmindful of the surrounding misery, and Indigence which were daily advancing to engulf them, unmindful of their responsibilities and their liabilities. He saw a mass of people disjointed, deranged, almost chaotic, having lost all initiative, confined and controlled by others and reduced to be mere hewers of wood and a drawers of water. He saw the futility of their entering the arena of political fight, themselves bound hand and foot, while the opponent was fully armed and determined to use his arm without compunction. Dayanand, therefore, started first to wield the Hindus into one united people, conscious of its present, mindful of its past, conscious of its strength to arise pure and strong from the prevailing welter and corruption, ignorance and internal strife, and stand on its own feet and take its proper place among the nations of the world. Then only would the people be able to make the strong cast of pride and Prejudice, and cease exploiting the ignorance and weakness of others. It would be possible only then for the Hindus not only to achieve liberty themselves but to fulfil their mission to rid other peoples of the materialistic mode of life which inevitably leads to exploitation of the weak by the strong.[74]

Dayanand, therefore, eschewed politics for the time being and devoted himself to teaching the people those eternal principles which form the basis of true religion, and free them from spiritual and social slavery, and instill national spirit in them and prepare them to regain their rights political, social and economic. Call this is a constructive programme for what you like, this work was absolutely essential to enable the people to gather strength to do their duty in this world and fit them for a higher and nobler life for which political freedom is as necessary as breathing is for life itself. He did not ask them at once to start fighting for their political liberty, knowing full well that they were weak and disunited. Progress, he knew well, was unity. A people cannot gain political freedom and remain slaves socially and spiritually. The chains of evil and debasing customs, and observances must be broken before a people can acquire strength to break political chains. This was the reason why he did not plunge headlong into the struggle for political independence, which cannot be won without strength of sinews and a will to conquer opposition.[75]

The Arya Samaj movment in Rajasthan hardly constitutes 15% part of all Indian movement while potentialities and possibilities were quite high. In comparison to Punjab, Haryana, Delhi and U.P. the movement could not flourish in Rajasthan. The geographical and social expansion of this movement has also been taken into account. In Rajasthan the Arya Samaj movement could spread among the high and middle castes of Hindus. It could also penetrate among the depressed classes, while it aimed to uplift them. Newly emerged urban intelligentsia was among the supporters of Arya Samaj. It's activities were based in urban areas but its influence was felt in the rural areas also. It became very popular among the Jat community of Shekhawati, Churu and Ganganagar areas adjoining to Punjab and Haryana. The peasant movements and freedom struggle of these areas were highly influenced by Arya Samaj movement. The Arya Samaj Movement played an important role in Rajasthan in creating a ray of hope at the period of the formation of political consciousness among the people. It created stir in the political backwater of Rajasthan and also initiated the formation of democratic institutions there. Finally, it developed favourable conditions for mass movements and freedom struggle in Rajasthan.

The Indian National Congress came into being in 1885 but it did not appear on the political scene of Rajasthan except Ajmer before Non-Cooperation movement. Therefore, the Arya Samaj movement bridged the political gap which existed in Rajasthan.[76] Among the valuable contributions of Arya Samaj to our national life, its educational work is perhaps the most popular and extensive and can easily claim for itself to be pioneer in the field of national education. It brought about a new awakening in the social and political spheres also through press. The social, religious and educational activities awakened the masses in Rajasthan. The people began to come out of their conservatism and religious darkness and the Arya Samaj movement made the people politically conscious about their rights and duties. It created spirit of self-respect, self-confidence, and self-esteem among the people and also generated a new consciousness in all spheres of national life. Thus, Arya Samaj became a means of political and national regeneration of the country in general and Rajasthan in particular.

The national consciousness created by the Arya Samaj immensely contributed to the rise and growth of nationalism in India in general and in northern India in particular. In Ajmer-Merwara the Arya Samaj during 1881 to 1947 remained influential socially and politically.[77] The Arya Samajists actively participated also in the movement led by Indian National Congress since inception. In the first session of Indian National Congress in December, 1885 one Arya Samajist Lala Murlidhar of Ambala (Punjab) participated actively, which opened the way to Aryasamajists of Ajmer-Merwara for political participation.[78] The leading Aryasamajists Harbilas Sarda and his associate Kayasth Mitthanlal founded the Congress committee in Ajmer in 1887. Harbilas Sarda and Ramvilas Sarda took part in Allahabad session of the INC in December, 1888. They also represented Ajmer in the Nagpur, Banaras, Calcutta and Lahore sessions of the INC.

Swadeshi Movement

Swami Dayanand was the first who propounded the concept of *Swadeshi* and *Swaraj*, which became the strong foundation of national and freedom movement. Annie Beasant in her book "India : A Nation" has mentioned that it was Dayanand who first raised the slogan "India is for Indians."[79] As an ardent advocate of Swadeshi, the Arya Samajists held that the ordinary requirement of every country should be supplied within that country. They were realising the bad economic condition of the country which was deteriorating day by day. They, finding that the British Government was not likely to come to take the industries of the country under the special protection, started the Swadeshi movement. It was essential for the reconstruction of the economy as well as the social and political unity of the country. Hence, swami Dayanand laid stress on the Swadeshi and he was regarded as the first advocate of this movement though it got its strength with political colour after the partition of Bengal in 1905.[80] The gradual growth of the Swadeshi movement can be traced everywhere in India under the guidance of leaders of the Arya Samaj. The preachers and leaders of the samaj, under whom the Swadeshi movement became the rallying cry of all-India, advocated in favour of Swadeshi and the national struggle for freedom began to extend from classes to masses.

Though, the Swadeshi movement was launched by the Indian National Congress but Arya Samajists all over northern India enthusiastically participated in it. The followers of Ajmer Arya Samaj were not exception to it; hence they too entered in the movement. Ramvilas Sarda after his return from Banaras Session of 1905 began to propagate and preach Swadeshi. Arya Samajist Seth Damodardas Rathi also played important role in the Swadeshi movement.[81] In 1908 Birdichand Mehta a worker of Ajmer Arya Samaj distributed a pamphlet to support the Swadeshi movement and to oppose the British rule in India. In the end of the said pamphlet '*Vedik Dharm ki Jai*' was printed, therefore suspicion went on Arya Samaj. Birdichand Mehta was arrested and was punished for two years prison along with a fine of Rs. 250.[82] National and political consciousness was visible everywhere in the city of Ajmer along with its towns.

Lala Lajpat Rai was the moving spirit of Swadeshi Movement in northern India particularly in Punjab and U.P.. His influence in Ajmer-Merwara and princely states of Rajputana was obvious. He delivered a series of lectures in order to promote Swadeshi movement in Punjab. In a meeting he appealed the Arya heroes to fly their own wings. He pointed out that unity was a great factor for the success of the Swadeshi movement.[83]

During the year 1906, he continued to tour and delivered lectures on the Swadeshi movement. While speaking at the Punjab Provincial Conference held at Ambala on 29th and 30th September of 1906, he said that the educated community of the Punjab should pay greater attention to the political movements (including Swadeshi) of the country and create real political environments among the masses for the success of the movement.[84] Referring the usefulness of the Swadeshi and Boycott movements in Bengal, he said, "They have raised the people to a consciousness of their power, they have taught the use of combinatioin and for once in the history of British India the industrial and the wage earning classes in this country seem to be realising that their destiny and their bread is in their hands - and not in the hands of those handful of people who lord it over them....[85] On March 27, 1907, he delivered a lecture in Allahabad on the New Spirit.

He drew attention of the people towards the Swadeshi movement and pointed out the means to be adopted to improve it. He advised the Indians to boycott British courts and start Swadeshi Panchayats for the adjudication of their disputes.[86] He presided at the All India Swadeshi Conference in Surat in 1907 and delivered a long lecture appealing Hindus and Muslims to unite themselves for the success of the movement.[87] At Cownpur, he delivered on the same topic on January 18, 1908, and said that there were three kinds of Swadeshi - Political, Social and Economic. Speaking on social and economic kinds of Swadeshi he said that the famine was due to the poverty of the country caused by want of arts and industries. Protective duties, according to him, were necessary, but the Indian Government being under the influence of European traders and merchants, was unable to improve them.[88]

The Swadeshi movement was first mass movement against the British rule in India. The efforts of Arya Samaj influenced and inspired the people to join national struggle. Being a Socio-religious organization the Arya Samaj did not involved directly in the political movement but its followers directed by the consciousness individually participated in the freedom movement. Some leaders and workers of Ajmer Arya Samaj joined the Indian National Congress and became part of active freedom movement. Thus, indirectly the Arya Samaj immensely contributed to the growth of freedom movement. The Swadeshi movement formally began on 7th August, 1905 and came to an end by mid 1908. It could not achieve its goal of getting the partition of Bengal cancelled. The Swadeshi Movement was only the first round in the national popular struggle against colonialism. The Swadeshi movement, thus, under the guidance of the Arya Samaj, became popular among the masses. It stimulated the idea of nationalism and the struggle for freedom began to extend from the educated classes to the masses. This movement, which owes its origin to Arya Samaj, became the popular weapon of the Indian National Congress after the partition of Bengal in 1905. Almost all the characteristic features that marked India's struggle for freedom upto 1947, may also be traced to the Swadeshi movement. This movement acquired an all India and national character almost immediately after its birth. It was the repercussion of this movement on Indian politics that gave rise to the Extremist or Nationalist Party under Tilak, Lajpat Rai, Khaparde and other leaders and readily changed the conception of political goal and the method to achieve it.

Revolutionary Phase

The oppressive character of the British imperialists compelled the youths and intellectuals to continue the anti British rule activities through secret societies and organisatons. Thus, the secret oganisatioins prepared the grounds for revolutionary activities. In 1907 the Indian National Congress was splitted, which created obstacle in the smooth growth of freedom movement under the Congress. Hence the political vacuum created by split gave space to the rise of revolutionary activities. Rajasthan also witnessed such activities.

Thakur Gopal Sigh of Kharwa was one of the prominent revolutionary of Rajasthan. He was *Istamarardar* (Jagirdar) of Kharwa in the British province of Ajmer-Merwara. He had strong leaning towards Arya Samaj. In true sense he was follower of Arya Samaj. Though, he was educated from Mayo College, Ajmer but he hated western culture and education.[89] In 1896 he was the chief guest at a function from 18 to 20 October organized by the "Kshatriya Anglo Sanskrit Middle School", Jobner. The said school was founded by Thakur Karan Singh as part of the Arya Samaj education mission.[90] The said school was renamed as 'Dayanand Anglo Vedic High School, Jobner' in 1911.[91] Thakur Gopal Singh of Kharwa firmly believed in armed revolution. He established contacts with Rash Bihari Bose and Sachindra Natha Sanyal. Before that he was also in contact of Shyanji Krishan Varma a staunch Arya Samajist and a noted revolutionary. He was settled in Ajmer as legal practicenor and was also member of Udaipur State Council. He was a staunch supporter of Swadeshi and in collaboration with Seth Damodardas Rathi he started a textile mill at Beawar to popularize *Swadeshi* goods. He was also suspect in Rand's murder case of 1897. But he managed to fly to England and he founded the India House in London in 1905 from where he was supporting and guiding revolutionary activities in India and abroad for the Independence of India. In 1906 V.D. Savarkar joined the India House and on 1 July 1909 one of Varma's disciple Madan Lal Dhingra shot dead Curzon wily in London.[92]

The names of Arjunlal Sethi, Keshrisingh Barhath, Gopal Singh Kharwa, Jorawar Singh Barhath etc. also appeared in Delhi Bomb Conspiracy case.[93] But in the absence of proper evidence none of the revolutionaries from Rajasthan was arrested. It is said that two prominent revolutionary viz. Vijay Singh Pathik allias Bhoop Singh and Jorawar Singh Barhat escaped from Delhi and went underground. The name of Thakur Gopal Singh Kharwa was prominent among the revolutionaries of Rajasthan of the pre-Gandhian era. He was in close contact of Ras Bihari Bose, Sachindra Nath Sanyal, Amir Chand and Awadh Bihari. Earlier he was in deep touch with Shyamji Krishna Verma and Damodar Das Rathi. In 1906 he also came into contact of Arbindo Ghosh and Swami Kumarnand when they visited Kharwa on the invitation of Thakur Gopal Singh. He was a sort of mini king of Kharwa, which he inherited as ancestral estate of *Jagir.* Among the feudal lords of Ajmer-Merwara province he was big *istimaradar* of top class. he was the only ruling prince of Rajasthan who sacrificed his life for the cause of freedom of India.

The Ajmer group of revolutionaries under Gopal Singh was unearthed during the trial of Nimaz and Kota murder cases. He was organizing revolutionary activities in Rajasthan and was also helping the revolutionaries out of Rajasthan. One criminal intelligence report mentioned that : 'Gopal Singh and Kesari Singh wee mixed up with the seditionists in British India and were furthering plots and conspiracies directly affecting British India. When the Thakur was called upon to explain he spun out and an evasive statement mouth after mouth, and meanwhile continued his plotting, and remained in possession of an extraordinary arsenal of fire arms and ammunition.[94] Through a contemporary writers account it is known that Kharwa remained the centre for revolutionaries. Thakur Gopal Singh used to collect arms for the revolutionaries and for the assistance in his revolutionary activities he appointed Bhoop Singh alias Vijay Singh Pathik, who soon became his right hand man.[95]

The story goes that when the first world war broke out in 1914 the revolutionaries under the leadership of Ras Bihari Bose and Sachinda Nath Sanyal planned an armed revolt in Northern India with the help of Indian armies of British and princely states of Rajputana. The date fixed for the action was 21 February, 1915. Ras Bihari Bose was supposed to attack Delhi on date by army detachment from Multan, Lahore and Meerut, while Gopal Singh and Bhoop Singh were assigned the duty to reach Delhi with the forces of princely states specially Jodhpur and Bikaner. A message to this effect was delivered by one Manilal to Gopal Singh subsequently Mani Lal turned to be Government approver and betrayed the cause and the plot fizzled out. On 26 June, 1915 the Chief Commissioner, Ajmere-Merwara served an internment order to Gopal Singh. He was ordered to leave Kharwa and report to Tehsildar at Todgarh, where he was detained. But on 10 July, 1915 he fled from Todgarh. He was charged with willfully disobeying the orders of Government and search warrant was issued in his name. However, he surrendered on 28 August, 1915 and was awarded sentence of two years simple imprisonment for breach of rules framed under the Defence of India Act.[96] He was put in Jail at Shahjahanpur in the United province.

The Kharwa estate was attached by the British Government and was put under the Court of Wards. The term of two years imprisonment completed on 4 September, 1917 but could not release. He too was released from jail in 1919 when general amnesty was given to the detainees after First World War. But till his death he remained under confinement of Government vigilance at Shahjhanpur (U.P.).

He was made the first president of Ajmer-Merwara Provincial Political Conference held at Ajmer on 20 March,

1920. In his speech on 28 March, 1920 in Ajmer he said : 'I have been interned and kept away from my place of birth and my personal province. People say that Rajputana is backward province, but at present a wave of political consciousness and awakening has blown and I have full confidence that a day will come when Rajputana will come in the fore front like our ancestors on the path of duty.' He further said : 'The traders of Europe came to earn profit and settled in Hindustan and with the help of tricks and cunningness were able to establish their rule. Why and how could these traders think of our benefit? They ruled till the mutiny of 1857, the British Crown took over the power in its hands, but whatever promises they made were not fulfilled.' He continued that : 'Whenever the people wanted political rights they were not paid heed. This led to an opposition between the rulers and the ruled. Frustrated with this repressive policy of the Government many revolution minded people took the path of the bomb and the revolver. I wanted to serve my country and the Government interned me and not only this, my estate was confiscated, Lord Chelmsford criticized me in public meeting saying that Gopal Singh was a blot on the name of *Istimarardars* of Ajmer and his family. What sort of behavior is this? Would we want to serve the Government after this behaviour? Many hindrances will come in way of achievement of goal, but we should not be afraid and our aim is to follow the path of dharma and duty. God is our helper.[97] Till his death he remained Tilakite a believer of extremist politics.

The revolutionary phase of Rajasthan during 1906-1915 created nationalist political consciousness. The only weakness of the revolutionaries of Rajasthan was the lack of organisation. Due to separate princely states boundaries with about 20 political and administrative units the conditions were not conducive in favour of formation of an unified organisation. But in the absence of any organisation the revolutionary activities kept pace with the political activities of British India. The rulers of Rajasthan opposed the formation of all type of organizations, while the residents of British provinces enjoyed a little freedom of expression and making of political associations. Thus, Ajmer was the only centre of national and freedom movement during the early phase, where Arya Samaj played a leading role.

Chandkaran Sarda a staunch Arya Samajist from Ajmer played an active and important role in the freedom struggle. He imbibed the values of patriotism and public service from his father Ramvilas Sarda. His father was disciple of Dayanand Saraswati. During his student life at Agra Chandkaran Sarda was active in the *'Arya Mitra Sabha'* and for the first time attended the session of Indian National Congress in 1911. In 1913 he attended the All India Arya Kumar Conference at Saharanpur where he met Lala Lajpat Rai. He became active in nationalistic activities after joining the legal profession as an advocate. In 1914 he launched an agitation for accepting the application in Hindi by the Ajmer-Merwara courts and consequently the Chief Commissioner conceded the demand.[98] In 1915 he founded the Home Rule League Committee at Ajmer. The Home Rule League Committee also established Reading Room to create public consciousness.[99]

Chandkaran Sarda beginning from anti-Rowlatt Act protest *satyagraha* remained in the fore front of freedom movement in Rajasthan Particularly at Ajmer till the attainment of freedom. His activities also got constant support from the Arya Samajists. Thus, he immensely contributed to the growth of mass consciousness.

The Arya Samaj also created public and mass consciousness in the princely states of Rajputana but due to their oppressive and coercive policy it could not translated into movement soon. This took more time in comparison to the British India.

The ideas which the revolutionaries spread tended to subvert the existing order in British India and in every native state. With a view to curbing their activities, the princely rulers were instructed to take necessary measures to prevent the seditious meetings, the infiltration of revolutionary literature and explosive material into their States.[100] On 6th August, 1909, Lord Minto, the Governor-General of India sent a letter to the rulers of princely states to this effect.[101] The princely rulers responded to this call enthusiastically by enforcing the order of their British masters. As such there were no organizations of modern nature. The Arya Samaj was the only oganisation which was propagating new ideas. Thus, the Arya Samaj became the prime victim of such oppressive rules. It is interesting to note that even before the said orders of 1909 the Jodhpur State acted against the Arya Samaj. In November, 1908 the Jodhpur Police removed the name-board on the Arya Samaj premises on the route of the Viceroy's procession through the town.[102] Though, the Arya Samaj could not begin any mass movement, but it created general mass consciousness in the princely states of Rajasthan which culminated into Peasant and Prajamandal movements with heavy mass participation.

It may be concluded that Swami Dayanand and Arya Samaj promoted the philanthropic activities to serve the cause of humanity. The Arya Samaj had devised various ways and means for the same. Swami Dayanand was the first who visualized the supreme usefulness of cow to humanity. Therefore, he initiated the cow protection movement. Swamiji gave serious attention on the education of masses. He was of the opinion that illiteracy and ignorance were the root causes of the degradation and subordination of India and its people. Therefore, the Arya Samaj took the mission of education sincerely. It was the impact of Arya Samaj movement that it awakened the broad masses. The mass awakening translated and transformed into the rise and growth of nationalism in India, which led to the freedom struggle.

Notes

1. Har Bilas Sarda, *op.cit.*, p. XVI.
2. *Ibid*, p. xv.
3. *Ibid*, p. xvi.
4. *Ibid*
5. Lajpat Rai, *op.cit.*, p. 129.
6. *Ibid*, pp. 129-33.
7. *Ibid*, p. 134.
8. Har Bilas Sarda, *op.cit.*, p. 213.
9. Devendranath Mukhopadhyay, *op.cit.*, p. 632 and J.T.F. Jordens, *op.cit.*, p. 215.
10. Lal Lajpat Rai the leader of Arya Samaj and originator of orphanage movement had enumerated that during the famine of 1877-78 about 52,20000 persons died of starvation. Lal Lajpat Rai had written a chapter entitled 'Famines and orphans' in his bok entitled 'The man and His word' (Ganesa & co., Madras, 1907). (This information has been taken from the Collected works of Lala Lajpat Rai, Volume two, Edited by B.R. Nanda, Manohar, New Delhi, 2003, pp. 275-280)
11. Lajpat Rai, *op.cit.*, p. 130.
12. Kenneth W. Jones, *op.cit.*, p. 235.
13. *Shrimad Dayanand Anathalaya, Ajmer, Varshik Vivran*, 1895-96, pp. 1-2.
14. *Ibid*, p. 3.
15. *Victoria Anathalaya, Bharatpur, A Report, 1908*, p. 2.
16. Lajpat Rai, *op.cit.*, p. 131.
17. *Ibid.*
18. *Ibid.*

19. *Ibid*, p, 132.
20. B.R. Nanda (Ed.), *The Collected works of Lala Lajpat Rai,* Volume two, op.cit., p. 269.
21. *Ibid*, p. 275.
22. Harbilas Sarda, *op.cit.*, p. xxxxi (Introduction).
23. *Ibid*, p. 459
24. Devendranath Mukhopadhyay, *op.cit.*, p. 585.
25. Harbilas Sarda, *op.cit.*, p.49.
26. Above Reference 24, p. 617.
27. *Ibid.*
28. *Ibid.*
29. *Ibid*
30. *Ibid*, J.T.F. Jordens, *op.cit.*, pp. 219-20.
31. J.T.F. Jordens, *op.cit.*, pp. 220-221.
32. *Ibid*, p. 221.
33. *Gaukarunanidhi*, 15th Edition, 1949, p. 1
34. J.T.F. Jordens, *op.cit.*, pp. 221-22.
35. Harbilas Sarda, *op.cit.*, p. 460.
36. Radhey Shyam Pareek, *op.cit.*, p. 105.
37. *Styarth Prakash*, Translated Chiranjiva Bhardwaj, op.cit., p. 34.
38. *Ibid.*
39. *Ibid.*
40. *Ibid.*
41. *Shrimati Paropkarini Sabha Ka Pratham Adhiveshan, Pratham Report, 1883*, Vedic Yantralaya, Prayag, 1884, p. 2.
42. Lajpat Rai, *op.cit.*, p. 138.
43. Indra Vidyavachaspati, *op.cit.*, Part I, pp. 166-72 and Radhe Shyam Pareek, *op.cit.*, p. 185.

44. *Dayanand Ashram Anglo-Vedic School ka Varshik Prativedan, 1889-1890*, Rajputana Press, Ajmer, 1890, p. 1. It seems that the objectives were identical to the D.A.V. College Lahore. Dr. G.C. Verma has written that : It was this small school, penned on 8th February 1888 with the late H.B. Sarda as its President, which ultimately became the famous D.A.V. College (Modern Education : Its Growth And Development in Rajasthan (18181983), p. 304 by G.C. Verma, Jaipur, 1984.
45. *Annual Report of D.A.V. High School, Ajmer, 1888-1922.*
46. *Ibid*, 1911-12, p. 5.
47. G.C. Verma, *op.cit.*, p. 304.
48. *Ibid*, pp. 304-5.
49. It was basically a Harijan basti, Arya Pratindhi Sabha, Rajasthan, Jaipur Arya Samaj Correspondence, Letter No. 73, 27th Feb., 1901.
50. *Arya Samaj Jaipur ke Sau Varsh*, Samarika, 1981, p. 67.
51. *Dayanand Anglo-Vedic High School Jobner, A Report*, Vedic Yantralaya, Ajmer, 1924, p. 4.
52. *Arya Pratinidhi Sabha, Rajasthan, File 16/A, letter no. 110 of 1937.*
53. *Arya Pratinidhi Sabha*, Rajasthan, A Report of High School, 1948, pp. 2-3.
54. *Ibid, File 1941-42, Letter No. 104 dated 10 June 1941, Director Public Institutions, Bharatpur.*
55. *Arya Samaj, Jodhpur, Ek Prativedan*, Vedic Yantralaya, Ajmer, 1915, pp. 34.
56. *Jodhpur Arya Samaj, A Report, 1946.*
57. Harbilas Sarda, *op.cit.*, p. 308.
58. *Paropkari, March, 1991*, p. 27 (Hindi monthly journal).
59. J.T.F. Jordens, Swami Shraddhanand, *op.cit.*, p. 55.
60. *Ibid*, p. 58.

61. Lajpat Rai, *op.cit.*, p. 145.
62. Satyadeva Vidyalankar, *Amar Shaheed Swami Shraddhanandji Maharaj ki Purn Pramanik aur Vistrit Jivani*, Delhi, 1933, p. 302 (Edited by Indra Vidyavachaspat). Indra Vidyavachaspati in his work the *Arya Samaj ka Itihas*, Dwitiya Bhag at p. no. 13 has mentioned that the Gurukul Kangri Vishwavidyalaya was inaugurated with 24 Brahmacharis.
63. *Gurukul Chittor ki Sankshipt Patrika*, p. 10.
64. *Shri Gurukul Chittor ka Arambhik Ashat Varshik Vritant*, V.S. 1984 se 1992, pp. 22-23..
65. *Udaipur Arya Samaj, File No. 7/930, A Report on Gurukul Chittor*, p. 2.
66. *op.cit.* reference No. 64, p. 39.
67. Harbilas Sarda, *op.cit.*, pp. XVIII-XIX.
68. *Ibid*, p. XIX.
69. *Ibid*, p. XX.
70. *Ibid*, pp. XX-XXI.
71. B.R. Nanda (Edit), *op.cit.*, Volume four, p. 246.
72. *Ibid*, pp. 245-46.
73. *Ibid*, pp. 246-47.
74. Harbilas Sarda, *op.cit.*, pp. XXIII-XXIV.
75. *Ibid*, p. XXIII.
76. Since 1938 the Congress began to support the Prajamandal movement in the princely states of Rajasthan.
77. *Prof. V.K. Vashishtha, Bhartiya Swatantrata Andolan mein Ajmer-Merwara mein Arya Samaj ka Yogdan*, Rajasthan History Congress, Proceeding Volume XXVII, 2012, p. 225,
78. *Ibid.*
79. Quoted from K.S. Saxena, *The Political Movements and Awakening in Rajasthan (1857-1947)*, S. Chand & Company, New Delhi, 1971, p. 112.

80. *The Arya Gazette*, 21 September, 1905.
81. Prof. V.K. Vashishtha, *op.cit.*, footnote no. 77, p. 227.
82. Ajmer Police Records.
83. The Paisa Akhabar, 13 December, 1905.
84. *The Punjabi*, 10-13 October, 1906.
85. *Ibid.*
86. *NAI, New Delhi, Home-Political Deptt. Proceedings, Part A, August, 1907, Nos. 148-235.*
87. *Ibid (Deposit), November, 1908, No. 7.*
88. *Ibid (D.C.I. Report), Part B, February, 1908, Nos. 105-112.*
89. Prof. V.K. Vashishtha, *op.cit.*, footnote no. 81, pp. 226-227.
90. *Kshatriya Anglo Sanskrit Middle School, Karngarh, 1891-96, Panchvarshiya Report*, Vedic Yantralaya, Ajmer, 1897, pp. 1-2.
91. *Dayanand Anglo-Vedic High School, Jobner, A Report*, Vedic Yantralaya, Ajmer, 1924, p. 4.
92. Brij Kishore Sharma, *Mass Movements & Freedom Struggle in Rajasthan (1818-1949)*, Book Treasure, Jodhpur, 2013, pp. 93-94.
93. On 23rd December, 1912 a Bomb was thrown on Lord Harding, the Governor General of India, in Chandni Chowk, Delhi.
94. *NAI, Foreign & Political Deptt., Secret I, March, 1917, Nos. 1-29.*
95. Ram Narayan Chaudhary, *Vertman Rajasthan*, pp. 27-28.
96. *NAI, Foreign & Political Deptt., Secret I, March, 1917, Nos. 1-29.*
97. Indira Vyas, *Freedom Movement in Rajasthan*, University Book House, Jaipur, 2004, pp. 75-76.
98. Satyadev Shastri (Edited), *Desh Bhakta Shri Kunwar Chandkaran ji Sarda, Sarda Abhinandan Pustika*, Vedic Yantralaya, Ajmer, 1948, p. 7.

99. *Ibid*, p. 52.

100. *NAI, Home-Poll - Deposit, October, 1909, No. 16.*

101. Letter dated 6th August, 1909, from Lord Minto to the Native Chiefs, Foreign Deptt., Abu Collection, U.O.R., Jaipur, NAI, Foreign & Political Department,F,No.178,1909.

102. *NAI, Home-Political (Confidential) Department, Proceedings, Part A, April, 1912, No. 4.*

6

Summary and Conclusions

The vibrant movements for social and religious reforms in the Nineteenth century were the first all-India response to the cultural and moral challenges posed by the colonial rule. The Indian intelligentsia unearthed the true and pure Hindu religion as they were of the firm view that the true nature of Hindu society and religion should not be evaluated from its prevalent forms because its true form lay buried under a mass of irrationalities and superstitions. Therefore, they called the people to return to the origin and purity of faith. They took their ideas from scriptures, Vedas, Upanishads, Bhagwat Geeta and other *shastras*. Through scriptural knowledge and philosophy they established the superiority of Hindu religion, culture and society.

These movements fostered a rational outlook and developed a logical and critical thinking. Even the attitude of those conservatives who continued to stick firmly to Indian tradition, was changed from uncritical acceptance to justification by reason. Thus, the cultural and religious consciousness combined with political and economic factors provided a powerful basis to the growth of nationalism.

Author has not come yet across any work of worth mention on Arya Samaj movement in Rajasthan. In the scenario of review of literature the relevance of the present study is self-explanatory. Moreover, the Rajasthan witnessed the early activities of Swami Dayanand Saraswati and Arya Samaj, and Ajmer became the centre of Arya Samaj movement but no work of worth mention on the history of Arya Samaj movement in Rajasthan has been done. Hence, the present study is a humble and modest effort in this direction. This study shall bridge gap existed in the knowledge of Arya Samaj Movement in Rajasthan.

The establishment of Arya Samaj organisations in Rajasthan proved a miracle because in the arch reactionary feudal setup it rise as ray of hope. Before the Arya Samaj there was not a single organisation founded on the modern lines. Indeed, in the background of the rise of nationalism the socio-religious reform movements played an important role in India, but in the context of Rajasthan these created general awareness. The people began to discuss their social, political and economic surroundings which impressed them to think beyond the existing situations. Hence, the establishment of Arya Samaj organisation initiated the process of modern thinking. Therefore, the present study may prove its worth.

The social, religious and educational activities awakened the masses in Rajasthan. The people began to come out of their conservatism and religious darkness and the Arya Samaj made the people politically conscious of their rights and duties. It created spirit of self-respect, self-confidence and self-esteem among the people and also generated a new consciousness in all spheres of national life. Thus, the Arya Samaj became a vehicle of political and national regeneration of the country in general and Rajasthan in particular. In this way the contribution of Arya Samaj has been evaluated and analysed in the present work.

At the age of 21 Moolshankar fled from his home to satisfy his thirst for true knowledge and enlightenment . Dayanand

Saraswati did not stay at a place for long and remained wandering from one place to other. In V.S. 1912 (A.D. 1855) he visited for the first time, the Kumbha fair at Haridwar. Here he met to so many sages and individual philosophers. He interacted with a lot of people and could know about the various sects of broader Hindu religion. Here he could also visualize the deficiency of his knowledge. During his visits of the above places of Himalayas he came into contact of various shades of sects and *Sadhus.* From Daronsagar Dayanand went to Moradabad via Sambhal and then crossing Garhmuktashwar. Then he took route to Farukhabad, Kanpur, Allahabad, Mirzapur and Banaras alosngwith Ganga. After this adventure from Banaras, on 26 March 26, 1857 he set out on journey to the hills, where the Narmada takes its rise. He kept wandering for three years on the bank of the Narmada and enjoyed the learned company of the *mahantas* and yogis. There he was advised that you study from Virjanand at Mathura your wishes will be fulfilled. That is where Dayanand arrived in November 1860. What frustrations and new discoveries made him at that stage give up that search for *moksha,* and take the road to Mathura in order to study grammar under the guidance of Swami Virjananda Sarasvati, the famous blind *guru.*

In fact Dayanand got a skill and tool in the education of grammar by which he may test the authority of scriptures that which one belongs to the creation of rishis and which one is composition of ordinary authors. By the end of March 1863, Dayanand had been with his *guru* virjanand, when his guru told him that his education was over and that he had nothing more to teach him. In April 1863 Dayanand left his *guru* and began his missioin to refute the evil religious practices and propagation of Vedas.

The Kashi Shastrarth (16November,1869) brought many changes in the thought and action of Swami Dayanand. He reached on the conclusion that he can succeed in his mission only by organised efforts, otherwise his individualistic works will not yield required results. After Kashi shastrarth Swami Dayanand finally rejected the idolatry and mythology. He further rejected polytheism and accepted monotheism. He stressed upon acquisition of true knowledge of God and observance of the moral laws as the will of God. He suggested the worship of God by *Agnihotra*.

Swami Dayanand also rejected the theory of Devine origin of *Varnas* and castes. He considered the caste a political institution made by the rulers for the common good of society, and not a natural or religious distinction. It was not based on birth rather was based on profession.

Swami Dayanand arrived in Calcutta on 16 December 1872. The Indian Mirror, noticing his arrival spoke of him as an iconoclast of a superior type, as a man of unbounded learning who had proved himself a name in Northern India. During his stay in Calcutta he met the galaxy of scholars, theologists, social workers, political activists and educationists.

Swamiji who was concentration on the religious issues until the Calcutta visit but there he could understand the importance of social and political reforms. His idea of establishing an organisation got matured and at the same time he could understand the importance of publication and printing. On 1 April 1873 Dayanand left Calcutta. Dayanand began to plan his future course of action and after a year his plan of action came into being in the form of the famous work Satyarth Prakash. It is a detailed discourse of Swami Dayanand Saraswati which became an organ of the establishment of Arya Samaj.

Dayanand Saraswati repeatedly stressed upon the fact that true happiness consists solely in giving up altogether the worship of idols and in serving the mother and other living gods. The hypocrite priests have created superstition for their personal ends. It is evil practices like idol worship that are responsible for the existence of millions of idle, lazy, indolent, and beggarly priest in India, who are mainly answered for this widespread ignorance, fraud and mendacity in the country. In the end Dayanand has said that we have thus briefly discussed the religion of the people of Aryavarta. Thus, Swamiji has refuted the ill and evil religious practices prevailing in the so called Hinduism, whom Swamiji called the Aryans.

In addition of the foregoing Swami Dayanand had also critically examined the Jainism, Buddhism and Charbak whom he considered atheists. In the same manner he has also examined the Christianity and Mohammedanism. Through his study of Vedas and shastras Swami Dayanand proved the superiority of Vedic religion. As has been already said that Swami Dayanand Saraswati has devised a complete system of ideal society along with social and political system in the Styarth Prakash. Thus, to implement his model and propagation of his ideas he felt urgent need of an organisation, which can play the role of an instrument of implementation.

Though the Calcutta visit had deep impact on Swami Dayanand from where his idea of founding an organisation became matured. But before this visit the idea of founding an organisation was already stirring in his mind. Swami Dayanand returned to Bombay on 29 January, 1875 and he revived his efforts for setting up an Aryasamaj. On 10 April 1875 (Saturday, Chaitra Shukla 5, V.S. 1932) the Bombay Arya Samaj was formally established.

From the study of twenty eight principles and rules the nature of the Arya Samaj organisation is very clear that it was a broad based organisation. It aimed to bring together all Hindus who agreed on the revival of Vedic religion. Looking to the moral degradation of Hindus the Arya Samaj aimed at moral upliftment of them. In totality it wished the religious, social and national advancement of the country. Basically, Arya Samaj wanted to reform the religion, society and polity. The same is clear from an important speech of Swamiji as follows : If you are able to achieve something for the good of mankind by Samaj, then establish a Samaj; I will not stand in your way. But if you do not organize it properly, there will be a lot of trouble in the future. As for me, I will only instruct you in the same way as I teach others, and this much you should keep clearly in mind : my beliefs are not unique, and I am not omniscient. Therefore, if in the future any error of mine should be discovered after rational examination, then set it right. If you do not act that way, then this Samaj too will later on become just a sect. That is the way by which so many sectarian divisions have become prevalent in India : by making the *guru's* word the touchstone of truth and thus fostering deep-seated prejudices which make people religion-blind, cause quarrels and destroy all right knowledge. That is the way India arrived at her sorry contemporary state, and that is the way this Samaj too would grow to be just another sect. This is my firm opinion : even if there be many different sectarian beliefs prevalent in india, if only they all acknowledge the *Vedas,* then all those small rivers will re-unite in the ocean of Vedic wisdom, and the unity of *dharma* will come about. From that unity of *dharma* there will result social and economic reform, arts and crafts and other human endeavours will improve as desired, and man's life will find fulfilment : because by the power of that *dharma* all values will become accessible to him, economic values as well as psychological ones, and also the supreme value of *moksha.* Thus, it may be said that the Arya Samaj organisation was broad based organisation free from sectarian and selfish interests for the betterment of human kind and humanity. But at the same time it promoted the national consciousness.

The arrival of Swami Dayanand Saraswati in Rajasthan has great significance because he brought a ray of hope in the arch reactionary feudal atmosphere. When he step out for the first time from the territories of Gujarat he arrived at Mount Abu in Rajasthan in the year 1852. He always considered his mission to embrace the whole of Aryavarta, and it was only natural that his interest should turn to the princely states, that other half of the country generally bypassed by the reformers.

The Rajasthan was the strong hold of princely states whom Swami Dayanand considered the Hindu states. Moreover, in his opinion the rulers of Rajasthan were the heirs of Vedic Kshatriyas. Therefore, his enormous expectations from the rulers of princely states of Rajasthan were obvious and justified. Thus, his attraction and inclination towards princely states of Rajasthan remained live till his death. Swami Dayanand visited Rajasthan four times after completion of his studies at Mathura under Swami Virjanand.

During the first visit to Rajasthan (1865-66) Swami Dayanand received dull response from the masses, rulers and *jagirdars*. It was due to lack of education and political oppression. The intricate social structure with lot of evil rituals and social inequality were the factors not conducive for new ideas.

Dayanand's second visit to Rajasthan (1878) too could not get required response. At Pushkar Swamiji created sensation among the conservative *pundits* and pandas but could not convince them with his ideas and also could not change their ideas and practices. His image emerged of a rebellious *Sannyasi*. Thus, he antagonised them. In the same manner at Ajmer Swamiji came into open confrontation with Christian missionaries. The Muslims and Jains were also offended by him. But, he could successfully recorded his presence in Rajasthan and his ideas began to penetrate in the mind of people here.

Thus, the third visit of Swami Dayanand to Rajasthan came to a conclusion which began in March, 1881 and ended in December. Obviously, it was a wandering of nine moth in Rajasthan and it had mixed results. He could not get any attention from the rulers of Bharatpur and Jaipur. Though, under the influence of Dayanand some Aryan organization known as *Vedic Dharma Sabha* came into being in Jaipur but remained unnoticed by and large. The Arya Samaj was founded about three months before the visit of Swami Dayanand but it could be strengthened by his presence in May, 1881. Thus, the first Arya Samaj organization was founded in Ajmer. The success of Swamiji at Masuda was unparalleled as a number of people adopted Vedic religion and among them the Jains were in sizable number. One thing is worthy to mention that the ruler of Mewar became the first who whole heartedly appreciated the ideas and thoughts of Swami Dayanand. He was so impressed that he requested the Swami to accompany him to Udaipur.

The foundation of the Paropkarini Sabha by Swami Dayanand Saraswati at Udaipur is worthy to mention as an extraordinary achievement of him. When he was in Meerut during July-September 1880, he made a will by which he appointed a society called the Paropkarini Sabha and frame its constitution and rules and got it registered. But during his stay at Udaipur he made another swikarpatra (will), cancelling the previous one. he got it registered in the office of the state Council according to law on 27th February, 1883.

The foundation of the Paropkarini Sabha in Udaipur was a great success of Swami Dayanand. The overwhelmed response of the Maharana, Council Members, officers, and employees towards Swami Dayanand inculcate mutual confidence. It is clear from the foregoing narration that Swami Dayanand deeply influenced the Maharana during his presence in Udaipur.

But after leaving Udaipur the influence of Swami Dayanand began to decline for three reasons. One, the Maharana was not an independent and sovereign ruler and was functioning under the subordination and supremacy (paramountcy) of the British. Therefore, he could not work on the advice and guidelines of Swamiji. Second, Swami Dayanand's ideas of *Swadeshi, Swabhasha* and *Swadharama* were not in consonance of with the British empire. He openly offended the Christianity which was flourishing in India under the patronage of British empire. In the eyes of the British Swami Dayanand was a kind of rebellious *sadhu.* Therefore, Maharana or any princely ruler could not afford to support Swamiji's ideas. Third, the people were hard believer of *Pauranik* religion based on mythology.

Swami Dayanand reached Jodhpur on 31st May, 1883, where he was received by Rao Raja Jawan Singh on behalf of the Jodhpur Darbar. Swami Dayanand decided to leave Jodhpur on the first October and on 27th September he asked Rao Raja Tej Singh to make the necessary arrangements for his departure. It was in these last days that he was struck down by the illness from which he was not to recover. On the night of the 29the September he took milk as usual which caused stomach pain and vomiting. He than suspected that someone has poisoned him. Swami Dayanand reached at Mount Abu on 21st October for treatment and from there he was brought to Ajmer on 26th October. In the evening of 30th October, 1883 Swami Dayanand knew that his end was near and he asked all the Aryas to come to his room to bid a final farewell.

It was Deepawali, 30 October 1883. Out of Gujarat Swami Dayanand began his journey form Abu in Rajasthan in 1852 and also breathed his last in Rajasthan. Thus, India's greatest Sadhu, seer and reformer of modern times expired.

It may be concluded that Swami Dayanand's visits and presence brought many positive effects on the life and thoughts of people. But he could not aqchieve his desired goal of making the rulers of Rajasthan at the helm of affairs of Arya Samaj to lead his reform movement. There were certain limitations of the rulers under the British paramountcy as they could not move indepently. His ideas were more revolutionary as he questioned hereditary rule and preferred a republican form of government. The qualifications of kings defined by Swami Dayanand were rigorously framed. He declared that the king has no absolute powers, he merely wielded them on behalf of the people, not as a representative of god, as was claimed. In the chapter - 6 of Satyarth Parkash entiltled 'Raja Dharama or Science of Government' has given a detailed discourse on 'Rajniti'. Swami Dayanand was of the view that if a king does not work for the welfare of his people, he should be dethroned. He always emphasized on the duties of rulars towards their subjects. He also stressed upon that a king should not waste public money on self indulgence. The king should not waste his time in amusement and sensual activities.

The ruling aristocracy of Rajasthan welcomed Swami Dayanand as a Vedic scholar and saint, but not his ideas due to a series of reason. The princely rulers disassociated themselves from their responsibilities towards their subjects and became responsible to their British masters, whom they tried to appease since their very existence depended on them. The British maintained the princely states to fulfill their own colonial purposes as all decisive political power was in British hands.

After the death of Swami Dayanand the members of royal houses, *Jagirdars* and members of the feudal aristocracy withdrew from his mission. It is of noteworthy that the members of newly emerged middle class entered into the Arya Samaj movement in Rajasthan. The earlier efforts of princes and *Jagirdars* could not went in vain and their importance as first step cannot be ignored. Thus, they too play their limited role in positive direction.

The princely states were puppet in the hands of British and Swami Dayanand was expecting more from them by considering them sovereign states. The princely rulers were being tempted by the western culture and learnt many vices from them. The colonial administrators induced the princely rulers into western culture. The nationalistic and *Swadeshi* thoughts of Dayanand might have presented the challenges before the British and their supporters. He denounced the profligacy of rulers, *jagirdars* and feudal aristocracy. None of them became true disciple of Swami Dayanand and few of them facilitated him in their areas out of curtsy and their *samskaras.* Since the inception they were taught to honour and worship *Sadhu*, Brahman and cow. Thus, Swami Dayanand was a Sadhu and also a Brahman. Therefore, it may be said that Swami Dayanand was welcomed by ruling aristocracy in Rajasthan but not his ideas.

Swami Dayanand established the authenticity and supremacy of the Vedas. He called on Hindus to go back to Vedas because only these contained the original and pure form of Hindu theology. He rejected the plurality of the Hindu Gods. He also denounced idol worship, superstitious practices and irrelevant ritualistic practices. Therefore, it is pertinent to discuss the impact of the Arya Samaj on religious reforms in Rajasthan. Arya Samaj initiated crusade against caste system, untouchability, social discrimination, slavery, *Sati,* girl infanticide, child marriage, unmatched marriage, polygamy, dowry, sex discrimination, pardha etc.. It encouraged widow remarriage, educational and vocational training of women, self-sufficiency of women, simple marriage rituals etc.. The educational scheme devised by Swami Dayanand was based on scriptures suitable to the indigenous conditions and need. After Swamiji the leaders of the Arya Samaj took the mission of establishing Vedic pathshalas and Gurukulas. Later on a progressive group within the Arya Samaj devised the Anglo-Vedic scheme of education.

Religious reform works of Arya Samaj were prominent as priority was given to them. The Christian Missionaries presented challenges before the Hinduism. Swami Dayanand devised a scientific form of Vedic religion based on *Arsha* literature and scriptures. He not only denounced the pauranik foundations of Hinduism but also criticized the pauranic religious practices. After his disciples took the mission of propagation of Vedic religion. They refuted all the superstitious practices and denounced the idol worship. Simple and scientific religious rituals were introduced by the Arya Samaj. The Sanatanists also began to be influenced from the Arya Samaj and they too introduced logical rituals by reforming the evil practices and rituals.

The social reforms of Arya Samaj were equally important. Through various means the Arya Samaj attacked the social evils. The removal of untouchability was an important programme of social reforms. Through the removal of untouchability activities the social unity could be achieved. Shuddhi movement initially envisage the shuddhi of *dalits* and later on through this a channel of reconversion of such people began, who embraced Christianity or Islam. After 1920 the Hindu Mahasabha and Sanatani organisations also adopted the programmes of *dalitoddhar* and Shuddhi. They also joined hands with Arya Samjists. The Arya Samaj also took an ambitious programme of women's emancipation. The Stree Arya Samaj took the lead in this direction. The evil of child marriage was confronted and Arya Samaj finally achieved its' goal by getting the Sarda Act passed in 1929. Various efforts were made to mitigate the problems of widowhood. The Vidhwa Ashrams and women homes were founded. The campaign of widow remarriage also got success which was also taken over by other Hindu organisations. The educational programmes of Arya Samaj created awareness among girls and women.

It may be concluded that Swami Dayanand and Arya Samaj promoted the philanthropic activities to serve the cause of humanity. The Arya Samaj had devised various ways and means for the same. Swami Dayanand was the first who visualized the supreme usefulness of cow to humanity. Therefore, he initiated the cow protection movement. Swamiji gave serious attention on the education of masses because he was of the opinion that illiteracy and ignorance were the root causes of the degradation and subordination of India and its people. Therefore, the Arya Samaj took the mission of education sincerely. It was the impact of Arya Samaj movement that it awaken the broad masses of Rajasthan. The mass awakening translated and transformed into the rise and growth of nationalism in India, which led to the freedom of India.

Bibliography

Arya, Anupama, *Religion and Politics in India : A Study of the role of Arya Samaj*, KK Paublication, Delhi, 2001.

Arya, Buddhiprakash, *Arya Samaj Ajmer ka Itihas*, Arya Samaj, Ajmer, 1993.

Agrawal, Hariprasad, *Rajasthan ki Azadi ke Deewane*, Beawar, 1953.

Baird, R.D. (Ed.), *Religion in Modern India*, Manohar, New Delhi, 1981.

Bayly, Susan, *Caste, Society and Politics in India from the Eighteenth Century to the Modern Age*, Cambridge University Press, Reprinted, 2011.

Bhartiya, Bhawanilal, *Navajagaran ke Purodha Dayanand Saraswati*, Vedic Pustakalaya, Paropkarini Sabha, Ajmer, 1983.

Bhartiya, Bhawanilal (Ed.), *Dayanand Shastrarth Sangraha*, Sonipat, 1969.

Bhartiya, Bhawanilal, *Deshbhakta Kunwar Chand Karan Sarda*, Paropkarini Sabha, Ajmer, 1981.

Brass, Paul R., *An Indian Political Life - Charan Singh and Congress politics 1937 to 1961*, Sage Publication India, New Delhi, 2011.

Chand,Tara, *History of the Freedom Movement in India*, Volume Two, Publication Division, Government of India, New Delhi, Reprinted, 1974.

Chandra, Bipan, *India's Struggle for Independence*, Penguin Book India, 2016.

Chaudhary, P.S., *Rajasthan Between the Two World Wars*, Sri Ram Mehra & Co., Agra, 1968.

Chaudhary, Ramnarain, *Adhunik Rajasthan ka Uthan*, Rajasthan Prakashan Mandal, Ajmer, 1968.

Dayanand Saraswati, *Satyarth Prakash*, English Translation by Chiranjiva Bhardwaja under the title Light of Truth, Arya Pratinidhi Sabha, New Delhi, 2015, Reprinted.

Dayanand Saraswati, *Sanskarvidhi*, Vedic Yantralaya, Prayag, 1884, Second Edition, (First published in 1877 by the Asiatic Press, Bombay).

Dayanand Saraswati, *Bhagavata-Khandanam*, Agra, 1864.

Dayanand Saraswati, *Vedaviruddhmatkhandana*, Bombay, 1875.

Dayanand Saraswati, *Advaitamat-Khandanam*, Banaras, 1870.

Dayanand Saraswati, *Panchamahayajnavidhi*, Bombay, 1875.

Dayanand Saraswati, *Gokarunanidhi*, Allahabad, 1881.

Desai, A.R., *Social Background of Indian Nationalism*, Popular Prakashan, Bombay, 5th Ed., 1976.

Dubey, S.N., *Religious Movements in Rajasthan : Ideas and Antiquity*, University of Rajasthan, Jaipur.

Gajrani, Shiv (Ed.), *Swami Dayanand,* Commonwealth, New Delhi, 2015.

Ghai, R.K., *Shuddhi Movement in India*, Commonwealth, Delhi, 1990.

Goswami, Sambodh, *Voicing the Unvoiced (Women's questions & Arya Samaj)*, Two Valumes, Yking, Jaipur, 2016.

Goswami, Sambodh, *Female Infanticide and Child Marriage*, Rawat, Jaipur, 2007.

Grover, B.L., *British Policy Towards Indian Nationalism*, National Publication, Delhi, 1967.

Gupta, S.K., *Arya Samaj and the Raj (1875-1920)*, Gitanjali, New Delhi, 1991.

Handa, R.L., *History of Freedom Struggle in Princely States*, Central News Agency, Delhi, 1968.

Heimsath, C.H., *Indian Nationalism and Hindu Reforms*, Princeton, 1964.

Jaffrelot, Christophe, *Religion, Caste and Politics in India*, Primus Books, 2018, Reprinted (First Ed. 2010).

Jain, Pratibha, Sharma, Sangeeta & Garg, Archana, *Liberation of Women - An Aryasamajist Perspective*, Project Report, Centre for Women's Studies, University of Rajasthan, Jaipur.

Jigyasu, Munshiram (Ed.), *Rishi Dayanand ka Patravyavhar*, Vol. Two, Gurukul Kangri, 1935.

Jones, Kenneth W., *Arya Dharm : (Hindu Consciousness in 19th Century Punjab)*, Manohar, New Delhi, 2006, Reprinted (First Ed. 1976).

Jordens, J.T.F., *Dayanand Saraswati : His Life and Ideas*, Oxford University Press, Delhi, 1978.

Jordens, J.T.F., *Swami Shraddhananda : His Life and Causes*, Oxford University Press, Delhi, 1981.

Jordens, J.T.F., *Dayanand Saraswati : Essays on His Life and Ideas*, Manohar, New Delhi, 1998.

Joshi, Sumnesh, *Rajasthan Mein Swatantrata Sangram ke Senani*, Granthagar, Jaipur, 1973.

Joshi, V.C. (Ed.), *Lajpat Rai : Autobiographical Writings*, University Publication, Delhi, 1965.

Kane, P.V., *History of Dharmashastra*, Vol. IV, Poona, 1973.

Khadgawat, Nathuram, *Rajasthan's Role in the Struggle of* 1857, R.S.A., Bikaner, 1967.

Lata, Prem, *Swami Dayanand Sarasvati*, Sumit, New Delhi, 1990.

O'mally, L.S.S. (Ed.), *Modern India and the West*, Oxford University Press, 1941 (Reprinted, 1968).

Majumdar, R.C. (Ed.), *The History and Culture of Indian People*, Vol. IX (British Paramountcy and Indian Renaissance), III Edition, Bombay, 1988.

Majumdar, R.C., *History of the Freedom Movement in India*, Vol. I-III, Calcutta, 1970-1971.

Mathur, V.D., *States People's Conference*, Publication Scheme, Jaipur, 1987.

Mimamshak, Y., *Rishi Dayanand Saraswati Ke Patra aur Vijnapan ke Parishisht*, Amritsar, 1958.

Mimamshak, Y., *Rishi Dayanand Ke Patra aur Vigyapan*, Amritsar, 1955.

Misra, B. B., *The Indian Middle Classes,* Oxford University Press, New Delhi, 1978.

Mukhopadhyaya, *Devendranath, Maharishi Dayanand Saraswati ka Jivan Charit*, Reprinted, 2013, Hinduaun City (First Published in Bangla in 1916 and Again Published in Hindi in 1933 translated by Pandit Ghasi Ram).

Nanda, B.R. (Ed.), *Collected Works of Lala Lajpat Rai*, 15 Volumes, Manohar, New Delhi, 2003-2010.

Natrajan, S., *A Century of Social Reform,* Asia, Bombay, 1959.

Mishra, S.C., *National Movement in a Princely State,* Pointer, Jaipur, 1993.

Palit, Projit Kumar (Ed.), *Swami Vivekanand and National Integration*, Delta, New Delhi, 2013.

Pandey, Dhanpati, *The Arya Samaj and Indian Nationalism (1875-1920)*, S. Chand & Co., New Delhi, 1972.

Pareek, R.S., *Contribution of Arya Samaj in the Making of Modern India 1875-1975*, Sarvadeshik Arya Pratinidhi Sabha, Delhi, 1973.

Parvati, C.T., *Mahadev Govind Ranadey : A Biography*, Bombay, 1963.

Rai, Lala Lajpat, *A History of the Arya Samaj*, Revised Enlarged edition (First Published in 1914, Longman Green London), Orient Longmans, New Delhi, 1967.

Reid, Graham J., *Arya Samaj as a Reformation in Hinduism with Special Reference to Caste*, Ph.D. Dissertation, Yale University, 1943.

Sarda, Har Bilas, *Life of Dayanand Saraswati, Paropkarini Sabha*, Ajmer, 1968, Reprinted, IInd Edition (First Edition 1945).

Sarda, Har Bilas, *Speeches and Writings*, Vedic Yantralaya, Ajmer, 1935.

Sarda, Har Bilas, *Shyamji Krishna Verma*, Vol. I-II, Vedic Yantralaya, Ajmer, 1954-1958.

Sarasvati, Swami *Satya Prakash (Ed.)*, Dayanand Commemoration Volume (Maharishi Dayanand Niruanshati Smritigranth), Paropkarini Sabha, Ajmer, 1983.

Saxena, G.S., *Arya Samaj Movement in India (1875-1947)*, Commonwealth, New Delhi, 1990.

Saxena, K.S., *The Political Movements and Awakening in Rajasthan (1857-1947)*, S. Chand & Co., New Delhi, 1971.

Sharma, B.K., *Mass Movements and Freedom Struggle in Rajasthan (1818-1949)*, Books Treasure, Jodhpur, 2013.

Sharma, Brij Kishore, *Social, Economic and Political Contribution of Caste Associations in Northern India (A Case Study of All India Jat Mahasabha)*, Har-Anand, New Delhi, 2008.

Sharma, G.N. & Vashishtha, *Political Awakening and Indian Freedom Movement : With Special Reference to Rajasthan*, University of Rajasthan, Jaipur, 1993.

Sharma, J.M., *Svami Dayanand : A Biography*, UBS Publishers, New Delhi, 1998.

Sharma, Sangeeta, *Women's Liberation : The Arya Samaj Movement in India*, Rawat, Jaipur, 2010.

Sharma, Suresh K. (Ed.), *Swami Dayanand and the Arya Samaj Movement*, Two Vols., VISTA, Delhi, 2009.

Shastri, Satyadev, *Deshbhakta Shri Kunwar Chandkaranji Sarda*, Vedic Yantralaya, Ajmer, 1948.

Shastri, Vishnulal, *Hand Book of Arya Samaj*, Tract Deptt. of the Pratinidhi Sabha, United Provinces, 1912.

Shyamlal, *Ambedkar and Dalit Movement*, Rawat, Jaipur, 2008.

Shyamlal, *Untouchable Movement in India*, Subline, Jaipur, 2002.

Shyamlal, *Untouchable Castes in India*, Rawat, Jaipur, 2010.

Shyamlal, *Studies in Social Protest*, Rawat, Jaipur, 2010.

Singh, Bawa Chhajju, *Life and Teachings of Swami Dayanand Saraswati*, Second edition Reprinted (First edition 1903), Jan Gyan Prakashan, New Delhi, 1971.

Singh, Sitaram, *Nationalism and Social Reform in India (1885-1920)*, Ranjit, Delhi, 1968.

Sisson, Richard, *The Congress Party in Rajasthan*, Oxford University Press, Delhi, 1972.

Tod, James, *Annals and Antiquities of Rajasthan*, Vol. I-III, London, 1920.

Upadhyay, Ganga Prasad, *The Origin, Scope and Mission of Arya Samaj*, Arya Samaj Chowk, Allahabad, 1940.

Upadhyay, Ganga Prasad, *Philosophy of Dayanand*, Allahabad, 1955.

Upadhyay, Ganga Prasad, *Swami Dayanand's Contribution to Hindu Solidarity*, Allahabad, 1939.

Upadhyay, Ganga Prasad, *Landmarks of Swami Dayanand's Teachings*, Allahabad, 1940.

Upadhyay, Ganga Prasad, *The Arya Samaj and Depressed Classes*, Allahabad, 1940.

Vable, D., *The Arya Samaj : Hindu Without Hinduism*, Vikas, New Delhi, 1983.

Vashishtha, V.K., *Rajputana Agency (1832-1858)*, Aalekh, Jaipur, 1978.

Vashishtha, V.K., *Bhagat Movement*, Shruti, Jaipur, 1997.

Vashishtha, V.K., *1857 Revolt in the Princely State of Jaipur*, Books Treasure, Jodhpur, 2008.

Vashishtha, V.K., *Role of Gandhi's Ideas in Mobilization of Adivasis of Southern Rajputana Princely States (1921-1948)*, IIAS, Shimla, 2014.

Verma, G.C., *Modern Educatioin : Its Growth and Development in Rajasthan 1818-1983*, Publication Scheme, Jaipur, 1984.

Vidyalankar, Satyaketu (Chief Editor), *Arya Samaj ka Itihas*, in Seven Volumes, Sarvadeshik Arya Pratinidhi Sabha, New Delhi, 1985-1988.

Vidyavachaspati, Indra, *Arya Samaj ka Itihas*, Pratham evam Dwitiya Bhag, Sarvadeshik Pratinidhi Sabha, Delhi, 1957.

Vyas, Indira, *Freedom Movement in Rajasthan*, University Book House, Jaipur, 2004.

Vyas, Prakash, *Rajasthan ka Samajik Itihas*, Panchsheel, Jaipur, 1988.

Yadav, K.C. (Ed.), *The Autobiography of Dayanand Saraswati*, Manohar, New Delhi, 1976.

Yadav, K.C. & Arya, K.S., *The Arya Samaj And the Freedom Movement, Volume - One : 185-1918*, Manohar, New Delhi, 1988.

Yagnik, Indu Lal, *Shyamji Krishan Verma*, Bombay, 1950.